Harry Potter's Folklore World

On Myth and Magic

*

Harry Potter's Folklore World

On Myth and Magic

★
★ *✱*

ROBERT B. WALTZ

edited by
Edward Cray and Susan O. Friedman

CAMSCO Music
1308 Brittany Pointe
Lansdale, PA 19446
800-548-FOLK

Loomis House Press
www.loomishousepress.com

ISBN 978-1-935243-84-7

Designed by Mark F. Heiman.

Cover photo: Gloucester Cathedral Cloister by Michael D. Beckwith, available under a Creative Commons 2.0 Attribution License (creativecommons.org) on flickr.com; modified for print.

To Sarah Cagley
Who Was There at the Beginning

See her with the dancers
And hear their feet all pound,
Ringing through the floorboards
As fiddle tunes resound.
Hearts thrill with the dancing,
Cloggers show us the old ways,
As the pickers keep alive
Graceful music of past days.
Let her keep on dancing
Even as she stays
Young-hearted all her days.

Contents

ACKNOWLEDGMENTS

This idea for this book came about rather casually, during a completely unrelated meeting. I was encouraging a fantasy-reading friend, Benji Flaming, to try the Harry Potter books, and two other Potter readers, Sarah Cagley and Catie Jo Pidel, became involved in the conversation. And they set me thinking.... The idea of a dictionary of folklore motifs in the Potter books began almost as a gag (my working title was "Harry Potter and the Ripped-Off Folktales"), but the more I thought about it, the more I came up with. Katryn Conlin tossed some ideas my way during this period of casual research, as did Jeff Rolfzen. Eventually it reached the point where I decided to share the results with the wider world. Of the crowd who was there at the time of that first meeting, I've spent the most time talking to Sarah, so this is her book. But the others all deserve a share of the credit.

Thanks as well to Elisheva Rosenberg (whose life bears some odd similarities to J. K. Rowling's, and who was my source for Slavic languages), Patricia Rosenberg, Paul Stamler, Ben Schwartz, David Engle, and Martha Galep, as well as my parents, Dorothy and Frederick Waltz.

I also owe substantial thanks to Don Nichols, who induced me to read the Potter books (I joined the craze about the time the *Prisoner of Azkaban* came out). Don also read an early draft of the book and made useful suggestions. As always, I owe much to Ed Cray, who has edited all three of my Folklore Series books, and who added much of value to this work — including nagging me to make it a more complete volume. Writers always thank editors, and almost always go on to say that the editor went above and beyond the call of duty — but in Ed's case, even that is understating my debt. He is a true friend as well as my editor.

And, of course, thanks to J. K. Rowling, for Hermione (perhaps my favorite character in all of literature), and Harry, and all the "gang."

Biblical texts are primarily from the King James or New Revised Standard Versions, or are my own rendering.

INTRODUCTION

"Hagrid… did you say there are *dragons* at Gringotts?"

Harry Potter himself, as he prepares for his first visit to the wizarding shopping district of Diagon Alley, has a hard time imagining the world he is about to enter. Think what it is like for those of us who can't see it! All the people in funny clothes, carrying wands, and causing… *things*… to happen.

Fantasy is one of the hardest forms of literature to set in context. If you write a contemporary crime novel, your readers know about the existence of police departments and forensic procedures and such. Write a western, and they know about cattle ranges and firearms and the like. You don't have to explain the world, just the characters and the plot.

In fantasy, there is absolutely nothing that can be taken for granted. Does the sun rise in the east? Why? Why not have it rise in the west? And why not make it purple? Because there are no rules at all, fantasy authors can create worlds that are very hard to explain and understand.

And yet, most of them don't. They use worlds that are mostly like ours. The main characters, e.g., are usually human beings and not gegnards or sysfifels. (What are gegnards and sysfifels? Well, that's the whole point!) Even when authors change the worlds, they change them in recognizable ways. The world of Harry Potter, for instance, is mostly our world — except that, for a few special people, magic works.

There is another interesting trick that fantasy writers use, often without pointing it out, perhaps without even noticing it. When their worlds do differ from the ordinary world, they often make changes of types that are familiar to us. Magic itself is an example. What is magic? *You* know what it is. You know it from all the other fairy tales and stories you grew up with.

Ultimately, most fantasies are grounded in our folktale tradition. The greatest fantasy writer of the twentieth century, J. R. R. Tolkien, knew this very well indeed; although the plots of *The Hobbit* and *The Lord of the Rings* are mostly original, very many of the character-types and plot themes are motifs well-known from folklore. "In *The Lord of the Rings,* his epic trilogy, he virtually created a new genre: one possessing obvious affinities with folk epic and mythology, but no true literary counterpart."[2] Tolkien in fact was looking at folklore and old stories and trying to mine out a "truth" that underlay them. In this he clearly succeeded; this is why his books have such a deep, rich texture. He even coined a phrase for this mixed set of sources: It is the "cauldron of story," to which authors add a little but from which they take much.[3]

The Harry Potter books are similar: Although the plot is, almost entirely, J. K. Rowling's, and although characters such as Harry, Hermione, Ron, Ginny, Neville, and Luna are entirely her creation, the world she invokes derives much of its vividness from the tales we already know.

Think of yourself as a new wizard about to ride your first broomstick. Exciting, perhaps unnerving — how do you *sit* on the thing? What makes it go? And how do you make it stop? Or aim where you want to go? There's no brake pedal, no steering wheel, no rear view mirror. There isn't so much as a seat belt — they didn't even have cushioning charms until 1820. What regulatory agency approved these things, anyway? Why are they allowed?

Are broomsticks really necessary to the plot? Not very. Most trained wizards can travel by apparition. For mass transit, there are portkeys — and surely the Hogwarts Express isn't the only wizarding train; it's simply not economically reasonable to run just one. Anyone with Floo Powder can use the Floo Network. The Knight Bus is available for anyone who can stomach it and can raise a wand. Advanced wizards such as Dumbledore and Voldemort can fly. And broomsticks aren't very safe; surely a sane society would invent something that it's harder to fall off of! Wizards ride broomsticks because... in our muggle world, witches are portrayed riding broomsticks. And, having accepted that fact, Rowling goes on to see where it leads her — and hence to Quidditch and the Quidditch World Cup and an international broomstick industry devoted to making faster and better brooms. (As seen in the notes in *Quidditch Through the Ages,* the broomstick industry has substantial resemblances to the automobile and aviation industries in the way it struggled toward mass production). That, in turn leads to people sometimes riding brooms when, rationally, they should use some other transport mechanism. (Why, for instance, did the Death Eaters ride brooms to Xenophilus Lovegood's home in *The Deathly Hallows?* Had they taken a faster means of transport, it would have been lights out for Harry and Company.)

Unlike J. R. R. Tolkien or Lloyd Alexander (who based his *Chronicles of Prydain* on Welsh myth) but like, say, C. S. Lewis in the *Narnia* books (which she seems to have admired[4]), Rowling does not seek to use and expand a single mythology. She borrows from everywhere. (She said herself, "I've taken *horrible* liberties with folklore and mythology."[5]) This bothers mythological purists, just as Lewis's eclecticism bothered Tolkien, and Wagner's *Ring* cycle troubles LeGuin;[6] Rowling's universe bristles with inconsistencies. (For starters, why is a school with so many bad teachers considered a good school?) But to her credit, Rowling has broken the Tolkien mold — so many fantasies after Tolkien were effectively set in Tolkien's universe that it has been labelled "Fantasyland."[7] Terry Pratchett's immensely popular "Discworld" fantasies are very largely spoofs on the Tolkien universe. Not so the Potterverse. Probably no important "genre" fantasy in the last half century has been so independent of Tolkien as the Harry Potter books. This is not to claim that there is *no* dependence. For one thing, there are all the doors he opened. Without Tolkien, probably no one would have taken Rowling seriously. Tolkien's influence opened a shelf for fantasy works — and allowed Rowling adult readers. And could Tolkien's deliberate hiding of direct Christian influence be responsible for Rowling's arguably doing the same?

The influence of Tolkien on Rowling is a matter of significant dispute; some of her disclaimers seem almost strident. It has been said that she "has a bizarre love-hate relationship" with Tolkien and C. S. Lewis.[8] Both Tolkien and Lewis were putting messages — Christian messages — into their stories. Rowling seems to be doing the same — many of the notes in this book will reveal that — but in a very different way. Her approach is unlike Lewis's explicit Christian fantasy or Tolkien's very subtle approach (so subtle that some people call it un-Christian); Rowling tells an explicitly Christian message but without hitting people over the head.[9]

Rowling's biggest single source, other than modern stories about witches, is probably Greco-Roman mythology she studied in college,[10] followed closely by British folklore — almost every creature that Harry learns about in third year Defense against Dark Arts, for instance, is attested in British folktales or some other mythological source. But she will use almost anything. Often in complex combinations which only take on meaning when seen together — the obvious example of this is the numerous deep, if extremely subtle, ways in which Christian messages seem to have informed her writings. (The Catholic Church once declared that Rowling is "Christian by conviction, is Christian in her mode of living, even in her way of writing."[11] She herself has said that her favorite painting is Michelangelo da Caravaggio's 1606 work "Supper at Emmaus," a drawing of the resurrected Jesus with certain of his disciples.[12])

Because Rowling is so eclectic, no single scholar is likely to discover all her influences. Rowling herself admits that about a third of her magic-based materials were *someone's* genuine beliefs;[13] if anything, that number is low. This book does not attempt to find all her sources, nor the books she consulted. Its goal is to identify as many items as possible which derive from folktales. It is not a Harry Potter encyclopedia; you won't find entries on the various characters, or even on important types of creatures such as dementors. Dementors are a product of Rowling's imagination; while there are Soul Eaters in some other fantasies, Rowling has said explicitly that dementors are based on her own emotions — in effect, they are depression made corporeal.[14]

The power of fantasy is subtle but deep. Sometimes it increases our understanding of folklore rather than vice versa — indeed, sometimes it encourages the study of folklore. Prior to the work of Lloyd Alexander, for instance, there were only two proper English translations of *The Mabinogion* (those by Guest and Jones/Jones). Alexander's *Chronicles of Prydain* were followed within a decade by translations by Ford and Gantz — and then by a thirty year hiatus until Davies produced another. So the fantasy had made the folklore more accessible in more ways than one.

Ursula K. LeGuin wrote, "For fantasy is true, of course. It isn't factual, but it is true. Children know it. Adults know it too, and that is precisely why many of them are afraid of fantasy."[15] There is much bad fantasy in the world, but the best — the work of the Tolkiens, the Alexanders, the LeGuins, the Rowlings — has much to teach us about ourselves and our heritage. It is my sincere hope that readers of Rowling's rich fantasies will be able to use this volume — which can be read either as a reference or continuously — as a first introduction to the even richer world of folklore and their own folk traditions.

Disclaimer

Literary critics of the Harry Potter books have offered all sorts of explanation of its contents. John Granger thinks it is "alchemical." Others have called it "demonic." Some compare it to C. S. Lewis; others (including J. K. Rowling herself) have vigorously denied this. My goal is *not* to engage in this sort of criticism. It is simply to study folklore. Yet, because the books have very strong Christian elements, and Christianity viewed from outside meets the criteria of "folklore," I have discussed the Christian elements — and because I've discussed Christian elements, I have also looked at material from other religions, living and dead. I have also compared it with genre fantasy, because that is where the adult copies of the Potter books are filed, and with medieval ROMANCE, because it inspired so much of the material in the Potterverse. This has at times led me to stray slightly into literary criticism, but that is not the primary purpose. This is supposed to be a book about folklore.

And, of course, this book is not authorized, prepared, approved, licensed, or endorsed by J. K. Rowling, Warner Bros., or any other individual or entity associated with the Harry Potter books or movies.

Reference Tools
Thompson Motifs

Folklore is such a vast field that many folklorists use a classification scheme to identify similar tales. The basic reference for this is Stith Thompson's *Motif Index of Folk Literature* and Antti Arne and Stith Thompson's *The Types of the Folktale*. This Dictionary makes us of Thompson motifs; they are identified with Thompson's name and a number, meaning that this item has a place in Thompson's list. The numbers themselves are shown in Bold Gray Type. A catalog of these references is located in the Index of Thompson Motifs.

Thompson's catalog is divided into two parts, tale-types and motifs. These are almost like verbs and nouns — tale-types tell *what* happened, motifs are characters or items in the plot. To distinguish the two, Thompson put a letter in front of the motifs (e.g. dragons are B11) while tale-types have just numbers (e.g. "tales of magic" are given numbers from 300 to 399, with "The ogre's (devil's) heart in the egg" being tale 302).

Determining where Rowling found her motifs is generally easy. She clearly borrowed werewolves (D113.1.1), but invented House Elves (although the latter are a lot like brownies). It's harder to tell if a tale-type is borrowed. This book includes examples of both, but material on tale-types is much more speculative — with much more first person guessing and fewer citations of sources. In writing the entries in this dictionary, it has sometimes been hard to draw the line between motifs and tale-types. Major tale-types are marked with an asterisk (*) to make things a little clearer.

It should not be assumed that every Thompson motif found in the Potter books has been indexed — the book omits J1705, "Stupid classes," even though Harry suffered through a number of those! The objective of this book is to look at the portions of the Potter series with true roots in folklore and fantasy.

Thompson organized the motifs into twenty-three broad categories, designated by letter. The general descriptions of each category are as follows:

A   Mythological Motifs (gods, creators, shaping of the Universe, calamities)
B   Animals (Mythical, Magical, creatures having human traits, friendly, fanciful)
C   Tabu
D   Magic (transformation, disenchantment, magic objects, manifestations)
E   The Dead (reconciliation, ghosts, revenants, reincarnation, the soul)
F   Marvels (otherworld journeys, marvelous creatures, extraordinary places)
G   Ogres (witches, trolls, horrid and cruel creatures; ogres defeated)
H   Tests (identity tests, marriage tests, tests of cleverness, tasks, quests)
J   The Wise and the Foolish
K   Deceptions (contests, bargains, thefts, escapes, captures, humiliations, seductions)
L   Reversal of Fortune
M   Ordaining the Future
N   Chance and Fate
P   Society
Q   Rewards and Punishments
R   Captives and Fugitives
S   Unnatural Cruelty
T   Sex
V   Religion
W   Character Traits
X   Humor
Z   Miscellaneous

Modern Fantasies and Citations

This book is designed to be read by anyone familiar with J. K. Rowling's Harry Potter series, either as a dictionary of folklore motifs or as a continuous text. But to understand why her sources matter requires context. So, although the main goal of this work is to locate Rowling's folklore sources, any analysis of sources must also look at *modern* materials. Therefore, in addition to describing the parallels between Rowling and true folklore, I have also set out to compare Rowling's use of folktales with the use made by other noteworthy modern fantasists. This attempt is by no means comprehensive. Although I have cited many books, I have devoted the most attention to four modern works which strike me as being both typical and as having high literary qualities. These four fantasy series are as follows:

Lloyd Alexander, "The Chronicles of Prydain" (*The Book of Three, The Black Cauldron, The Castle of Llyr, Taran Wanderer, The High King*). The underpinning of this series is Welsh mythology. It tells of how a fatherless young man, Taran, grows from boyhood as a lonely Assistant Pig-Keeper to love and honor in Prydain.

Kevin Crossley-Holland, The "Arthur" Trilogy (actually four books, *The Seeing Stone, At the Crossing-Places, The King of the Middle March, Gatty's Tale/Crossing to Paradise*). This is underpinned on the King Arthur legend. It tells of how a young esquire, Arthur, learns how to make his way in the world, and also relates the story of his friend Gatty.

Ursula K. LeGuin, *The Earthsea Trilogy* (now many more than three books, but the main ones are *A Wizard of Earthsea, The Tombs of Atuan, The Farthest Shore*). A young man, Ged, proves to be a great mage; the books tell parts of the "Deed of Ged" as he brings evil and then good into the world.

J. R. R. Tolkien, *The Hobbit* and *The Lord of the Rings*; also *The Silmarillion* and others. These books have some underpinning, mostly linguistic, from Icelandic, Norse, and Old English mythology; also, Tolkien used the sounds of Welsh and Finnish for his Elvish languages. They tell of the end of the Ages of the Elves in Middle-Earth, as the free peoples of the world fight first Morgoth the Great Enemy and then his servant Sauron, the maker of the One Ring.

Citations to modern fantasy are not very detailed (mostly because so many editions, with so many different paginations, exist). Citations to folklore sources are in the endnotes, with the books cited being listed in the bibliography. Cross-references between articles are shown in SMALL CAPS, e.g. "see also Meeting DEATH ON THE ROAD" means that there is more information under the entry "Meeting Death on the Road," which (since the word DEATH is in small caps and the word Meeting is not) files alphabetically under "Death," not "Meeting."

There is, in all of this, the question of authority — that is, what is a "genuine" part of the Potterverse. There are at least three possible sources: the books, the movies, and the other material offered by J. K.

Rowling. Rowling's various offerings *explain* the books — but the canon is simply the seven primary Harry Potter books, plus the by-blows of *Beedle the Bard, Fantastic Beasts,* and *Quidditch through the Ages.* I have not sought out every comment Rowling has made about her characters' lives. (For example, Rowling has said that Hermione chose a legal career, working in the Ministry of Magic.[16] It seems evident that Hermione went on to be either a Headmistress of Hogwarts or a scientist.)

Book Shorthand

Odds are that the reader will know the titles of the Potter books and will have no trouble recognizing them. But, just in case, I have used the following short names:

The *Philosopher's Stone* = *Harry Potter and the Philosopher's Stone* (published in the U.S. under the unenlightened title *Harry Potter and the Sorcerer's Stone)*

The *Chamber of Secrets* = *Harry Potter and the Chamber of Secrets*

The *Prisoner of Azkaban* = *Harry Potter and the Prisoner of Azkaban*

The *Goblet of Fire* = *Harry Potter and the Goblet of Fire*

The *Order of the Phoenix* = *Harry Potter and the Order of the Phoenix*

The *Half-Blood Prince* = *Harry Potter and the Half-Blood Prince*

The *Deathly Hallows* = *Harry Potter and the Deathly Hallows*

Beedle = *The Tales of Beedle the Bard*

Quidditch = *Quidditch Through the Ages* (credited to Kennilworthy Whisp)

Fantastic Beasts = *Fantastic Beasts and Where To Find Them* (credited to Newt Scamander)

An Opening Chapter:
Folklore, Literature, and the Genre of Harry Potter

This book is mostly about the folklore motifs in J. K. Rowling's work, not about her plots. But her plots also have traditional roots, so it might be worth a few words.

Many authors claim that all successful stories can be broken down into a few basic types. *Forbes* columnist Nick Morgan, for instance, lists "The Quest," "The Stranger in a Strange Land," "Rags to Riches," "The Love Story," and "The Tale of Revenge." All of these can be found in the Harry Potter books (for example, the search for the Horcruxes is a quest; Harry's entry into the wizarding world makes him a stranger in a strange land; his orphan upbringing and entry into wealth and fame is an example of rags to riches; his relationship with Ginny is a love story, and his relationship with Draco Malfoy is largely motivated by revenge). But the fact that these elements are all found in the Potter books shows that they aren't really independent stories; rather, they are plot motifs — subplots.

Hero tales in particular are often based on a few common motifs. This position was most forcefully stated by Joseph Campbell, and is described in the entry on the PRICE — but while the PRICE appears in the Potter books, there are other elements as well. Campbell did not, however, invent the idea of a Standard Hero Tale; the first to propose that the common elements of hero tales were "elemental ideas" seems to have been Adolf Bastian, and Adolf Bauer helped popularize it.[17]

Robert A. Heinlein once claimed — probably in an attempt to shock — that all mainstream plots belong to just three categories: "Boy Meets Girl," "The Brave Little Tailor," and "The Man Who Learns Better."[18]

Of the three types, "Boy Meets Girl" hardly needs explanation; it is so common that Thompson doesn't even bother assigning it a number.

"The Brave Little Tailor" is Thompson motif 1640. It is named after #20 in the Grimm collection, "The Valiant Little Tailor" (compare Grimm #114, "The Clever Little Tailor"). A tailor sees seven or more flies land on his bread and jam, swats them all, and goes out boasting "Seven at one blow!" People hear him and are amazed at his exploits, and so call on him to deal with whatever their problem is (e.g. a marauding giant). The tailor manages, by trickery, to defeat these real adversaries as well, and so becomes a hero. The tale became known in English due to its inclusion in Andrew Lang's *The Blue Fairy Book,* and Katherine Briggs listed three English variants on Thompson 1640, "John Glaick, the Brave Tailor" (Peterhead, Scotland; the refrain is "Weel done! John Glaik, Killt fifty flees at ae straik"),[19] "Johnny Gloke," and "Jack the Giant-Killer."[20] The basic idea is that someone not naturally equipped or expected to be a hero becomes one.

"Learning Better" is a much more murky concept; many of the examples are modern. But the folktale of "Why the Sea is Salt"[21] appears to be a survival of an ancient tale of the Scandinavian king Froda (the same name, incidentally, as Tolkien's "Frodo"). Froda tried to create a happy nation by having the magic mill grind out the people's needs — but overworked the giants who ran the mill, and suffered for it.[22] In Asbjornsen and Moe's anthology, Froda's story became a tale of a mill which ground out whatever the owner wished — but would grind until stopped, so, when an owner acquired it without learning the trick required to turn it off, it turned the sea salt. There is a Japanese equivalent of this tale, "The Magic Mortar," in which the mortar, which had been stolen by the rightful owner's brother, is told to grind out riches — but instead grinds out salt until it sinks the brother in the newly-salty sea;[23] in the Gypsy tale "Why the Sea is Salt," the object is a magic apple, but again, we see an evil brother lost at sea.[24] The tale of Midas is also an instance of learning better; the most common moral of these tales is "Be Careful What You Wish For."

Critics claim that plots using elements other than Heinlein's three are not few — it has been pointed out that a large part of LeGuin's work, for instance, consists of incomplete persons managing to unite with what they lack. (This is a major element in the psychology of Jung.) Ged, for example, is reunited with his "shadow" in *A Wizard of Earthsea.* The motif of the shadow-self shows its enduring power in tales such as Robert

Louis Stevenson's *The Strange Case of Dr. Jekyll and Mr. Hyde*. Another variant on this is the common folktale theme of a commoner marrying a nobleman; here, the "shadow," or complement, is the representative of another social order.[25]

Still, there is a great deal of truth in Heinlein's argument. If you think about Shakespeare, all the Great Tragedies are tales of Men Who Learned Better (if too late) — Lear learned that he couldn't ordain love, Othello learned that Desdemona was true and Iago false, MacBeth learned that prophecies don't always mean what we take them to mean, and Hamlet, if nothing else, learned that there is such as thing as "too dang complicated." *Henry IV, Part I*, by contrast, is in large part a tale of a Brave Little Tailor — Henry V (who is the true hero of the play rather than his father Henry IV) was not born to be king: he matures in the story from an irresponsible young man, the flighty son of someone who was properly only an earl, to be a prince who, in time, will be capable of defeating all of France.

Probably most successful fantasies are based on "The Brave Little Tailor," or on its close relative "The UGLY DUCKLING." Bilbo in *The Hobbit* and Frodo and Sam in *The Lord of the Rings* are all Brave Little Tailors, ordinary people (or, at least, people-like beings) who achieve far beyond what seems possible. Taran in Alexander's *The Chronicles of Prydain* is an Ugly Duckling; so is Ged in the Earthsea books. Tolkien, in particular, has no "Boy Meets Girl" at all, and although a few characters Learn Better (Boromir in particular), they are not important to the plot.

The Man Who Learns Better can be pretty obnoxious in isolation. (As Ursula K. LeGuin once remarked, "Nobody who says, 'I told you so' has ever been, or will ever be, a hero."[26]) This is what many people dislike about Lewis's Narnia…. But it can be powerful in combination.

Rowling clearly uses all three of Heinlein's motifs. Boy Meets Girl is obvious. Harry is a Brave Little Tailor from the start — but the key to the whole series arguably comes near the end of *The Deathly Hallows*, when Neville becomes a Brave Little Tailor by slaying Nagini.

The Deathly Hallows reveals Snape as a Man Who Learned Better — and, indeed, reveals Dumbledore as having Learned Better in his youth. Voldemort's failure is that he never did learn better — not even when Harry stared him in the face at the very end and appealed to him to do so. In a way, Voldemort was like Milton's Satan, who preferred to be wrong but in control to being right but a servant.

On the other hand, none of these types really accounts for Hermione Granger, whose intelligence is as necessary for the success of the enterprise as is Harry Potter's bravery. (Rowling herself has said that "they couldn't do it without Hermione."[27]) Hermione's relationship to Harry is almost as Merlin's was to King Arthur — and yet, Dumbledore is also Merlin.... Or perhaps Hermione is Athena to Harry's Odysseus. This would give a Classical Greek element Rowling's plot — in *The Odyssey*, Odysseus was "the man of twists and turns"[28] and "never at a loss,"[29] but it was Athena, the Goddess of Wisdom and Crafts,[30] who (for instance) called upon Zeus to say "the exile must return,"[31] induced Telemachus to seek his father,[32] guarded Odysseus as he left Calypso's island,[33] inspired Penelope to set out Odysseus's bow,[34] who regularly set the stage for Odysseus's triumphs. There is a resemblance between the trio of Harry, Hermione, and Ron and the classical trio of Odysseus and Diomedes who, backed by Athena, raided Troy in the night[35] and later stole the Palladium to allow the overthrow of Troy[36] — like Diomedes, Odysseus, and Athena, Ron is the brawn, Harry the trickster skilled with his hands and quick in a crisis, and Hermione the genius with many skills and crafts.

A strong case could be made the Hermione, not Harry, is the true heroine of the Potter books. Harry was born (or at least chosen at the age of one) to be a hero. Hermione wasn't. Yet she, and she alone, *always* stands by Harry. Both are UGLY DUCKLINGS, but for Hermione, this is more unexpected. W. H. Auden, in an essay called "The Quest Hero" (one of the great defenses of *The Lord of the Rings,* but with much that applies to Rowling also), pointed out that there are people who are *meant* to be heroes, and particularly endowed for it: Achilles (not that he did a very good job of it), Beowulf, Roland; in *The Lord of the Rings,* Auden points to Aragorn and Gandalf as "natural" heroes. But there are also people who are not meant to be heroes but manage it anyway.

As an example of these "accidental" heroes, Auden looks at *The Magic Flute.* The "typical hero" is Prince Tamino, who of course succeeds in fulfilling his quest at a high cost. "But beside him stands Papageno, who is, in his own way, a hero too."[37] Not a *heroic* hero; he explicitly denies his ability to face the tasks that Tamino undertakes. But he is humble enough to admit his defects, and contributes in the end to success, and is rewarded with Papagena — not a princess, indeed a comic like Papageno himself, but a love fit for him; he "asked only for a nice little wife and his birds."[38] Auden points out that the hobbits in Tolkien fulfill this role — not mighty, not destined to greatness, but called upon: "You may be nobody in particular in yourself, yet, for some inexplicable reason, through no choice of your own… it is on you… that the task falls."[39] *That* is true heroism — the heroism of Hermione, and of Harry, and even of Neville. Little as they are, they are brave tailors indeed.

There is an even older quip than Heinlein's, anonymous, which claims that there are only three story plots in the world, and the Eternal Triangle is two of them. That is, stories such as Tristan, Isuelt, and Mark;[40] or Arthur, Lancelot, and Guinevere, in which two suitors contend for one lover. Rowling uses this as well — consider Krumm, Ron, and Hermione; or Hermione, Lavender Brown, and Ron (and why in the world doesn't Rowling realize that Hermione deserves better than Ron?). But it is not an overarching plot element. There is no evidence that Voldemort ever loved anyone other than himself. (Dumbledore, we know from Rowling's comments outside the books, did.) Perhaps it was Voldemort's inability to find love and have children that led him to so desire immortality.…

Orson Scott Card once claimed that science fiction is the only true religious literature left. In this he distinguished *religious* literature from *inspirational* literature, in which the religious truth was simply assumed, not explored. So *"Real* religious literature… does something entirely different. It explores the nature of the universe and discovers the purpose behind it. When we find that purpose, we have found God.…"[41] Rowling arguably finds this purpose in her praise of the power of love.

Rowling's theology, if such it can be called, is non-orthodox, having a hint of the Pelagian heresy in it. It may be easiest to explain this un-orthodoxy by comparison between the climax of *The Deathly Hallows* and *The Lord of the Rings*. In Tolkien, Frodo goes into the Sammath Naur to destroy the Ring — and fails, and catastrophe is averted only because of Gollum. It is salvation by grace: "For by grace you have been saved through faith… not because of works, lest anyone should boast" (Ephesians 2:8). Also, Frodo comes away with three permanent injuries, from knife, sting, and tooth, all the result of moral failings.[42] In the *Deathly*

Hallows, the basic situation is similar: Harry goes alone to the Forbidden Forest to perform a necessary but very difficult task — in his case, to confront Voldemort and (he thinks) die. *And Harry does not fail.* He goes to the Forest and does what needs to be done. "This, perhaps, is the most disturbing, and potentially threatening, concept in Rowling's universe: that each individual is completely responsible for his or her own fate."[43] This is the essence of Pelagianism: that individuals had the power and ability to choose good and evil themselves; that there was no original sin[44] or "total depravity." Pelagius declared, "In the freedom to choose good or evil lies the pre-eminence of the rational soul.... There would be no virtue in him who perseveres in the good if he had not had the possibility of going over to evil."[45] This so offended Saint Augustine of Hippo that he developed his counter-doctrine based on predestination, infant damnation, and human depravity — doctrines found in the Catholic Church and especially in the Calvinist branches of Protestantism.

Rowling's Pelagianism is interesting because Pelagianism is a *British* heresy, and the only major heresy of the early church to still be widespread (although not in any organized denomination).[46] Pelagius, the founder of the sect, came to Rome from Britain some time in the period 390–400; some think he was from Roman Britain, others, from Ireland.[47] His leading follower Coelestius was almost certainly Irish.[48] So this might be a particularly tempting doctrine to a British author.

This is not to claim that Rowling is trying to offer an introduction to Pelagian Christianity, as Tolkien was trying to offer a Catholic introduction. Certainly she is not offering a Pelagian allegory in the sense that C. S. Lewis offered an Anglican allegory in *The Lion, the Witch, and the Wardrobe.* But Rowling has admitted the Christian content of the work, and even declared it "obvious." It certainly is to those who are willing to see it — but there is more than just standard Christianity. "Harry's apotheosis [is] about man reaching his destination rather than falling short of it";[49] unless we claim that Harry *is* Jesus, it is a Pelagian ending. Whether Rowling knows anything about Pelagianism, the general ideas were likely on her mind.

Why do these stories resonate? It has been suggested that most great children's books are "utterly bound up in the medieval."[50] But this is balderdash. The medieval era was a time of disease, dirt, highway robbery, political insurrection, and uncaring nobility lording it over oppressed peasantry. No one would want to go back there. That sense of the old arises not because children's books are medieval but because many of them, including the Potter books, are ROMANCES — in the medieval sense that they are tales of great things, of heroes and of vast threats and of happy endings from the brink of disaster. ROMANCES are probably the most popular literary form of all time; it is a curiosity of the modern era that the ROMANCE has been fading. We have moved from myth and ROMANCE — tales of characters we would *wish* to be — to tales of ordinary life, and even of lives less than ordinary.⁵¹ But the ROMANCE always comes back.

Rowling's work has many typical ROMANCE characteristics. It is highly episodic, and ROMANCES (especially the Arthurian romances) tend to feature jumbles of incidents piled together. It involves a great theme (in the medieval ROMANCES, often love or some sort of quest; in the Potter books, the defeat of Voldemort). Success almost always hangs by a thread at the end — the happy ending is what J. R. R. Tolkien calls a "eucatastrophe." The ending of a romance must, as J. R. R. Tolkien put it, allow for either *eucatastrophe* or *dyscatastrophe*. Orfeo may rescue Heurodis — or he may fail, and even be taken himself. Sir Gawain may lose his head in the Beheading Game. Floris and Blancheflour, instead of both surviving, may both be killed.⁵²

But there seems to be more. Here we plunge into what Carl Jung called the "collective unconscious," which contained many "archetypes" of concepts found in myth and story.⁵³ Psychology has changed much since Jung's day, so we cannot place too much weight on this. Still, it does seem as if there are tale-types which are particularly appealing to many people.

An archetype, according to Jung, often involves a higher "selfhood."⁵⁴ (Although, interestingly, autistics, who seem to have a damaged sense of self,⁵⁵ often find these archetypes even more appealing than ordinary people.) An archetype, in Jung's view, was an unusually specific but entirely internal thing; LeGuin wrote, "I won't find a living archetype in my bookcase or in my television set. I will find it only in myself: in that core of individuality lying in the heart of the common darkness."⁵⁶ "The great fantasies... speak *from* the unconscious *to* the unconscious, in the *language* of the unconscious — symbol and archetype."⁵⁷

A typical example of a plot archetype is the need to face one's own "shadow." This concept is of particular importance to LeGuin; she makes it explicit in *A Wizard of Earthsea,* where Ged is helpless against his shadow-thing until he confronts it directly — and both overcomes and joins with it. But she got the idea from Hans Christian Andersen,[58] and the theme goes back at least to the Norse *Egill Skallagrimsson's Saga,* which shows several instances of brothers where one is joyful and one dour or otherwise complementary.[59] Some have also seen it in the Arthurian tale of Balin and Balan, two brothers who, unrecognized, fight and slay each other.[60] It has also been suggested that Tolkien's Gollum and Frodo fit this pattern; it is also in the ending of Card's "Ender" books, and arguably even in Dante's pairing of himself and Virgil; the whole thing is somewhat reminiscent of the DOPPELGÄNGER.[61]

We see this directly in the resolution to the Harry Potter books. As the books themselves point out, Harry and Voldemort are much alike: orphans, parselmouths, brought up among muggles. Yet one is good and one vile. Harry must overcome his shadow. "NEITHER CAN LIVE WHILE THE OTHER SURVIVES."

The number of well-known archetypes found in Rowling probably goes far toward explaining the power of her work. Some of these will be explored on the following pages.

A Summary of
THE SEVEN PRIMARY HARRY POTTER BOOKS

Please note that these summaries are not intended as a substitute for reading the books. Much that is important is left out, and of course the summaries give away the endings. They are offered primarily to folklorists who have not read the Harry Potter books, and secondarily to readers who need a brief reminder of what happens in each particular book.

HARRY POTTER AND THE PHILOSOPHER'S STONE

Eleven-year-old Harry Potter, an orphan, has grown up in the home of his mother's sister and her husband, Vernon and Petunia Dursley, and their son Dudley. Harry, small but agile, is thoroughly oppressed by his relatives until a series of envelopes arrive in the mail. Vernon Dursley will not let Harry see them, but takes the family into hiding. They are preparing to spend the night in a deserted cabin when a giant man bursts in, declares that he is Rubeus Hagrid, and announces that he has come to take Harry to the magical boarding school known as Hogwarts — for Harry (as certain of his adventures have shown) is a wizard. As a new student, Harry is to take a train from Platform 9¾ to go to school. Unable to find the platform, he is befriended by the Weasley Family — who are amazed to meet him; it turns out that Harry is famous among wizards because the infamously evil Lord Voldemort had been unable to kill him; indeed, Voldemort's attempt to do so has apparently destroyed the "Dark Lord."

Finally safe aboard the Hogwarts Express, Harry becomes fast friends with his new classmate Ron Weasley. Upon arriving at Hogwarts, Harry and Ron are among those recruited into Gryffindor House, one of the school's four "houses" or dormitories and the one which most actively encourages good deeds and heroism. He also becomes friends, after a battle with a troll, with Hermione Granger, the smartest student in the class. He gets along with most of his teachers as well — but utterly loathes Severus Snape, the Potions master, who returns the loathing with interest.

Harry quickly becomes enamored of the wizarding activity of broomstick-riding, and finds himself recruited to Gryffindor's Quidditch team — Quidditch being the most famous wizarding sport, played on broomsticks by two teams of seven. But the Quidditch contests quickly turn ugly as someone is trying to knock Harry off his broom.

This is not the only mystery at Hogwarts in this year. Something is being hidden on the campus. After much sleuthing, Harry, Ron, and Hermione determine that it is the Philosopher's Stone, which can bring immortality — and that someone is trying to steal it. Needing to stop the theft, and unable to find anyone to help them, the three at the end of the year set out themselves to save the stone. They find their way into a guarded chamber, and lull the guardian, the three-headed dog Fluffy, to sleep with music. Then their real adventures start. Several Hogwarts teachers have set up traps for the unwary. Hermione is able to outwit most of the traps, and Ron wins a chess game against living pieces, but at last Harry must go on alone as Hermione tries to summon help. Harry comes face to face with the turbaned Professor Quirrell — whose turban hides Lord Voldemort. Harry manages to hold him off. Quirrell dies and Voldemort escapes without his minion. But Harry has had his first experience of his destiny. It will not be his last confrontation with the Dark Lord.

HARRY POTTER AND THE CHAMBER OF SECRETS

Harry expects that his magic will win him better treatment in the summer — but he is forbidden by wizarding law to use magic outside school, and his relatives still oppress him. A strange creature, a House Elf named Dobby, gets him into trouble with the Dursleys. So it is with happiness that he is rescued by the Weasleys and returns to Hogwarts, where all his friends are. New to Hogwarts is Ginny Weasley, the younger sister of Harry's friend Ron, who clearly suffers from a case of hero worship toward Harry. A series of tragedies quickly begins. Something briefly stops Harry and Ron from reaching Hogwarts; they have to fly in using a modified car, bringing trouble to Ron's father who rebuilt it.

Various people and animals are attacked and petrified — not turned to stone, but rendered immobile and unable to communicate. There are also threats written on the walls while Harry hears strange noises in the pipes.

Meanwhile, Harry discovers a diary that, somehow, seems to be alive. It was written by an earlier Hogwarts student named Tom Riddle, and Riddle describes a mysterious time half a century ago. Then, as now, rumor had it that "the Chamber of Secrets had been opened." Students died. Eventually it was concluded that the guilty party was none other than Harry's friend Hagrid. It was regarded as accidental — one of Hagrid's many strange pets had been held directly responsible; Hagrid had been allowed to stay at Hogwarts, but he was no longer permitted to practice magic.

The goings-on at Hogwarts are sufficiently serious that Lucius Malfoy, the father of Harry's worst school enemy Draco Malfoy, threatens to close the school. Hermione is one of those petrified. The diary disappears. And then — so does Ginny Weasley.

Harry, Ron, and Hermione had been concocting plans — and potions — to try to figure what was happening. They had done this in Moaning Myrtle's bathroom — a water closet haunted by the ghost of a girl who had died half a century ago. It is not a pleasant place. But Hermione, just before her petrification, had left a key clue: "Pipes." The Chamber of Secrets is accessed via the pipes in Myrtle's bathroom; she was one of the victims, fifty years earlier. Voldemort had enchanted a path so that only a Parselmouth — a speaker of snake language — could open it. But Harry, like Voldemort himself, is a Parselmouth. Harry and Ron, pushed by Professor Lockhart, the incompetent Defense against Dark Arts teacher, enter the Chamber, home of the Basilisk set there by Voldemort. Harry, helped by the phoenix Fawkes, finds Ginny, defeats the basilisk, destroys the evil diary, and is able to return to the upper world, where Hermione, Ginny, and the rest are restored to life and mobility. Harry then asks Dumbledore, the Headmaster, about other secrets, but Dumbledore answers only some of the questions; others will have to wait…. Harry does succeed in freeing Dobby from servitude to the Malfoys, winning himself a lifelong friend.

Harry Potter and the Prisoner of Azkaban

Once again the book opens with Harry in Durance Dursley. His situation is so extreme that he "blows up" his Aunt Marge and flees the Dursley home. But he is not punished; the magical government is afraid for him. Sirius Black, who had been a friend of Harry's father but who is believed to have betrayed him to death, has escaped from the Wizard prison Azkaban. He is thought to be looking for Harry. The Ministry of Magic is therefore willing to forgive a lot once they know Harry is safe.

And it is a good year at Hogwarts. Harry's friend Hagrid has a new title, Care of Magical Creatures teacher; the teacher of Defense Against Dark Arts, Remus Lupin, proves to be an excellent instructor who gives Harry special lessons in dealing with dementors, those guardians of Azkaban who give Harry particular trouble.

But there are secrets about Lupin. One is that he was a friend of Harry's father, and of Sirius Black, in school. Another dark secret is that he is a werewolf.

Hagrid, although fond of magical creatures, is not popular with some students. When he is teaching about hippogriffs, Draco Malfoy acts up and pretends that the injury he receives is very severe. Buckbeak the hippogriff is put on trial for its life, and Hagrid, no negotiator, ruins his beloved animal's chances; it is sentenced to death.

The year is dominated by Dark Arts lessons, Quidditch, the fact that Hermione seems to be taking twice as many classes as is humanly possible — plus fears about Sirius Black. Finally Harry is lured to meet Black, who seems half-mad with the desire to find Harry.

But it is not a desire to hurt Harry that Black feels. Rather, he is Harry's godfather, and wishes to renew the acquaintance. Furthermore, he wishes to have revenge on Peter Pettigrew, the man who — while pretending to be the friend of Harry's father James — had in fact betrayed him. The acts blamed on Black were in fact Pettigrew's fault. Lupin and Black have trapped Pettigrew, who until this time had been concealing himself as Ron's pet rat Scabbers — but before they can offer proof of Pettigrew's guilt, he escapes. Black is captured and immediately condemned to die at the hands of the dementors. But Headmaster Dumbledore and Hermione have one more trick to play. Hermione has been using a time turner — a device for going back in time — to take extra classes. Now she and Harry use it to free Sirius and let him escape on Buckbeak. Unfortunately, Black is still regarded as a criminal, and Peter Pettigrew is still free — and the Hogwarts Divination teacher has received a prophecy that these events foreshadow that Voldemort is about to return, his powers intact and even increased....

HARRY POTTER AND THE GOBLET OF FIRE

The book opens with Harry and Hermione visiting the Weasleys and being rewarded with the chance to see the Quidditch World Cup — the top championship in the wizarding world's top sport. But after the contest, Death Eaters (the followers of Voldemort) display their increasing boldness by showing their emblem of the Dark Mark over the camp; there is a period of confusion and chaos.

All that is forgotten when the students return to school, for it is announced that this will be the year of the revived Triwizard Tournament — a three-part competition between the top students of three schools. Only the oldest students are allowed to enter, so Harry, Ron, and Hermione are excluded. Much hilarity ensues as young students try to enter their name in the Goblet of Fire, which is to choose the contestants. But things turn deadly serious when the names are announced: Cedric Diggory of Hogwarts, Fleur Delacourt of Beauxbatons, and Viktor Krumm of Durmstrang — and Harry. Somehow, someone had managed to place his name in the Goblet of Fire as belonging to a fourth school.

Harry quickly finds that Professor "Mad-Eye" Moody, the new Defense against Dark Arts teacher, is at once highly competent and very helpful in dealing with the requirements of the event.

The tasks are spread out over a year, and Harry does well at the first, in which he uses his broomstick to snatch an egg from a dragon. In the second, rescuing his friend Ron from where he is trapped at the bottom of the Hogwarts lake, he needs help from Dobby, but shows nobility by insisting on taking all the hostages, not just his own, back.

The final task is a maze. It appears to be a simple hedge, but it is guarded by various magical guardians. The first wizard to reach the center and touch the cup wins the prize.

Cedric and Harry arrive simultaneously, agree the event is a tie, and touch the cup together. But triumph turns to tragedy as they are transported to a graveyard. Cedric is immediately killed. Harry is bound and made part of a ritual of necromancy as Peter Pettigrew — using Harry's blood and other ingredients including Pettigrew's own flesh — brings Voldemort back to life. The Death Eaters come, and Voldemort prepares to kill Harry. But Harry, by magic he does not understand, is able to hold him off long enough to escape and return to Hogwarts to warn Dumbledore and others. Only — before anything can be done, the false Mad-Eye Moody, who had disguised himself as a professor and engineered the whole thing, is killed in another of those acts of too-swift wizarding "justice." Voldemort's secrets are safe, and the Dark Lord is again loose in the world — and only Harry, Ron, Hermione, Sirius, and Dumbledore know it....

Harry Potter and the Order of the Phoenix

Probably the grimmest of all the Potter books, for Harry finds himself disbelieved and distrusted, and responds with hostility and adolescent tantrums even toward his closest friends. The Ministry of Magic, rather than admit that Voldemort is loose, tries to have Harry convicted of underage magic when he is forced to use his skills against a dementor; it also appoints an overseer, Dolores Umbridge, to look into conditions at Hogwarts.

Umbridge also teaches Defense Against Dark Arts — and refuses to teach anything useful.

The only ones who seem willing to fight Voldemort are a mysterious group called The Order of the Phoenix, which includes Dumbledore, the Weasleys, Sirius, Remus Lupin and a few others — including even Professor Snape, despite his continued sneering hatred of Harry — but which commands little political power. Gradually, Hogwarts is overtaken by rules and restrictions that make it all but impossible to learn. In despair, some of the students turn to Harry himself to train them against the Dark Arts. After much persuasion, he takes charge of a group called Dumbledore's Army, which prides itself on refusing to take Umbridge.

At night, Harry is having nightmares about trying to reach a certain mysterious place. The nightmares are real, because at one point he witnesses himself attacking Mr. Weasley — and Mr. Weasley is attacked at the very place and time of the dream. In certain circumstances, Harry is reading Voldemort's mind.

Finally Umbridge catches up with the D.A., and Harry dreams that Sirius is in danger. He insists upon going to the rescue, and a handful of other students — Hermione, Ron, Ginny, Neville Longbottom, and Luna Lovegood — are all who are prepared to go with him. They are trapped in the Ministry of Magic — for the dream had been sent by Voldemort, who wants to know the full content of a prophecy made about him at the time Harry was born, and which only Harry can access.

Fortunately, certain members of the Order of the Phoenix arrive in time to turn a one-way battle into a near-draw. But Sirius dies in the fighting. Later, Voldemort tries to take over Harry's mind; eventually the prophecy is destroyed and Dumbledore chases Voldemort off. But Dumbledore — who heard the prophecy when it was made — has to tell Harry the truth. Harry and Voldemort are inextricably linked; "Neither Can Live While the Other Survives." Harry must kill Voldemort — or be killed, and let Voldemort rule.

At least one good thing comes of it: Voldemort has been openly revealed as back. The wizarding world is on guard, and Harry's honesty and sanity are no longer in question.

Harry Potter and the Half-Blood Prince

With the lines of battle finally drawn, it is time for Harry to learn the truth. Dumbledore shows up at the Dursleys' door — one of his hands burned and withered — to personally take Harry to the Weasleys' so that he can prepare for term. And, as the schoolyear progresses, Dumbledore takes to showing Harry preserved memories in his Pensieve — memories that show how Voldemort became Voldemort.

In his classes, Harry has found himself turning into a genius with potions, having inherited an old potions book belonging to "The Half-Blood Prince" which (along with some very evil spells) contains many extremely useful potions tips. It causes Hermione to become jealous and suspicious — but it also earns him a small supply of Felix Felicis, or liquid luck.

Among the many memories (one of them Dumbledore's own) which Harry sees (indeed, one which he uses Felix Felicis to recover) is one in which Tom Riddle, the boy who came to be Voldemort, asked about *Horcruxes.*

Horcruxes seem to be the key to Voldemort's behavior. It is possible to take part of a Soul and embed it in an object for safekeeping. This guards the existence of the maker of the *horcrux* — but also damages him, for a *horcrux* can only be created by murder. And Voldemort has gone farther than most — he wanted to have seven *horcruci* so that he could survive even if one was destroyed.

And one has been destroyed; it was the diary Harry ruined in the *Chamber of Secrets.* Dumbledore had found and destroyed another — a magic black ring that had belonged to Voldemort's grandfather; it was this that cost the Headmaster the use of his hand. Now Dumbledore is seeking more. Toward the end of the year, he asks Harry to come with him as he seeks to destroy a third. They find a cave in a small island, where Voldemort has set a trap around a bowl containing a locket. The bowl's contents must be drunk to reveal it — and Dumbledore drinks and becomes deathly ill.

Harry had already been worried. There had been random attacks on — someone, and Harry is sure Draco Malfoy is up to something. He turns out to be right. Even as Harry and Dumbledore are seeking the locket, Malfoy opens an entrance to Hogwarts using a magic Vanishing Cabinet he has repaired. So Hogwarts is attacked while Dumbledore is away — and even when Dumbledore returns, he is very weak. Malfoy finds him, but cannot bring himself to kill him. It is Severus Snape — who, as a student, had called himself the "Half-Blood Prince," whose Potions book Harry had used — who comes up behind Malfoy, who says the Avada Kedavra that kills Dumbledore.

And the locket proves a false *horcrux.* A *horcrux* had been there, but someone named R.A.B. had taken it away. So Harry, Ron, and Hermione are left with the knowledge that there are many more *horcruci* to destroy — and, without Dumbledore's guidance, they know neither where nor how to look.

HARRY POTTER AND THE DEATHLY HALLOWS

As the final book of the saga opens, Harry is once again staying at the Dursleys, but his seventeenth birthday is approaching. On that day, he will finally be allowed to practice unlimited magic — but he will also lose the special protection that comes from being under the care of a relative. It may have been grudging, limited, dreadful care, but it had given Harry a chance to survive. In July, all that will change. So the plan is to take Harry to some other well-protected place. Many members of the Order of the Phoenix will escort him — and indeed be disguised as him. It is a reasonable plan, but it almost fails; Mad-Eye Moody is killed and Harry once again finds himself in battle with Voldemort. He barely survives. After a brief interlude when he witnesses the wedding of Ron's older brother Bill, he, Ron, and Hermione set out secretly to find the missing *horcruci*.

It is a miserable time; they have no home, and no place to rest in a world increasingly dominated by Voldemort, and have few skills for surviving on their own. They manage to rescue the *horcrux* stolen by R.A.B., but have no way to destroy it, and the evil it emanates is so strong that it leads Ron to abandon Harry and Hermione. Disaster is averted when Ron is guided back, and someone leads them to the Sword of Gryffindor, which can destroy the *horcrux*.

Although briefly captured by Voldemort's minions, the trio escapes — and rescues others. From a goblin, Griphook, they learn how to steal another *horcrux* from Voldemort's vault in the goblin-run bank, Gringott's. It is very difficult, and in the end they are detected. They have the *horcrux*, but have lost the sword that can destroy it — and Voldemort now knows where they are and what they seek. They need to destroy the *horcrux* and find two others, one of which they believe is at Hogwarts and the other which is the snake Nagini that Voldemort keeps with him; then they must destroy Voldemort himself. There is little choice; they must go to Hogwarts — where they find that Neville Longbottom has been leading a quiet resistance to the rules imposed by Voldemort and his subordinates. But they arrive too late. Voldemort is there, demanding that Harry Potter be turned over to him, but the larger share of the teachers and students choose to resist. As the battle proceeds, Harry determines that the missing *horcrux* is probably the Diadem of Ravenclaw. As he seeks it, Ron and Hermione destroy their one *horcrux* by going to the Chamber of Secrets and using basilisk venom. They all go to the Room of Requirement to find the Ravenclaw diadem — to be intercepted again by Draco Malfoy. Fortunately, the *horcrux* is destroyed in the altercation.

Voldemort, meanwhile, is unhappy. He has captured the great Elder Wand, the most powerful wand known, and one of the Deathly Hallows that give the book its title. But the wand does not work well for him. He determines that he must kill Severus Snape to take full ownership. But the dying Snape gives Harry his memories — and they show that Snape has been on Dumbledore's side ever since Harry's parents were slain, and that one part of Voldemort's soul, instead of becoming a *horcrux*, has lodged *inside Harry*. Harry must go before Voldemort, and die at Voldemort's hands, if Voldemort is to be slain.

Voldemort has demanded Harry's surrender. Alone, Harry sets out to surrender his life. He is taken, briefly mocked, and subjected to the killing curse.

But when Harry awakens in a formless place, something very odd happens. The spirit of the dead Dumbledore comes to him and tells him that he is not dead, and can still save the world. Harry goes back to his body, but does not reveal that he is alive. Voldemort starts his march of triumph on Hogwarts — and takes and torments Neville Longbottom. Neville, the clumsy butt of many jokes, redeems himself fully by slaying Nagini, the snake that is the last of the horcruxes. Voldemort is alone, with no protection left. He is slain by Harry, who uses no stronger curse than "expelliarmus," the wand-removing spell, and the world is cleansed.

Dictionary of Folklore References

Six (or so) Articles for Each Potter Book

Although I hope this entire dictionary will prove useful to you, the list below is intended to give a "shortcut" to major themes in each of the Harry Potter books.

Harry Potter and the Philosopher's Stone
Broomsticks
Fluffy
Hermione
The Mirror of Erised
The Philosopher's Stone
Harry's Scar
Two-Faced Figures

Harry Potter and the Chamber of Secrets
Basilisk
The Chamber of Secrets
Cornish Pixies
Dobby
House Elves
Petrification
The Phoenix
The Voice That Only One Can Hear

Harry Potter and the Prisoner of Azkaban
Animagus
Boggarts
Kappas, Grindylows, Redcaps
Peter Pettigrew's Finger
Remus
Werewolves
The Whomping Willow

Harry Potter and the Goblet of Fire

Blood
Gillyweed
Labyrinth
The (Enchanted, Merpeople's) Lake
The Ugly Duckling

Harry Potter and the Order of the Phoenix

The Door of Death
Hagrid and the Half-Giants
Hogwarts, the Edifice
The Inner Circle
Neither Can Live While the Other Survives

Harry Potter and the Half-Blood Prince

Horcruxes
Immortality
Killed His Father and Married His Mother
Love Conquers All
The Soul
Things Bought at Too High a Cost

Harry Potter and the Deathly Hallows

The Afterlife and Catching a Train
"And Give His Life as a Ransom for Many"
The Deathly Hallows
The Last Battle
The Taboo Name/The True Name
The Price
The Resurrected Hero

The Tales of Beedle the Bard

Babbitty Rabbitty (for "Babbitty Rabbitty and her Cackling Stump")
Meeting Death on the Road (for "The Tale of the Three Brothers")
The Fountain of Fair Fortune (for the tale of the same name)
Horcruxes (for "The Warlock's Hairy Heart")
The Hopping Pot (for "The Wizard and the Hopping Pot")

Achilles's Choice

In the Trojan War legend, Achilles had the choice: A long, dull life which would end with him being forgotten — or a short but brilliant life which brought him everlasting fame. He of course chose the fame.[62] (We see this, in a sense, today, when athletes have to decide whether to use steroids — improving their results but risking their health or playing football for fame with almost guaranteed brain injuries.)

There is a real similarity here to the choices made by Harry (who at least seemed to be offered the option of a long life as Voldemort's ally) and Voldemort. See Things Bought at Too High a Cost.

Acromantula

Aragog, Hagrid's first monster pet, whom we meet in the *Chamber of Secrets* and see buried in the *Half-Blood Prince*, is an acromantula — a giant, intelligent, talking, deadly spider. It's Ron's worst nightmare, "Spider's body made larger," Thompson A2301.2.

Probably the best-known intelligent spider of folklore is Anansi, the "trickster spider in West African tradition who became the executive or representative of the supreme god, but was eventually put down by the chameleon"[63] (Thompson A522.7, "Spider as culture hero"). "His exploits form cycles of popular stories and they are relished as far away as the West Indies."[64] Many examples come from Jamaica, although he seems to have been humanized there: "Annancy is a legendary being whose chief characteristic is trickery.... His appetitive is voracious, and nothing comes amiss to him, cooked or raw."[65] Interestingly, all the Jamaican

Annancy stories end with the line *Jack Mantora me no choose any.* The line is explained as being a sort of apology to hearers: "This story of mine is not aimed at anyone."[66] Could the name *Jack Mantora,* which is phonetically very close to "Acromantula,*"* be derived from that name? "Acromantula" sounds Latin, but is not; it has been proposed that it is a twist on "Arachnid," the scientific name for spiders, but this involves a very substantial phonetic shift. "Acromantula" is also very faintly reminiscent of the Greek word ακρομανης, *akromanes,* "on the brink of madness," which fits in well with the fact that it seems impossible to restrain the behavior of acromantula.

That a spider would be deadly is no surprise; although venomous spiders are in fact rare, and even the bites of poisonous spiders are rarely deadly because they insert so little venom, in Somerset it was said that "if a big black spider comes into the house it is a sure sign of death."[67] (Compare the clicking of the Death Watch Beetle,[68] which clicks in a way somewhat reminiscent of the way the acromantula produce speech.)

Horace SLUGHORN very much wanted Aragog's venom, because it was useful in potion-making. This seems to have been known to Muggles; spiders were widely used in British medicine — eating a spider was considered helpful for several conditions, and cobwebs made bandages; in addition, keeping an imprisoned spider was supposed to be a curative.[69] In other parts of Europe, it was thought that they could cure even the plague.[70] Killing spiders was thought to bring bad luck: "If that you would live and thrive, Let the spider run alive."[71]

Accursed Wanderers: see The MARK OF CAIN.

The AFTERLIFE AND CATCHING A TRAIN

In the *Deathly Hallows,* Harry "dies" (temporarily, anyway) and ends up in a blank, formless place which eventually takes the shape of King's Cross Station. But, originally, it is a place that is not a place.

It does give the impression of being underground, which is fitting for the place of the afterlife. But so is the formlessness. In Hebrew myth, Sheol (the original afterlife) was probably originally thought of as a nothing place ("There the wicked cease from troubling; there the weary are at rest" — Job 3:17), although this has been disputed. In the *Odyssey,* Odysseus visits Hades and finds it a place where there is nothing for the shades to remember. They are nothing but "drifting, listless spirits."[72]

The Norse Niflheim, ruled by the goddess Hel, was a cold, befogged place that housed the dead spirits that did not go to Valhalla.[73]

Thus the Potterverse's unsubstantial afterlife has a venerable tradition. Catching a train appears to be a genuine invention. But in Catholic legend, when Jesus was crucified, he is said to have come to Limbo (hence the words "he descended into hell" in the traditional form of the Apostle's Creed) and taken the virtuous pagans to Heaven[74] — almost like taking a train. C. S. Lewis allows the damned to visit Heaven on a sort of bus. Plus there are folk songs, such as "The Gospel Train," telling hearers to "Get On Board, Little Children."[75]

In a way, Harry's creation of his after-world resembles even more J. R. R. Tolkien's concept of "sub-creation," in which a created being (a human) can nonetheless create, or at least imagine creating, new worlds or changes within the existing world.

Harry's choice of whether to return to the living world has a number of partial parallels — e.g. Ged has to be forced to leave the land of the dead in LeGuin's *The Farthest Shore*. But it is perhaps most reminiscent of the question asked of Galahad after he has achieved the grail in Malory's *Morte d'Arthur*: does he wish to go back to the mundane world? Galahad, having no earthly ties, decides not to go back. Harry, by contrast, loves Ginny and Ron and Hermione; he returns to his body to save them.

The "Abode of the Dead" is Thompson motif E480. The "choice between life or heaven," which Harry has to make when he decides to leave the undefined place, is V311.3.

See also UNDERGROUND ADVENTURES.

Age: see OLD AGE

AGRIPPA

One of the famous wizards whose chocolate frog card Harry collects on the Hogwarts Express in the *Philosopher's Stone*. Unlike most of those other wizards, Agrippa was a real person, well-known in the Muggle world. The question is, *which* real person. History is full of important Agrippas. The first, whose fame in effect brought the others to fame, was Marcus Vipsanius Agrippa (63–12 B.C.E.), who was the right-hand man of the Roman Emperor Augustus; it was Agrippa who won the battle of Actium that guaranteed Augustus control of the Roman Republic.[76]

One of Agrippa's daughters was Vipsania, the wife of the emperor Tiberius; another was Agrippina I (died 33), the mother of the future emperor Gaius (Caligula).[77] Gaius's sister was Agrippina II (died 59), who was the wife of the Emperor Claudius and the mother of Nero by a different husband.[78] Two kings mentioned in the New Testament, (Herod) Agrippa I[79] and his son (Herod) Agrippa II,[80] were named for Marcus Agrippa.

There is also the Menenius Agrippa who appears in Shakespeare's *Coriolanus* and talks the people out of a revolt with the so-called "parable of the belly."[81]

But the Agrippa of the frog card is probably Heinrich Cornelius Agrippa von Nettesheim (1486–1535), a German alchemist, astrologer, and magician who dabbled in philosophy and spent time as a courtier. Unlike his near-contemporary Paracelsus, who also had a chocolate frog card, there is no hint that Agrippa was any sort of scientist. He wrote (in Latin) *De occulta philosophia,* "The Occult Philosophy," the final edition of which was published in 1533; in it, "his point of departure is that magic is the supreme science and constitutes the true path to the knowledge of God and nature."[82] He also wrote *De incertitudine et vanitate scientiarum et artium, atque excellentia Verbi Dei, declamatio invectiva,* "On the Uncertainty and Vanity of the Arts and Sciences: An Invective Declamation," a general attack on knowledge (it favored divine inspiration).[83]

Supposedly Agrippa was one of the models for Goethe's *Faust.*[84]

ALBERIC GRUNNION

One of the famous wizards whose chocolate frog card Harry collects on the Hogwarts Express in the *Philosopher's Stone.* There does not ever seem to have been an actual person by this name, but the name "Alberic" is interesting, since it is clearly related to "Alberich." Alberich was the king of the dwarfs in Norse legend who had access to many highly magical objects — e.g. he gave Sigfried his magic sword Balamung and an invisibility cloak.[85] Richard Wagner, however, made him a much more ordinary character — an evil dwarf who cursed the Nibelungen hoard.

The name "Grunnion" does not seem to mean anything; there is a type of fish known as a "grunion," but the spelling is different.

AMULETS

There are, in the Harry Potter books, a number of unique magical objects — the PHILOSOPHER'S STONE, the Goblet of Fire, the Sword of Gryffindor, the Diadem of Ravenclaw, the Sorting Hat — plus, of course, all three of the DEATHLY HALLOWS. All of these are described as having unique properties. Such objects are often known as "amulets" in the literature of fantasy[86] — and Thompson notes a dozen or so folkloric amulet motifs. Other sources call them "talismans."[87] The curiosity about such items is that it seems to be impossible to replicate them, and they often have no known creator. We know who made the Philosopher's Stone, and Dumbledore's Deluminator, but most of the others just appear.

Amulets have a venerable history. The Palladium was said to guard Troy, so that its theft was required before the city could fall.[88] The Stone of Scone, on which the Kings of Scotland were crowned, was said to have amulet-like powers — hence its later name "The Stone of Destiny."[89] The Black Crochan (for which see the DEATHLY HALLOWS) was an amulet of sorts. The Holy Grail was, well, the Holy Grail of amulets.

Amulets have a bad tendency to drive plots toward the status of a game — "you must find the Wizarding Wand to be able to enter the Cave of Charlemagne to find the Jewel of Justice which will open the Rock of Revenge...." Amulets of this type have been sarcastically labelled "plot coupons."[90] We see a hint of this in *The Deathly Hallows* as the characters seek the HORCRUXES — most of which, we note, are also amulets (or were, before Voldemort corrupted them). This shows the strong interdependence of amulet tales.

Ancient Runes: see under BEEDLE THE BARD

"AND GIVE HIS LIFE AS A RANSOM FOR MANY"

Many religions involve someone being sacrificed for others — this is the whole basis for such barbaric rites as the Aztec version of human sacrifice.[91] The quotation which gives this section its name is from Mark 10:45 (compare Matthew 20:28): "For the Son of Man came not to be served but to serve, and to give his life as a ransom for many." The parallels between Harry's passion[92] and Jesus's are frequently close:

"he was to dispose of Voldemort's remaining links to life, so that when at last he flung himself across Voldemort's path, and did not raise a wand to defend himself, the end would be clean." Compare Isaiah 53:7–8: "Like a lamb that is led to slaughter, and like a sheep that before its shearers is silent, so he did not open his mouth. By a perversion of justice he was taken away.... For he was cut off from the land of the living" (also quoted in Acts 8:32).

"This cold-blooded walk to destruction would require a different kind of bravery." Harry goes through emotional torture as he prepares to die, and cries out to his parents and friends, who come to guard him. How like Jesus in Gethsemane: "Then an angel from heaven appeared to him and gave him strength. In his anguish he prayed more earnestly, and his sweat became like great drops of blood falling down on the ground" (Luke 22:43–44, although this passage is not in fact part of the Gospel, being a later interpolation). But while that incident is a unique insertion in Luke, the idea of Jesus's suffering before he is taken is found in all the passion narratives: "He said, 'Abba, Father, for you all things are possible; remove this cup from me; yet, not what I want, but what you want'" (Mark 14:36).

Harry goes to his death without any living companion. Similarly Jesus: "All of them deserted him and fled" (Mark 14:50).

Harry says only two words before Voldemort: "You weren't." Similarly, Jesus is mostly silent at his trial: "Pilate asked him again, 'Have you no answer? See how many charges they bring against you.' But Jesus made no answer, so that Pilate was amazed" (Mark 15:4–5).

And, of course, both Jesus and Harry come back from the dead — although it happens faster in Harry's case.

See also THINGS BOUGHT AT TOO HIGH A COST.

AND LEAD US NOT INTO TEMPTATION

The words "And lead us not into temptation" are the familiar form of one of the phrases of the Lord's Prayer (Matthew 6:13, Luke 11:4 as given in the King James Bible). It is worth noting that Tolkien was thinking of this phrase when he wrote the climax of *The Lord of the Rings,* when Frodo is in Mount Doom and trying (failing) to destroy the One Ring.[93] In fact, this scene was meant to be an exemplum (illustration) of "And lead us not into temptation, but deliver us from evil." Tom Shippey argues[94] that this is one of the greatest strength of *The Lord of the Rings,* in that it shows evil both from the inside (temptation) and the outside (external evil from which we must be delivered).

In the very first Potter book, we find temptation given visible form in the MIRROR OF ERISED — and we are told that people lose themselves in it, just as Tolkien's ring (and its predecessor, the Nibelungen ring) could take over the soul.[95] Harry meets other temptations — at the end of the *Philosopher's Stone,* Voldemort addresses Harry for the first time, and tells him, "Better save your own life and join me."

This is not the last time someone will try to tempt Harry into something. Nor is Voldemort the only tempter. Consider the underwater scene in the *Goblet of Fire,* where Harry might be tempted to win and get on with the contest rather than trying to save the other precious people.

The whole business of temptation scenes seems largely inspired by Jesus and the Temptation, when Satan shows him "all the kingdoms of the earth" (Matthew 4:1–11). There are some linguistic similarities between the Biblical scene and the Temptation of Harry by Voldemort. Most of these folkloric temptations fail (if they fail) because the Tempter offers the Temptee what *the Tempter* wants — typically power (as in both the cases of the Devil and Voldemort; similarly, the One Ring seems to offer power rather than, say, friendship). What might have happened had Voldemort offered Harry a reunion with his parents? But evil does not understand good… (on this point see DEEP MAGIC AND DEEPER MAGIC and THINGS BOUGHT AT TOO HIGH A COST).

Ancient tales about the dangers of temptation are common — indeed, many mythologies start with a successful temptation. This includes, in fact, the Bible, where Eve is successfully tempted (Genesis 3:1–6 — where the tempter, we note, is a serpent, the creature most associated with Voldemort). The Greeks had a near-parallel: Pandora was tempted into opening her box, and so set many curses loose on the world.[96] The Trojan War arose because Paris was tempted by the most beautiful woman in the world.[97] The Cupid and Psyche myth is also built around a temptation (Psyche being urged to see her lover's face),[98] and has gone into many folktales such as "East of the Sun and West of the Moon"[99] and the less common "The Enchanted Pig;"[100] also the Middle English ROMANCE "Partenope of Blois."[101] The Bluebeard legend sees Bluebeard deliberately tempting his wife to enter the room in which the dead bodies are kept.[102] The fall of the Arthurian kingdom, in the late forms of the legend, is also attributed to yielding to temptation: First Arthur wanted Guinivere, then Lancelot desired her (and maybe Mordred did as well), and all took her up in turn.

Thus yielding to temptation is a very common folklore motif. But Christianity turns it on its head, as Jesus resists temptation and immediately thereafter begins his public ministry. Rowling follows this in having Harry largely resist temptation — where Tolkien's Frodo, e.g., failed. Once again Rowling takes the mostly Christian viewpoint.

Temptation ultimately proved fatal to both Dumbledore and Voldemort. Dumbledore was tempted to see his family and so use the Resurrection Stone; Voldemort was tempted to extend his life. Which temptation is more inherently "moral" must be left as an exercise for the reader (although Dumbledore clearly pursues his temptation in a more ethical manner). It is fascinating that neither dies at once. (Similarly those tempted by the Rings in Tolkien — and also Adam and Eve. Eating the Forbidden Fruit did not cause them to die at once; it caused them to become mortal.) Evidently death by temptation is slow — and, perhaps, painful.

AND THEY ALL LIVED HAPPILY EVER AFTER

This is a curious motif of relatively recent folktales — and false, in the sense that everybody dies eventually. Many early folktales have unhappy endings. The first report of (not-yet-called-King) Arthur is that he won a battle at Badon but died at Camlann.[103] Sir Gawain loved Dame Ragnall above all others — only to have her die young.[104] Beowulf kills Grendel but dies in battle with the dragon, leaving his kingdom to be destroyed[105] — a sort of gloom that pervades almost all Anglo-Saxon literature; the hero may win this fight, but *wyrd* (fate) will catch up eventually. Nor did this idea die with the Norman Conquest; the "Gest of Robyn Hode," the earliest substantial tale of Robin Hood, ends with his death by treachery.[106] And almost everybody who fights in the Trojan War has an unhappy homecoming.

In the modern tales, Alexander's Taran gives up immortality in order to fulfill his (self-defined) duty. Shallow critics have maintained that Tolkien's *The Lord of the Rings* has a purely happy ending because all eight "good" characters of the Fellowship survive — indeed, at least four and probably five of eight end up in the immortal realm. But, to Tolkien, this is a tragic ending — Frodo can no longer stay in Middle-Earth. Galadriel calls it the "long defeat" — Sauron is overcome but the Elves leave Middle-Earth and their works fade away. Similarly, LeGuin's Ged survives and saves the world but loses all he had lived for. (For this theme, see the PRICE.)

Rowling's surviving characters, on the other hand, do live Happily Ever After. This is the one of the first (well, alphabetically the first; chronologically the last) of a number of indications that the Harry Potter books have an extreme degree of optimism, more like Christianity than folktale. In the Harry Potter universe, even the people who die live in another form (note Dumbledore's two *different* types of appearance after his death), just as in Christianity.

Rowling's universe also has an interesting aspect in that the world is not fundamentally changed by the events in the story. In both Tolkien and Alexander, the world is diminished — in both, magic is effectively eliminated; also, in Tolkien, the Elves leave Middle-Earth. Similarly, "From the time of Chaucer onwards, the Fairies have been said to have departed or to be in decline." The quasi-technical term for this increasing "mundanity" of the world is "thinning."[107] Marion Zimmer Bradley also played with this in *The Mists of Avalon;* Arthur's magic world no longer connects to this world. Thinning also takes place in LeGuin's Earthsea, although we only see this fully worked out in her later follow-ons. Some have regarded thinning as a standard part of fantasies; it is an indication of Rowling's independence of vision that the Potter books show no hint of it.

ANIMAGUS

Although all competent wizards in the Potter universe can transfigure themselves, only a handful — the animagi — can do it natively and apparently without use of wand or incantation. These transformations are always to a particular animal.

This motif is not common in recent fiction — of the major authors cited here, only Tolkien really uses it, and the animagus involved, Beorn, is a minor character; indeed, there are hints that Tolkien wanted to transform him from a skin-changer to a berserker.

But animagi are common in folklore; the Greek goddess Hecate, who was in charge of sorcery and magic, was sometimes credited with the ability to transform into a dog,[108] and Proteus was so good at changing shape that his name gave us the word "protean."

The tale of the Animal Brothers-in-Law is Thompson 552/B314. In this tale, three sisters, unable to find husbands, marry beast-men. The beasts can all transform into humans at times, and all give the girls' brother a token which he can use to call them. He is then able to perform great feats with their help.

There is an instance of beast-transformation in the Scandinavian legends which Tolkien knew so well: *Hrolf Kraki's Saga* features a character named Böthvarr Bjarki, whose surname means "Little Bear" and whose parents both have bear names. According to Tom Shippey, he seems to have been a man who could become a bear.[109]

A variation on this idea is the literal skin-changer, in which a creature both human and animal leaves behind an actual animal skin as it becomes human — and a human can fix it in human form by stealing the skin. The most common version of this, according to Thompson, is probably the swan-maiden — although some of the versions have the odd motif of swan-women shedding their skins to go into the water. (And doing so isn't smart, since it obviously gives someone the chance to steal the skin and force marriage on the woman.) In the Burmese tale "The Snake Prince," which is much like the English story of "Beauty and the Beast" combined with the temptation in the story of Cupid and Psyche, we see a character who becomes a snake when he puts on his skin, a human when it is taken off[110] (Thompson B646.1, "Marriage to person in snake form"). But we also see the skin-changing in the tales of Silkies/Selkies, the Seal Folk. Some legends make them seals by day and human by night, but usually they shed their skins (Thompson D1025.9, "magic seal skin"). Like the swan maidens, the women are said to be extraordinarily beautiful, with shining black hair and magic eyes. Although the legends are known mostly from the Orkneys and Shetlands, there are some traces in Scotland — one legend says that the MacDonalds are descended from a selkie. Williams, pp. 102–103, says that an early MacDonald chief was allowed to wed Fionna, the daughter of the King of the Seals, but only if he never spoke an angry word to her. They had a son, but one day MacDonald spoke harshly to her. She kissed her babe and returned to sea. Heartbroken, he brought up the boy, from whom the MacDonald chiefs are descended. Then, when the boy came of age, he made his son the chief and sailed away into the west, never to be seen again. One of the most beautiful of the Scots ballads is "The Great Silkie of Sule Skerry," in which the selkie declares,

> I am a man upon the land,
> I am a selkie in the sea,
> And when I'm far and far frae land,
> My home it is in Sule Skerry.[111]

Hardwick reports that the Irish thought of seals as "'the souls of thim *[sic.]* that were drowned at the flood.' They were supposed to possess the power of casting aside their external skins, and disporting themselves in human form on the sea-shore. If a mortal contrived to become possessed of one of these outer coverings belonging to a female, he might claim her and keep her as his bride. This seems to point to the origin of the stories about 'mermaids' and some similar sea monsters."[112]

See also TRANSFIGURATION, and note the prevalence of the theme of changing body-types in Ovid's *Metamorphoses*.

Curiously, Voldemort's many powers and his close affinity with serpents do not seem to include the ability to become a snake. This is the more surprising since snake transformations are relatively well-attested in fantasy, and the people who can perform the feat are frequently notably evil. Involuntary transformations into a snake are also well-known in folk song, being found in "Tam Lin" (Child #39), "Kemp Owyne" (Child #34), "Allison Gross" (Child #35), "The Laily Worm and the Machrel of the Sea" (Child #36), and sundry Danish ballads.[113] The French legend of Melusine/Melusina/Melisande involves a woman who was transformed into a half-human, half-snake for one day a week.[114]

Although Muggles have found ways to replicate many magical feats, this one is likely to prove beyond them. The selkie conversion from seal to human did not involve a very great difference in the size of the animals; it is at least possible that it followed the most basic law of physics, the law of conservation of mass/energy. This clearly is *not* true for animagi, since Peter Pettigrew turned into a rat and Minerva McGonagle into a cat, both much smaller than the human being. This implies that the body is not simply "rearranged" but somehow rebuilt. Obviously the method of this is beyond our speculation.

See also Sirius BLACK, WEREWOLVES.

Aragog: see under **ACROMANTULA.**

Argus Filch: see under **HERMIONE.**

ARITHMANCY

As with most Hogwarts subjects which might involve actual logical *thinking,* we never see Arithmancy in action. So it's not entirely clear what it is. The name is based on the Greek roots αριθμος, *arithmos, number* (whence, obviously, "arithmetic") and μαντεια, *manteia, prophecy, the power of prophecy.* The most likely meaning is *prophecy based on numbers.* The curious fact, in that case, is that Hermione never seems to use Arithmancy to make a prediction. One might suspect, therefore, that Arithmancy is really what we might call "magical theory" — constructing a logical, mathematical, scientific framework for magic (something which is patently necessary but of which there isn't even a faint hint in the tales as we have them).

In the Muggle world, however "Arithmancy" is indeed used to refer to prophecy based on numbers — an area more often known as "numerology."[115] Another name is "Gematria," and this version of arithmancy is actually used in the Bible. In Rev. 13:18, we read that the "Number of the Beast" is 666. And this was only the beginning; "The Talmudic, Midrashic, and Cabalistic literatures developed and used for the interpretation of the Scriptures a sort of numerology called Gematria (אירטמג), a Hebraized form of γεωμετρία, which sought to discover the hidden sense of the Hebrew text through the numerical values of the letters of the alphabet."[116]

On the other hand, Dumbledore would surely have approved of the fact that הבהא, *ahabah, love,* has the same value, 13, as דחא, *echad, one,*[117] which could be interpreted as meaning God ("the one") is love, or that love is the first thing.

Similar sorts of calculations occur in many cultures. The Roman historian Suetonius knew another Greek arithmantic calculation about Nero (who clearly got around), noting a nasty poem that said

> Count the numerical values
> Of the letters in Nero's name,
> And in "murdered his own mother":
> You will find their sum is the same.[118]

Νερων, *Neron, Nero,* has value 1005, and so does ιδιαν μητερα απεκτεινε, *idian metera apekteine, own mother murdered.*[119] And Nero did in fact eliminate his own mother Agrippina the Younger.

See also PROPHECIES FULFILLED ONLY BECAUSE SOMEONE TRIES TO PREVENT THEM.

Atonement: see under "AND GIVE HIS LIFE AS A RANSOM FOR MANY" and THE PRICE.

AVADA KEDAVRA

"Death by pointing" is Thompson Type D2061.2.3. In the Potterverse, the power to do it comes from the words "avada kedavra." Apparently Muggles learned the words "avada kedavra," but learned them slightly wrong and made them into an incantation, "abracadabra." Then they had to *explain* it — which was tricky, since it was recorded in a Roman text, perhaps by Quintus Serenus Sammonicus, but the language was not Latin.[120] It was often engraved on amulets in a triangle shape:[121]

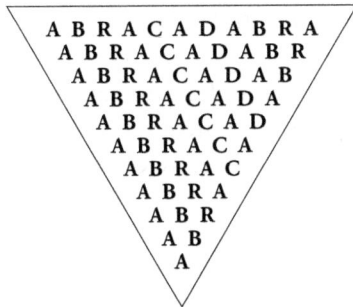

```
A B R A C A D A B R A
  A B R A C A D A B R
    A B R A C A D A B
      A B R A C A D A
        A B R A C A D
          A B R A C A
            A B R A C
              A B R A
                A B R
                  A B
                    A
```

Note that the top edge of the triangle reads "Abracadabra," the right edge reads "Abracadabra" backward, and the left edge reads all the letter "A." (This is because the word has an odd number of letters, and five of those letters, distributed symmetrically, are the letter "A.")

It's worth noting that B and V are closely similar phonemes — e.g. Greek β used to be pronounced as a "b" sound but now carries a "v" sound; if a classical Greek had heard "avra kadavra," he would have written "abra kadabra." So to get from "Avada..." to "Abra..." is a trivial change.

There are at least three explanations for what the original word was. One explanation makes it a cabbalistic charm, made up from the Hebrew elements **AB** (father), **B**en (son), and **R**uach **ACAD**sch (Holy Spirit),[122] i.e. בא ב ר שדק. This is probably the most Christian explanation.

A second explanation makes it a distortion of a different Hebrew construction, *arba-echad-arba, four-one-four,* the idea being to give the symbolic number nine.[123]

A third possibility is that it is a distortion of an Aramaic phrase such as *avra k'davra, I will make as I say* or *Let what I say come to be* — not so much a spell as an affirmation of power.[124]

There was a malicious Singhalese spirit known as "Dala Kadavara,"[125] but that is probably unrelated.

It will be evident that none of these explanations is particularly convincing. Which might explain why Rowling herself said that *abracadabra* means "let the thing be destroyed."[126]

The words "kedavra" is similar to "cadaver," which is an interesting twist. "Cadaver" is of course an English word for a dead body — but it is also the *Latin* word for a corpse, and most wizarding spells are in somewhat banged-up Latin. "Avada" isn't a Latin word, but it has some similarities to some interesting Latin words: *aveho, to carry away,* or *avide, eagerly, readily,* etc. So *Avada Kadavra* might be a twist on "I want you to be a corpse" or "They will carry off your corpse."

It is perhaps ironic to note that "Abracadabra" amulets were listed as "an infallible receipt for the cure of an ague"; it was said that over a hundred people at Wells, Somerset were cured by this means.[127]

Babbitty Rabbitty

This tale is a combination of many different themes. The king who hires a charlatan to learn magic is a minor variant of "The Emperor's New Clothes," which is by Hans Christian Andersen (Thompson K445). The idea of a charlatan using tricks to pass himself off as a magician is real, as the history of alchemy shows (see an example under the Philosopher's Stone); it is also a key element of *The Wizard of Oz*. See also Animagus for the issue of Babbitty's transformative ability. The offstage helper is a frequent motif, not confined to magic; consider, e.g., the story of Cyrano de Bergerac. For witch hunts, see the entry on Wizards. "The Magician and His Pupil," a tale in which the pupil is apprenticed to a mage and has to try to escape him, is Thompson tale 325, although in that tale the apprentice's magic works, as it does not in "Babbitty."

The most original part of the printed version of "Babbitty" may be Dumbledore's notes, regarding Lisette de Lapin and the rabbit which allegedly advised King Henry VI. There is, of course, no record of a rabbit who advised Henry VI. (There *is* the case of the Roman Emperor Gaius/Caligula, who made his horse consul, i.e. a high state official,[128] but even that did not involve actual advice.) But if any English king had done such a thing, it would be Henry VI. England has had a number of mentally troubled kings — Henry VII and Henry VIII were obvious sociopaths, and Richard I also showed signs of that. John and Edward II displayed symptoms of autism. Henry V and Richard II were megalomaniacs. Henry III was pretty stupid, as were most of the Stuarts.

But only two English kings were regarded as patently mad: Henry VI and George III. And George III lived after Beedle's time (and there is some debate about just how crazy he was anyway). About Henry

VI, there is no doubt. "The only [English king] to be crowned king of France; and arguably the worst, who inherited two kingdoms and lost both."[129] Our records for this period are few (meaning that, just possibly, there could have been a rabbit counselor), but we know that during the summer of 1453, Henry VI fell into a catatonic state which lasted for about fifteen months.[130] He did recover temporarily, but he seems never to have been quite the same,[131] and there were later spells of madness. We cannot, at this distance, diagnose his malady, but it is noteworthy that his grandfather, the French King Charles VI, suffered from violent madness,[132] as well as from delusions such as a belief that he was made of glass, so it is not entirely impossible that Henry suffered similar illusions.

Interestingly, if de Lapin (whose name *means* rabbit) had lived a little earlier, she might have introduced rabbit-kind to England; rabbits are not native to Britain.

The idea of rabbits being associated with witches is unusual in England, perhaps because they didn't arrive in the country until the late Middle Ages, but hares are reported to be a common familiar of witches.[133]

The name "Babbitty Rabbitty" is a three-syllable feminine rhyme, but what suggested the first name "Babbitty"? Very likely a "bairn's rhyme," or a children's game from Scotland. "Babbity Bowster" is quite well-known, and has been cited since at least 1828. A typical version begins,

> Wha learnt ye to dance, Babbity Bowster, Babbity Bowster?
> Wha learnt ye to dance, Babbity Bowster brawly?
> Ma mither learnt me to dance, Babbity Bowster, Babbity Bowster,
> Ma mither learnt me to dance, Babbity Bowster brawly.[134]

Which translates as

> Who taught you to dance, Babbity Bowster, Babbity Bowster?
> Who taught you to dance, Babbity Bowster bravely/handsomely?
> My mother taught me to dance...

BANSHEE

We don't meet a banshee in the Potter books, but in the *Chamber of Secrets* Gilderoy LOCKHART refers to banishing the Bandon Banshee. In the *Prisoner of Azkaban,* when Seamus Finnegan faces the BOGGART in Defense against Dark Arts, what he sees is a banshee — described as a woman with very long black hair and greenish skin on a skeletal frame. In the *Goblet of Fire,* Seamus compares the sound made by Harry's golden EGG to the cry of a banshee, and suggests Harry might have to fight one — without saying why this was so difficult.

If anyone in Harry's class should fear a banshee, it is certainly Seamus, since the banshee is primarily Irish (the name is used in Scotland, but the Scottish banshee is "simply a fairy woman"; she does not have any particular mythological function.[135] The original word was probably *bean sidhe* (Irish Gaelic) or *ban sith* (Scots Gaelic) a name meaning "woman of the fairies";[136] alternately, the root is *bean sí,* with similar meaning. It is a "female spirit that, in folk belief, is heard to cry when the death of a member of an Irish family is imminent. [Compare the GRIM.] The designation means 'other-world lady,' and the banshee is invariably a solitary being. Her cry is described as plaintive and very much like that of a keening woman of this world."[137] She usually cries near the place where the victim is to die. It is sometimes said that only the Irish, or only those with traditional names starting with Ó or Mac, have banshees. (It has been suggested that, after centuries of intermarriage, most people descend from someone in these families, so banshees can now follow almost anyone.[138]) It is further said that the cry of the banshee cannot be stopped by walls or the thickest blankets. A few accounts describe a banshee as beating a drum rather than shrieking.[139] There are various irreconcilable descriptions of the banshee's appearance — young or old, beautiful or a hag; some accounts say her eyes are bloodshot with weeping for those she is concerned with. She supposedly "bears nothing but goodwill from those she would protect"[140] — indeed, having a banshee was regarded as a mark of status.[141] Thus it is far from clear why Gilderoy LOCKHART would wish to banish a banshee, or why Seamus feared it so (unless it was that he feared that it would announce his own death); they bore bad news but did not cause it.

The Scots had an equivalent of the Banshee, known in the Gaelic as the Caoineag; unlike the Banshee, it stayed hidden even when keening.[142]

It has been suggested that the banshee was originally a princess of the native people of Ireland, but the meaning changed as Christianity gained influence.[143]

BASILISK

Knowledge of Latin is evidently widespread in the wizarding world — after all, the spells are mostly in Latin (they aren't *all* in Latin, but Reagin, pp. 39–40, declares that "Counting conservatively, there are about 140 spells in all seven books. Of these, 72 are either Latin, Latin-derived, or Latin in part.") — but whoever named the basilisk didn't pay much attention to Greek, because βασιλισκοσ, *basiliskos*, means "*little* king." (A plain old normal-sized king is a βασιλευς, *basileus*). A catalog of dragon-like creatures points out that "small dragons are [attested] — the basilisk is a famous example."[144] The basilisk is said to be "the King of the Small Serpents (the Dragon being King of the Larger Serpents)."[145] The monster of the *Chamber of Secrets,* however, is more than a little oversize — according to *Fantastic Beasts,* a basilisk can grow to be fifty feet long. The use of such an incorrect name is all the more peculiar because, according to *Fantastic Beasts,* Herpo the Foul, who created the basilisk, was himself Greek. (His name, in fact, is the same as the Greek verb ἕρπω, *herpo, to creep or crawl,* which gave us such words as *herpetologist,* one who studies reptiles. *Herpo* is the first person singular, meaning his name should be translated as *I creep.*)

How little was a classical *basiliskos*? Well, Aesop (one of the first sources to use the word) used it for the golden-crested wren![146] (The crest, which looks a little like a crown, may have suggested the name basilisk; some portrayals of the basilisk show it with a crest or even a crown.)

The serpent form of basilisk is mentioned by Pliny and in the LXX, the Greek translation of the Old Testament, in Psalm 90/91:13 and Isaiah 59:5. In both instances, the Hebrew seems to refer merely to a poisonous snake; it has been speculated that the Greek word originally meant a cobra.

Folklore going back to Pliny has it that a basilisk was born of a cock's egg (not quite as crazy an idea as it sounds, given the way most birds' plumbing works, but let's not get into that). *Fantastic Beasts* says that a basilisk was incubated by a toad; other folklore suggests that a snake did the job. The resulting creature combined the traits of serpent and bird, with head and feet of a cock, and perhaps wings, but a serpent's body. Its gaze and its breath were both poisonous — a fact alluded to by Shakespeare on at least two occasions. (Shakespeare, in *King Henry VI,*

Part II (Act III, scene ii, lines 52–53 [p. 648] in the Riverside edition) says, "Come, basilisk, And kill the innocent gazer with thy sight." In *Richard III,* Anne Neville wishes she had a basilisk's eyes to kill Richard; when he says, "Thine eyes, sweet lady, have infected mine," she shrieks back, "Would they were basilisks, to strike thee dead!" (Act I, scene ii, lines 149–150 [p. 716] in the Riverside edition). Sadly for the truth of this completely non-historical play, it appears that Edward Prince of Wales, Anne's husband, was killed in battle, not by Richard, and there are slight but significant indications that Richard and Anne were happily married.) There are a few mentions of an ability to turn to stone (see PETRIFICATION), but is not one of its normal abilities. Its primary enemy was the weasel (more evidence that it was small — probably pigeon- or chicken-sized); also, the crow of a cock could be fatal to it. Christians sometimes equated it with the antichrist.

Voorzieninghen raedt,   Booſheyt wederſtaet,

"The Basilisk and the Weasel," woodcut attributed to Wenceslaus Hollar (died 1677). Source: Wikimedia Commons.

Most folklorists say that a basilisk is the same as a cockatrice, which is mentioned, e.g., in *Romeo and Juliet.* It would appear that the wizarding world distinguishes them, however, since in the *Goblet of Fire* we read that a cockatrice disrupted the Triwizard Tournament of 1792 (the contestants had actually been called upon to deal with the thing). Perhaps, in the wizarding world, a basilisk is large and a cockatrice small.

The *Chamber of Secrets* says that "the Basilisk flees only from the crowing of the rooster." This is an interesting phenomenon, because the crowing of a rooster was known to rout the undead. In the ballad "The Grey Cock," (Child #248) for instance, we hear the girl beg her rooster, "say, don't you crow before day," so that her dead love can stay with her, but "the cock prov'd false, and untrue he was, For he crew an hour o'er soon," and she is forced to send her love away before daybreak. In this version, the danger is not the actual cock-crow but the arrival of the light, but other versions make the cock-crow itself the threat.

(Children Found in) Baskets: see The Unwanted Child.

Beedle the Bard

Beedle the Bard is the wizarding Mother Goose — the source to whom all the great fairy tales are attributed.

The introduction to *Beedle* (p. ix) states that Beedle lived in fifteenth century Yorkshire. Scholars have exerted great ingenuity to try to defend this statement in the face of very strong evidence to the contrary.

For starters, the fact that the tales are attributed to Beedle should not be interpreted as evidence that Beedle was a real person, or — if he *did* exist — that he in fact collected or told the stories attributed to him. Collections of folk tales in other languages prove this. Mother Goose, the reputed source of English fairy tales, was not real, and the stories attributed to her in fact came from many different sources. A few examples will make this clear. "Cinderella" is known throughout Europe, but the version you probably have heard is from Charles Perrault.[147] "Little Red Riding Hood" is best known from the version published by Charles and Wilhelm Grimm, even though Perrault had a version (as the Grimms had a "Cinderella"). "Hansel and Gretl" and "Snow White" are purely Grimm tales. "Sleeping Beauty" is another known from both Perrault and Grimm. "Beauty and the Beast" is usually told in a form based on Jeanne-Marie Leprince de Beaumont, but the basic Cupid and Psyche story goes back to Roman times — and shows up in many other guises such as "East of the Sun and West of the Moon." Few would recognize any version of "Rapunzel" other than that by the Grimms, but some connect the story with that of St. Barbara, which was well-known in the version of Christine de Pisan — one of the first women to make a living from literature. "Rumplestiltskin" is the Grimms' name for a character known in an English story as "Tom Tit Tot." "The Ugly Duckling" came out of the head of Hans Christian Andersen. The point is, although moderns tend to know fairy tales from collections (those by Andrew Lang being probably the most famous in English), the stories are much older, and usually weren't found together.

The name "Mother Goose" as a teller of folk tales goes back to seventeenth century France, when a book refers to a tale which is like a "conte de la Mère Oye" — a "story of Mother Goose."[148] The name seems to have come into English in 1729 when Charles Perrault's fairy tale book *Contes du Temps Passé (Tales of Past Times)* was translated with the title *Mother Goose's Tales.*[149] The name was popularized by a book called *Mother Goose's Melody,* which lists no author but was printed around 1765.[150] This book, however, was a collection of rhymes rather than tales, and even those rhymes generally came from older sources.

None of which tells us anything about Beedle, of course. But it tells us what his forerunners *might* have been like. And it tells us why the details reported about him — that he was a bard, that he lived in Yorkshire, that the original written version of his tales were in runes — are all themselves folklore.

Even his name shows signs of being a pseudonym. It is, obviously, much the same as the word "beadle," an official in the Church of England responsible for public announcements and church organization. The term "beadle" derives from the Old English verb *bēodan, to proclaim, announce, command.* Thus Beedle the Bard, by analogy, would be "Proclaimer the Poet." The most probable meaning is 'one who assembled' (an audience, or group of pupils), so 'teacher, academician'; but the term is suggestive rather than precise."[151]

Beedle's tales are not the work of bards. Neither are Muggle fairy tales. Bards were Celtic performers who usually sang to the harp; their productions were generally metrical, and Beedle's tales are not.

There is of course a slight chance that Beedle's tales were "translated" out of poetic versions in ancient runes, but the runic version gives every sign of being a later creation intended to enhance the antiquity and authority of the tales. For one thing, the tales are patently too modern to have been written in Middle English, which was the language of fifteenth century Yorkshire.

On the whole, based on the tiny bits of information we have, it appears likely that the Hogwarts subject "Ancient Runes" is actually Old English (or some other early Germanic language such as Old German or Old Norse or Gothic[152]) anachronistically written in the earlier Teutonic runes. The decision to use runes may have been because there seems to be a belief that runes were somehow more "pagan" and "magical" than the Latin alphabet which arrived with Christianity. Brøndstedt, p. 195: "The runes were thought by the Germanic people, and the Northerners too, to possess occult powers…. This concept is reflected in the Norse myth of Odin, wisest of the gods: even he is not credited with inventing the runes but rather with finding them and releasing from them their magical powers." But even if this is true of the original "Futhark" runic alphabet of 24 letters, it does not apply to the 33 letter "Futhorc." J. R. R. Tolkien declared that the runes are "so closely *if accidentally* associated with pagan traditions" (Tolkien-Sigurd, p. 25; italics added), by which he seems to mean that the runes were not really associated with paganism but just happened to survive mostly in pagan settings.

Thus we may assert with absolute certainty that, if Beedle the Bard existed, the extant tales are not his. Indeed, there are many who assert that *The Tales of Beedle the Bard*, rather than being ancient folklore, are in fact the work of a forger of relatively modern times — perhaps the twentieth century.

Below Ground: see **UNDERGROUND ADVENTURES.**

BEZOAR

This one is absolutely real. "Also known as madstones, or magical gut rocks, bezoars were rock-like formations that developed within the innards of ruminants (cows, horses, buffalo, deer, etc.). Just as a grain of sand becomes embedded in an oyster to form a pearl, hair balls, small rocks, or dirt masses that were ingested while eating grasses, that or bits of metal or other foreign materials, calcified inside the stomachs of ruminants to produce gut rocks. As medicine, these stones were highly valued by frontiersmen."[153] They varied in size and shape, and were produced in different parts of the gut. They had some slight ability to absorb materials, which may have led to the belief in their medical value. They were thought, e.g., to be able to cure rabies (hence the name "madstones"). Rowling's contribution to the story of the bezoar, then, is simply to increase their efficacy.

The Black Crochan: see under **The Deathly Hallows.**

Blast-Ended Skrewts: see under **Manticore.**

Sirius Black (and family: Regulus, Andromeda)

The ancient and noble (in their own minds, anyway) House of Black tends to name their children after astronomical features: Sirius and Regulus Black are both named after stars, their relative Andromeda has a name which is a person's name but which is also the name of a constellation, and Internet sources say that others in the family have names such as Arcturus (a star), Pollus (star), Cassiopeia (constellation), Cygnus (constellation), and Orion (constellation).

So do the names Sirius and Regulus have any significance? In one sense, it is not surprising, if one is to name a child after a star, to call him Sirius; Sirius (α Canis Major) is the brightest star in the sky (excluding the sun, of course).[154]

But there are two other interesting points. One is that Sirius is one of the relatively few stars to have a Greek name (most star names are Arabic, although the constellations seen in the northern hemisphere were named by the Greeks, it was the Arabs who named most of the stars); "Sirius" (Σείριος, *Seirios)* is first mentioned in Hesiod's *Works and Days,* believed to be from around 700 B.C.E.[155] The other is that Sirius is the brightest star in *Canis Major,* the constellation whose name means the first/main/big dog. Sirius itself is called the "Dog Star" because it is the brightest name in that constellation.[156] So Sirius Black is a name which, in a way, means a "big black dog." And Sirius Black is an Animagus who turns into — a big black dog.

The name "Regulus" is harder to explain. It is a star, α Leonis, the brightest star in the constellation Leo — but it is not one of the brightest stars in the sky; it is only #21 on the bright star list. But it is another star with an interesting name — "regulus" is the diminutive for Latin *rex, king,* so *regulus* is a "little king," a "kinglet." (Yes, this is the precise Latin equivalent of the Greek Basilisk. Regulus is very unusual in being a star with a Latin name). So the proud Black family might have used the name "Regulus" to suggest that their second son, being a Black, was also noble, even regal. The diminutive form probably was suggested by the fact that Regulus is a second son — but Regulus was also shorter and less handsome than Sirius; he really was a *littler* Black.

Finally, Regulus the star is sometimes called *cor leonis,* "heart [of the] lion," and Regulus Black proved to be lion-hearted in his resistance to Voldemort.

See also the True/Taboo Name.

Blood

At the end of the *Goblet of Fire,* Voldemort uses a variety of disgusting ingredients to bring himself back to life: Tom Riddle Senior's bones (compare Thompson P203, "Game with bones of ancestor"), Wormtail's hand. But he uses Harry's *blood: "B-blood of the enemy... forcibly taken... you will... resurrect your foe."*[57] Voldemort doesn't want Harry's DNA — hair or saliva or flesh could provide that. That isn't sufficient. It is blood he requires. "Resuscitation by blood," in fact, is Thompson Type E113, and "Blood as Magic Drink" is D1041.

We of course do not know why Voldemort demanded this. It might just be that he likes using blood in spells — recall that the cave door that guards the horcrux in the *Half-Blood Prince* is paid in blood. But it is worth speculating. And the speculation starts right in the Bible. We are told that "The blood is the life" (Thompson E714.1); as early as Genesis 9:4, Noah (who is being given the right to eat animal food) is told not to eat "flesh with its life, that is, its blood." Deuteronomy 12:16 expressly forbids eating blood, and there are many variations on this theme. We see a few references to this even in the New Testament; the Council of Jerusalem (Acts 15:20) forbids the consumption of blood even as it lifts almost all other requirements of the Mosaic Law. Most of the rules in the Pentateuch are primarily ritual; based on its prohibition to Christians, the banning of blood seems to be done on moral grounds.

But there is more. In Leviticus 17:11, we read that blood makes atonement, and this theme is taken up in the New Testament: Jesus's blood is "the blood of the covenant" (Matthew 26:28 and parallels). Ephesians 1:7 says that we have redemption through Jesus's blood. Hebrews 10:19 says that the blood of Jesus takes us into the sanctuary.

Revelation 7:14 refers to washing in the blood of the lamb (Jesus). In all, there are 91 references to blood (αιμα, *haima*) in the New Testament (apart from Luke 22:44, which is a later addition; see "AND GIVE HIS LIFE AS A RANSOM FOR MANY"). References occur in thirteen books of the New Testament (Matthew, Mark, Luke, John, Acts, Romans, 1 Corinthians, Ephesians, Colossians, Hebrews, 1 Peter, 1 John, Apocalypse), by nine or ten different authors; about thirty of these references are to the blood of Jesus, usually as a sacrifice or cleansing agent or in the context of the eucharist and the consumption of the body of Christ.

It is often stated that the Holy Grail became holy because it was used to catch the blood of Christ on the cross, although this may have originated as a misinterpretation. For the Grail catching the blood of Christ, see Moorman, p. 62; Larousse, p. 207. Usually, however, it was simply the cup used at the Last Supper. Loomis, p. 25, suggests that the confusion arose because "le *saint* graal," "the *holy* grail," was sometimes shortened to the *sankgreal,* which appears to contain the element *sang, blood.* One version of the grail legend has Joseph of Arimathea make the grail and place it at the foot of the cross to catch the blood that dripped down.[158] This idea of ritual catching of blood survives in the ballad of "Lamkin" (Child #93); Lamkin catches, in a bowl, the blood of a woman he has murdered.[159]

A folktale about Cain says that he not only killed Abel but drank his blood (Thompson Type D1812.3.3.7). Another said that the blood of virgins (or perhaps children) could cure leprosy (F955.1);[160] we see this in action in the romance of Amys and Amelis (for which see DOPPELGÄNGER).

Thus there is every reason to think that Voldemort's ritual is a deliberate perversion of Christian doctrine: As Jesus's blood, voluntarily offered up, gives life to the believers, so Harry's blood, involuntarily taken, gives life to Voldemort. Voldemort is restored to his hollow life by the body and blood of his followers and enemies. And yet, Harry's blood still cleanses and (so Voldemort thinks) protects him.

To be sure, blood has many other places in folklore — Thompson's list of blood motifs is two pages long and includes hundreds of items. "Sorcerers regarded blood as one of the most potent ingredients in spells and used it to obtain control over others, to subdue demons, to draw magic circles, and to drink in certain initiation ceremonies."[161] Agreements with Satan were expected to be signed in blood[162] (Thompson M201.1.2; also D1273.0.1) — although anyone who has ever tried writing with blood will find it very tricky to do (the author, after suffering a minor injury, tested it as an experiment; blood does not flow well and makes a poor ink).

The blood of those who were murdered was said to cry out for revenge. We see this first in the blood of Abel ("your brother's blood is crying out to me from the ground"; Genesis 4:10), but also in the folktale of Hugh of Lincoln (which became the basis of Chaucer's *Prioress's Tale*),[163] and versions of the ballad "Sir Hugh, or The Jew's Daughter" also sometimes shows blood crying out for revenge.[164] Places where unholy blood was spilled were regarded as permanently blighted.[165] And Lady MacBeth was not the only one to find that the blood of a murder victim could not be washed away.[166]

See also DRAGON'S BLOOD, which has magical but not ethical significance.

BOGGART

Very rarely used in modern fantasy, but a genuine creature of folklore. "A mischievous Brownie, almost exactly like a poltergeist in his habits."[167] They are primarily known in northern England. "'Boggart,' by some writers is regarded as the Lancashire cognomen for 'Puck' or 'Robin Goodfellow.' Certainly there are, or were, many boggarts whose mischievous propensities and rude practical jokings remind us very forcibly of the eccentric and erratic goblin page to the fairy king."[168]

In a way, boggarts are a sort of a reverse brownie: A figure usually associated with a particular place, and usually engaged in nastiness — but occasionally known to do a good turn for the home's owners.

Sometimes they preferred to harass a particular family rather than a place. One Yorkshire tale has it that a boggart so tormented a family that they decided to move out. So they packed up their possessions and left their empty house — and a voice from a milk jug declared that the boggart was still with them. So they turned around and headed back to their home — better to be tormented at home than on the road.[169]

Boggarts could also live outdoors, haunting, for instance, a pit or well or lane.

It is generally believed that the bogle (Scottish for "ghost") and "bo-gey/bogy" are variants on the boggart,[170] as is the "bugaboo." In addition, C. S. Lewis mentioned "Boggles" among the followers of the White Witch in *The Lion, the Witch, and the Wardrobe,* although their nature is not explained.

There are also English legends of the brownies/hobgoblins which are relevant. Leather reports, "Brownie is the name now used in Her-efordshire for Robin Goodfellow, the Puck of the Midsummer Night's Dream. We have the Welsh form of the name in the 'Pwcha' farm, at Michaelchurch Eskley. Brownie, now all but forgotten, was a domes-tic elf, sometimes useful and hard-working, helping the maids with household tasks, more often mischievous, even evil and malicious. As elsewhere, the Brownie and the Bogie reduce themselves to different humours of the same uncanny thing."[171] Leather goes on to tell of a man who set aside a legacy to keep a bell ringing forever to placate or drive off a brownie who had tormented him.

"'What is a Boggart? A sort of ghost or sprite. But what is the mean-ing of the word Boggart? Brand says that 'in the northern parts of En-gland, ghost is pronounced *gheist* and *guest.* Hence *bar-guest,* or *bar-ghe-ist....*' Brand might have added that bar is a term for gate in the north, and that all the gates of York are named 'bars,' so that a *bar-gheist* is literally a gate-ghost."[172]

Boggarts in the Potterverse are seemingly of the indoor variety. Their ability to understand their victims' worst fears seems not to be known in Muggle tales (although Lewis in *The Voyage of the Dawn Treader* has a faintly similar idea in the island where dreams come true). However, various shape-shifting British bogeys, such as the "Hedley Kow," would take on a shape that they would assume their victims would find most irritating[173] — e.g. a fleeing sheep to a shepherd. From there it is a small step to a demon that would take on the form its victim most feared.

The idea of chasing off a malefic creature with laughter or insults is rare in British tradition but known in the east. Apollonius of Tyana told of scaring off an "ampusa" with insults. Marco Polo was told that ghúls could be chased off in the same manner. Even Martin Luther knew a story about laughing at devils.[174]

See also HOUSE ELVES.

BONFIRE

"All over Europe the peasants have been accustomed from time immemorial to kindle bonfires on certain days of the year, and to dance round or leap over them. Customs of this kind can be traced back on historical evidence to the Middle Ages, and their analogy to similar customs observed in antiquity goes with strong internal evidence to prove that their origin must be sought in a period long prior to the spread of Christianity."[175]

Some have suggested that bonfires were first kindled as part of a solar celebration, based on the belief that fire was a small, escaped part of the sun.[176] However, the rarity of bonfires in parts of Britain is widely considered an argument against this.[177] At Hogwarts, they still have the fall bonfire on Hallowe'en, but for Muggles, the "bonfires which once blazed on Hallowe'en are now lit on 5 November [Guy Fawkes Day] to commemorate the failure of the Gunpowder Plot in 1605."[178]

The origin of the word "bonfire" is disputed, but many of the ideas connect it with magic. A fourteenth century writer claimed it was a "bone-fire"; others think "bonfire" is partly derived from French, a *bon* fire or good fire; there is also the idea of "need-fire" to cure cattle of diseases.[179]

BOWTRUCKLE

These little creatures are guardians of trees. Rowling's description does not much resemble any other such creature, but compare Tolkien's "Ents," plus the Aërico mentioned in the entry on the Whomping WILLOW.

The dryads/hamadryads of classical mythology are sometimes said to guard trees, but they are primarily the *spirits* of the trees: kill the tree and the dryad dies too. They are not really separate beings.

BROOMSTICKS

The *idea* of witches, i.e. those who can perform natural magic, is widespread (e.g. they are mentioned in the Bible; see the entry on WIZARDS, which suggests that they are a response to some deep human desire to explain natural phenomena).[180] But the Bible never mentions them riding broomsticks. Indeed, detailed descriptions of witches are few; "Unmistakably wicked as she is, the witch presents no clear-cut picture to the folk."[181] The idea of broomsticks and broomstick-riding is Thompson G242.1, and is mentioned in several folklore manuals,[182] but background is largely lacking. Nor were broomsticks the only means of flight: "Modern… writers take for granted that a witch's magic flight requires a broomstick, but folk tradition mentions other means too, including pitchforks, staffs, plant-stems, hurdles, bowls, and pig-troughs."[183] Simpson and Roud mention, as possible sources for witches riding brooms, a chapbook about a trial in 1612, which shows a woman, a man, and the Devil on broomsticks, and Reginald Scot's 1584 book which describes witches carrying (but not riding) brooms at a Sabbat.

Brooms did have a role in witchcraft, to be sure — e.g. a witch could throw water over her shoulder with a broom in order to induce hail.[184]

The Slavic ogress Baba Yaga, well-known from the tale of Vasilisa the Fair, was sometimes said to ride in a kettle or mortar and pestle, followed by a magic iron broom which swept away her tracks, but she did not herself ride the broom.[185]

There was significant folklore about brooms (also known as besoms) which is not related to their use in witchcraft. For instance, it was said to be unlucky to buy them in May or make them at Christmas.[186]

Interestingly, brooms could also *detect* witches; in Lancashire, it was said that putting a broom in a doorway would cause a witch to pass by the house.[187] Thompson Type B272.7.1 is "beam across door protects from witch." Also, the plant known as broom, from which brooms were sometimes made, was "most potent against witches and spirits."[188]

The Tale of the Three Brothers: see Meeting DEATH ON THE ROAD.

Carpets, Magic/Flying: see FLYING CARPETS.

CATS

Cats are commonly listed as the "Familiar" of witches in British folklore: "any old woman in medieval Europe who kept a cat for company, especially if it were black, might be a target for accusations of witchcraft."[189] "The most common witch-familiars in the British Isles are cats, hares, and occasionally red deer. These animals have taken the place of wolves which, having been eradicated, may no longer serve the purposes of the witch."[190] The reason cats are desirable familiars is that they are often said to have magical wisdom (Thompson B121.3). In a way, the surprise is not that there are cats in the Harry Potter books but that they are so few. As a figure of magic, they seem to go back to ancient Egypt — Bast was a cat deity,[191] said by some moderns to represent the sun in which cats like to rest.[192] It was said of Freya, the Norse goddess of beauty and love, that "When she goes on a journey she sits in a chariot drawn by two cats."[193] The Hindu goddess of birth, Shasti, is said to ride a cat.[194] In Thailand, they are supposed to guard temples; in China, they are said to be cursed because they did not weep at the death of the Buddha. Some eastern legends regard cats as shape-shifters. Tibert the Cat is one of the adversaries of Reynard the Fox in the latter's beast-tales.[195] Cats are so familiar in Ireland that there are eight words for felines.[196] In Zoroastrianism, they were said to be allied with Ahriman, the evil power.[197]

Interestingly, cats are not mentioned at all in either the Hebrew Bible or the Greek New Testament. The only Biblical mention is in the apocryphal/deuterocanonical Letter of Jeremiah (verse 22; sometimes called Baruch 6:22), where bats, swallows, and cats descend upon certain evildoers. This would seem to imply that the early Jews didn't approve of cats — but they didn't approve of dogs, either.

The only cats of significance in the Potter sequence are Crookshanks and Mrs. Norris — and no one likes Mrs. Norris except Filch. Mrs. Norris's ability to turn up to spy on wrongdoers is reminiscent of cat folklore — but it's also somewhat reminiscent of Lewis Carroll's Cheshire Cat, all or part of whom regularly appears and disappears. Nor is the Cheshire Cat the only important feline in Carroll's *Alice* books; Dinah (the actual cat of Alice Liddell, named for the song "Vilikins and his Dinah") motivates the *Through the Looking Glass* in particular, and also appears in *Alice's Adventures in Wonderland*.

Mrs. Norris shows us the bad side of cats; the good side is Crookshanks. Crookshanks gives no evidence of being Hermione's Familiar, but he does seem to have something of a folklore aspect — there is a lot of Puss in Boots in Crookshanks, who cannot talk but otherwise seems to have near-human intelligence. Incidentally, Crookshanks has his finest hour in "Cat, Rat, and Dog," chapter 17 in the *Prisoner of Azkaban*.

CENTAURS

The centaurs are an element of classical mythology (Thompson B21) — although, frankly, the Potterverse centaurs are a lot more like C. S. Lewis's than the creatures of Greek myth. The Greek centaurs were carnivores (they preferred their meat raw)[198] who lived on Mount Pelion, and most of them were brutal[199] — Chiron was the noteworthy exception, but he and Pholus, although centauroid in appearance, had a different ancestry.[200] The primary story told of Greek centaurs is of their war with the nearby Lapiths.[201] There are also tales of them attempting to rape human women. It was another centaur, Nessus, who arranged for the death of Heracles by causing Deianira, Heracles's wife, to give him a garment coated in the (poisoned) blood of Nessus.[202]

There is no tradition of centaurs in British folklore; Rowling's version appears to be entirely derived from classical legend and/or from Lewis.

It is interesting that folklore often views human/animal crossbreeds as relatively ineffective, with their freedom of action largely restricted by the animal part of their nature.[203] Note how generally ineffective Rowling's centaurs are. They have (they claim) extraordinary intelligence, but (except for Firenze) they never *do* anything. It's as if they don't care if

Voldemort wins. They claim this as a virtue. Could it be that it is instead an artifact of their nature?

The fact that classical Centaurs ate meat is significant. Modern apes are mostly vegetarian, and horses are hay-burners. Humans by contrast eat a lot of meat. It is believed that this change from a vegetable to an omnivorous diet was necessary; the human brain requires a tremendous amount of energy, and plants alone could hardly supply it. Meat had to be included. Hence a centaur, which is a horse with a human brain, also would have to adjust its diet. Could lack of a sufficient food supply be part of the reason for their ineffectiveness?

The CHAMBER OF SECRETS

The Chamber of Secrets is a cavern, associated with a pool, in which a monster lives. This has significant similarities to one of Geoffrey of Monmouth's tales of MERLIN. King Vortigern is trying to build a strong tower, but the building keeps failing.[204] At last Vortigern is advised to call upon Merlin, who says that there is a pool under where Vortigern is trying to build the tower, and under it, two dragons[205] (Thompson B11.3.4). The pool and the beasts are excavated, and the dragons fight.

Scandinavian folklore includes sagas in which an old king (Thrain the Viking, Karr the Old, etc.) is buried with his hoard, and a later adventurer comes down via a rope or some other means to reach it; often the old king's ghostly warriors, or a monster, will fight the intruder. Possibly these tales later evolved into versions where a monster guarded the treasure. These later versions underlie the story of Sigfried/Sigurd and the dragon[206] — and hence, indirectly, Smaug the Dragon in Tolkien's *The Hobbit*. (Is it possible that Salazar Slytherin was buried in the Chamber of Secrets? It would fit.)

There is a happier version of this tale of monsters under the earth, the motif of the "Sleeper Under the Hill." A number of great kings are said to be asleep, waiting for their time. Arthur and Merlin are both among the leaders said to be at rest — the latter both in folklore and, more recently, by C. S. Lewis in *That Hideous Strength* — as are Charlemagne and Frederick Barbarossa.[207] In classical mythology, Epimenides was said to have slept for fifty-seven years in the earth.[208] There is also the tale of the "Seven Sleepers of Ephesus" (Thompson D1960.1) — soldiers who, as Christians, hid in a cave to avoid fighting a pagan battle or a persecution, then emerged centuries later, by which time the Empire had turned Christian and they were welcomed as witnesses to the idea of resurrection.[209]

CHESS

There are a number of references to chess in the Potter books, notably in the *Philosopher's Stone,* where Ron's skill at the game enables Our Heroes to get past the enchanted chess set. This is not the only instance in the Potter books of animated chess pieces, although it is certainly the most important. Moderns who are asked about living chess pieces will surely think first of Lewis Carroll's *Through the Looking Glass,* but we find an earlier instance mentioned briefly in the Mabinogion in the tale of "Peredur." There is also a *flying* chess set in the Dutch *Roman de Walwein* ("Romance of Gawain"),[210] although it's not clear if these pieces are alive in the same sense as those in the Potter books. Probably, though, Carroll is enough to explain all post-nineteenth-century mentions of living chess pieces.

CHIMAERA

In the *Order of the Phoenix,* Hermione fears that Hagrid will acquire a chimaera. In *Quidditch,* we are told that a chimaera ate Dai Llewellyn, a great Quidditch player (for whom a ward at ST. MUNGO's is named). Neither book describes the creature, but it is clearly deadly. In *Fantastic Beasts,* we are told it has the head of a lion, the body of a goat, and the tail of a dragon.

They are said to be rare, but the implication is that there are several of them. This contrasts with the classical Chimaera (χιμαιρα, *chimaira*); there was supposed to be only one of them, "which took its shape from both a goat and a lion. In some versions it is said to have had the hindquarters of a snake and the head of a lion on the body of a goat, and in others it is claimed that it had two heads, one of a goat and one of a lion; it breathed fire. It was the offspring of Typhon and Echidna"[211] — making it a sibling of Cerberus,[212] the archetype of Fluffy. Because it was so often mentioned in classical literature (in the *Iliad,* the *Aeneid,* and in Ovid), the Middle Ages adopted it; Saint Brendan was supposed to have seen one on his voyage,[213] Milton refers to chimaera in Hell, and Spenser says that it mated with Cerberus to produce the "Blatant Beast."[214]

According to *Fantastic Beasts,* only one Chimaera has ever been killed — by a wizard on a flying horse who fell off the beast due to exhaustion soon afterward. The Greek Chimaera was slain by Bellerophon, who did it with the aid of the flying horse Pegasus.

CIRCE

> Once they'd drained the bowls she filled, suddenly
> she struck with her wand, drove them into her pigsties,
> all of them bristling into swine — with grunts,
> snouts — even their bodies, yes, and only
> the men's minds stayed steadfast as before.
> So off they went to their pens, sobbing, squealing,
> as Circe flung them acorns, cornel nuts and mast,
> common fodder for hogs that root and roll in mud.[215]

This account from the *Odyssey* is the earliest tale of Circe, one of the famous witches whose chocolate frog card Harry collects on the Hogwarts Express in the *Philosopher's Stone.* When a party of Odysseus's men visit her on her island, she traps them and turns them to pigs; it is only because one of them, Eurylochos, hides and spots her spell that Odysseus is warned and is able to use an herb to foil her magic and force her to restore his men.[216]

As is often the case in Greek legend, the rest of Circe's story is somewhat uncertain. One account makes her the child of Helios (the sun) and the nymph Perse,[217] and hence the sister of Pasiphae the wife of Minos;[218] another story says that Hecate the witch-goddess was her mother.[219] She liked to transfigure visitors, often making them into wolves, lions, or pigs.[220] After Odysseus over-awed her, he reportedly spent a month or more with her and fathered a son, Telegonus (or perhaps more than one son, but Telegonus was the most important).[221] Telegonus was later said to have killed his father Odysseus, after which Odysseus's son by Penelope, Telemachus, married Circe.[222] She was said to have made him immortal.[223] Prior to this, she had been responsible for transforming Scylla into a monster; they had been rivals over Glaucus, one of the Argonauts.[224]

Since much of Circe's magic involved making her victims drink, it seems likely that, in the Potter universe, she would have been famed for potions. Or, of course, TRANSFIGURATION. Like Morgana, another famous witch with a complicated history, one suspects her chocolate frog card was… interesting.

Note: Although the name is spelled "Circe" in English, and so is usually pronounced *Sur-see,* the Greek is Κιρκη, which should be pronounced *Kirkeh.*

CLIODNA

(Also spelled Cliodhna, Clíodna, Clidna.)

One of the famous witches whose chocolate frog card Harry collects on the Hogwarts Express in the *Philosopher's Stone.* She is called a "druidess," but she was an Irish diety: "Goddess of beauty who fell in love with a mortal named Ciabhan of the Curling Locks [other sources give him other names, e.g. Aonghus]. They fled from the wrath of Manannán Mac Lir and landed in Glandore, Co. Cork. While Ciabhan went to hunt, Cliodhna was lulled asleep by beautiful music played by Manannán [Iuchna], who then sent a great wave to sweep her back to the Otherworld."[225] Carraig Clíodna in County Cork bears her name.[226]

"She is notorious for appearing as a seductress to tempt young men. Certain Munster families claim her as their banshee."[227] One account says that she was associated specifically with the McCarthys.[228]

It is suggested that the name "Clíodna" means "the territorial one."[229] She is said to have had fair hair. She was also regarded as a poetic muse.[230] She was said to lead fairy dances, and to sometimes appear as a rabbit[231] — perhaps an early ANIMAGUS?

The Invisibility Cloak: see under **The DEATHLY HALLOWS.**

Cockatrice: see **BASILISK.**

Companions: see **The INNER CIRCLE.**

CORNISH PIXIES

In the *Chamber of Secrets*, Gilderoy LOCKHART's first sort-of-lesson involves letting lose a flock of Cornish Pixies. Does it matter that the pixies are Cornish? It probably does, because in folklore, they're called Cornish *Piskies.* (Occasionally written "Pigsies."[232]) "Piskies are Cornish sprites. Unlike most fairies, they lead solitary lives, although they are quite merry and enjoy playing pranks on mortals. 'Pisky-led' is a Cornish expression which describes someone who is bewildered or lost."[233] On the other hand, "The Cornish Piskie… is older, more wizened and meagre than the sturdy, earthy pixies of Somerset and the white, slight, naked pixies of Devon."[234] Those which wore clothing seem to have worn primarily green. They were known to use lights to lead drunken mortals into moors and bogs. The name (which most think is a variant on "pixy," although some disagree) is probably related to "Puck" of *A Midsummer Night's Dream.*[235]

Pixies can be driven off by turning a piece of clothing inside out or, like brownies, by being given clothing[236] (although this may be because they run off to show it to the other fairies[237]).

Various tales make Piskies the reincarnated souls of some sort of dead people (unchristened children, druids),[238] but there is no evidence of this in the brief account in the *Chamber of Secrets*.

Thompson F200.1 is Pixies/Piskies.

Crookshanks: see under CATS.

CRUEL PARENTS AND UNWANTED MARRIAGES

> "Oh cruel were his parents that sent my love to sea,
> And cruel, cruel was the ship that bore my love from me.
> Yet I love his parents, since they're his, although they've ruined me.
> I love my love because I know my love, he loves me."[239]

The lines are from the ballad of "A Maid in Bedlam," but the motif is incredibly common — Malcolm Laws, in his catalog of British ballads, lists 39 items under "Ballads of Family Opposition to Lovers."[240] Sometimes the family forcibly marries the girl (it's usually a girl) to another man. Sometimes they have the man pressed to sea ("The Banks of Dundee"[241]). Sometimes they lock her up ("Locks and Bolts"[242], "The Iron Door"[243]). Or they exile her to some place he cannot reach ("The Suffolk Miracle,"[244] "Betsy is a Beauty Fair"[245]). Sometimes they kill him ("Lovely Willie,"[246] "Edmund in the Lowlands Low"[247]). On the other hand, sometimes the girl and her lover elope, or they somehow convince the parents to repent, or they manage to find each other despite the opposition. Or one or both may commit suicide ("Farewell, Dear Rosanna"[248]) or die of love ("American Woods"[249]).

Does any of this amount to anything? Perhaps not, but observe that Voldemort's grandfather was violently opposed to his daughter's love. Not a good start to a marriage. Or a life....

CRYSTAL BALL

The crystal ball is regarded as an offshoot of the scrying mirror; see under the MIRROR OF ERISED. Although there was a crystal-gazer recorded in England as early as the reign of Elizabeth I, (This was Dr. John Dee (1527–1608/9), a fairly good mathematician whose intellect was clouded by a fascination with pseudoscience — he was an astrologer, alchemist, and magician as well as a (failed) crystal-gazer). The crystal ball is regarded as a "modern cliché."[250]

Compare also J. R. R. Tolkien's *palantíri,* which are crystal spheres with the ability to see at a distance. Crossley-Holland's "Seeing Stone" is not a crystal sphere, but it is a crystal which serves much the same purpose.

There is an interesting connection between crystal balls and magic mirrors, found in the Grimm tale of "The Crystal Ball."[251] A young man has come to rescue a princess who is trapped twice, once in an ugly body and once in a prison. Her true beauty can only be seen in a magic mirror. And she can only be freed by a crystal ball that defeats the magician. But the ball, while magical, does not appear to have scrying powers.

The Dark Lord

This title is not very folkloric — most sources say that the name, at least as used in Rowling's sense, goes back only to Tolkien. (Which makes Voldemort's use of the title somewhat anachronistic.) It isn't catalogued as a motif by Thompson. Of course, the idea of a Dark Lord — a malignant being with magical powers whose goal is to take over the world — is older. It has been claimed that Alberich in Wagner's Ring cycle is an earlier example of the same thing.[252] But while Alberich is a real character in the Nibelung cycle, Wagner has reshaped him; in the original myths, he is more the master of craftsman who supply magical objects — a Haephestus rather than a Hades.

On the other hand, the idea of an evil parody of the gods is an ancient one in Christian thought, and is one of the several conceptions of Satan. Indeed, Satan is sometimes called "The Dark One," but this has a rather different implication than "The Dark Lord." Compare also Lucifer's title of "The Prince of Darkness."

Note that Satan is often depicted as human-but-not-quite (having horns, a tail, and cloven hooves) — and Voldemort also seems to be not quite physically human at the end. Satan's non-human nature was said in folklore to be undisguisable (you could always tell the devil by looking at his feet); it is not clear if this applies to Voldemort.

Meeting Death on the Road

Beedle the Bard's "Tale of the Three Brothers," found in both the *Deathly Hallows* and *Beedle,* is built on two very basic folkloric motifs. The first, the "Victorious Youngest Son," is Thompson L10. The second, "Meeting Death on the Road," Thompson 763, is even more familiar, because it is the heart of one of Chaucer's masterpieces, "The Pardoner's Tale." Three roisterers are drinking when they see a dead man's corpse on its way to burial. Offended at his death, the drunks determine to go out and slay Death. Finding an old man, they accuse him of being Death. He says that he is not, but if they go a little ways, they will find death easily enough. They follow his instructions — and find a treasure. Although they agree to share the wealth, the three men conspire against each other, and as a result, all end up dead. Chaucer's direct source, if he had one, does not seem to have survived, but there are many related tales.[253] Rowling has admitted that "The Pardoner's Tale" was an influence on *The Deathly Hallows*.[254]

Medieval artwork very often showed death as an actual living person — images of "the Dance of Death" or "Danse Macabre" were famously common during plague eras, when the feeling was that death was always present.

"Death and the Abbot," woodcut by Hans Holbein showing Death personified.
Source: Wikimedia Commons.

It is interesting that all three of the Peverells, whom Xenophilus Lovegood claims were the three brothers of Beedle's tale, have names which involve a sort of meeting with death on the road. "Ignotus" is a variant on "Ignatius," and St. Ignatius was martyred in 107 as a Christian, taking a long road from Antioch to Rome to be executed[255] — and he went voluntarily to his death; he turned back attempts to rescue him.[256] Note that Ignotus was the brother who, in the end, did not resist death.

Cadmus in Greek mythology was the founder of Thebes, who created its population when he sowed dragon's teeth and was threatened by the quarrelsome men who sprang from them.[257]

Antioch is the most forced of the interpretations, but the name derives from the various Seleucid kings Antiochus, most of whom perished violently in civil wars; the Seleucid Empire, more than perhaps any other in history, was a plaything of rulers who did nothing but fight each other until there was nothing left to fight over. They spent a *lot* of time meeting, or fleeing, assassins on the road.

See also Door of Death, The Grim.

Death Portents: see The Grim; also Banshee.

Death, Return/Resurrection from: see The Resurrected Hero.

The Deathly Hallows

"Hallows. In Celtic Irish mythology, the kingly regalia that were widely recognized as symbols of true sovereignty."[258]

The idea of a special set of linked treasures is hardly new. Welsh legend gives King Arthur his own "Hallows." He had more of them — they were known as "The Thirteen Treasures of Britain"[259] — but the list is interesting. Three of the items were:

Arthur's sword, usually Dyrnwyn, Caliburn (a name supposedly derived from Welsh *Caladfwch*.[260]), or Brounstell. This was said to be a flaming sword, and was unbeatable. If we try to compare Arthur's Hallows with Rowling's, this "unbeatable weapon" is surely equivalent to the Elder Wand. Arthur's sword came into English as Excalibur, but with its traits changed. Alexander had it as "Dyrnwyn."

Gwenn, the Cloak of Arthur, was an invisibility cloak. This shows up in Alexander as Doli's power of invisibility as well as in the Potterverse. The *cap* of invisibility is Thompson F4555.5.3 (and is used to sneak into a bedroom in K1349.10). The Arthurian universe also has a ring of invisibility, mentioned in Chrétien de Troyes's *Yvain;* see below.

Arthur had a cauldron that was never empty (compare Thompson D1472.1.7, "magic table supplies food and drink," and D1652.1, "inexhaustible food"). Folklorists, however, think Arthur's cauldron to be a conflation of two items: The cauldron of plenty (Thompson K81.3, "inexhaustible food") and the cauldron of resurrection. The bottomless cauldron — which sounds rather like the "Hopping POT" of Beedle the Bard's story — appears in Irish myth as Dagda's cauldron of plenty[261] (Dagda, or The Daghdha, a leader of the Tüatha Dé Danann, also had a staff which could kill or bring back to life, thus combining two hallows in one[262]); in Alexander the cauldron is Gurgi's Wallet of Food. Some think that the Holy Grail was originally a cauldron of plenty;[263] legends say that it fed Joseph of Arimathea and his family for a time. The Cauldron of Resurrection is much like the Resurrection Stone; the description in *Branwen Daughter of Llŷr* says that the Welsh cauldron belonged to Llassar Llaes Gyngwyd,[264] and if a man is slain, the owner is told to "cast him into the cauldron, and by tomorrow he will be as good [at fighting?] as ever — but he will be without speech."[265] In Alexander, this becomes the Black Crochan, although Alexander's cauldron is much more wicked than Arthur's or Llassar's (Alexander also made the Welsh Annuvin into a more evil place than it is in the *Mabinogion*).

Geoffrey of Monmouth's version of the Arthurian legend, which led to the whole modern falderal of Camelot, gives Arthur three particular treasures: The shield Pridwen[266] [Prydwenn, "Prydain"=Britain], the sword Caliburnus,[267] and the lance Ron (probably a short form of Welsh Rhongomyniad).[268] Hm. Could that be where Ron Weasley got his name? After all, his preferred Hallow was the weapon....

Both the Cloak of Invisibility and the Invincible Sword are known from the English "Jack Tales" (Jack the Giant Killer, etc.),[269] and they go back at least to Perseus's Cap of Invisibility and Adamantine Sword.[270] Grimm #97, "The Water of Life," features a magic sword and an inexhaustible loaf of bread. Sigfried in the *Niebelungenlied* also has an invisibility cloak,[271] although it isn't exactly used for the highest of purposes. In Scottish folklore, ravens could be induced to supply a crystal which would render invisible anyone who put it in his mouth.[272] In Celtic myth, Caswallawn had an invisibility cloak which he used to steal the properties of Manawydan.[273] There is also a ring of invisibility in Plato (the "Ring of Gyges," in the *Republic*), as well as in the ROMANCE of *Ywain and Gawain,* and in its French ancestor *Yvain* by Chrétien de Troyes,[274] as well as in a tale of Reynard the Fox,[275] plus of course in Tolkien. Tolkien's ring, as originally conceived, is much like the Scandinavian ring of Andvari the Dwarf, which rendered the user invisible but still left his shadow visible.[276]

Although the Hallows of Britain number over a dozen, a set of three magical objects is more typical (see under THREE) — so much so that "The Three Magic Objects" is one of the descriptions of Thompson theme 566.[277] Harry's set can even be compared to the Trinity — the Father, in charge of justice and power, is the Elder Wand; the Son, the first fruits of the resurrection, is of course the Resurrection Stone, and the Holy Spirit, which moves invisibly, is the Invisibility Cloak. A forced analogy? Sure. But you would be amazed at the number of forced analogies to the Holy Spirit in Christian literature. Even recipes for gunpowder have been based on the Trinity.

Beedle the Bard's story of how the three brothers received the three Hallows (for which see Meeting DEATH ON THE ROAD) also bears some resemblance to the "Three Magic Objects" tale, since the three objects are given to three different people.

It seems highly unlikely that the symbol for the Deathly Hallows is derived from Euclid's famous geometry book *The Elements* — but a variant of it is in there. Book IV, proposition 3 is "To circumscribe a triangle equiangular with a given triangle about a given circle"; proposition 4 is "To inscribe a circle inside a given triangle." The equilateral triangle (or even the isosceles triangle) is a special case of this, and from there, it is an elementary secondary proposition to

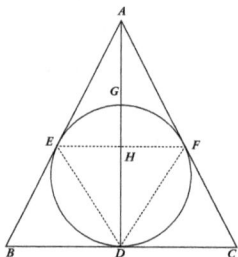

show that the bisector AD not only cuts the triangle ABC into equal halves but also the inscribed circle. So the Deathly Hallows *could* derive from a two thousand year old geometry text. Or, perhaps, vice versa.

DEEP MAGIC AND DEEPER MAGIC

This isn't a folklore motif, but it is perhaps worth noting. Rowling's plot derives from the fact that Lily Potter saved Harry's life with her love, and that love is something Voldemort — despite his immense technical skill — never understands.

The idea of Something the Bad Guy Doesn't Comprehend is a common enough notion — Tolkien (based, perhaps, on ideas from Boethius's *The Consolation of Philosophy*)[278] tells us that Sauron cannot imagine the plan to destroy the Ring; he doesn't understand the idea of not wanting power (see under THINGS BOUGHT AT TOO HIGH A COST). C. S. Lewis shows this concept in *The Magician's Nephew*; Jadis (the White Witch), when she urges Digory to take an Apple of Life home to his mother instead of bringing it to Aslan, and when she steals an Apple herself, cannot understand that the end does not always justify the means — and that using the wrong means can destroy the end.[279] Lewis also briefly mentions the idea in *The Screwtape Letters,* in which the demon Screwtape "laments the inability of the [Intelligence] department to penetrate the purposes of the enemy."[280]

This is sound Christian doctrine, but it feels as if Rowling's version has another part, this one taken largely from another of C. S. Lewis's Narnia books, *The Lion, the Witch, and the Wardrobe*: The "Deep Magic from the Dawn of Time" (which gives traitors to the White Witch to punish) and the "Deeper Magic from Before the Dawn of Time" (in which Aslan/Jesus cannot be made to stay dead). Voldemort makes something that might almost be an allusion to this: "Dumbledore invoked an ancient magic, to ensure the boy's protection as long as he is in his relations' care. Not even I can touch him there...."[281] Voldemort understands the power of evil. But Dumbledore knows the deeper magic of love — and, with it, triumphs from the grave. Rowling was not directly imitating Lewis, but the idea seems similar.

As for the deep magic itself — is it folklore? Depends on what you think of the Christian message....

DEMIGUISE

These creatures are mentioned briefly in the *Deathly Hallows* and in *Fantastic Beasts* as creatures whose hair can make invisibility cloaks. They are said to look like apes. The name is indicative; "demiguise" means, in effect, "half visible."

Although the term "demiguise" is not in use outside the Wizarding world, there are a number of tales of creatures somewhat like this — that is, of humanoid creatures that can turn invisible or otherwise vanish. Most major cultures have at least one type of creature which can disappear in this way; fairies are one of the more common examples in British lore.

DIRICAWL

The Diricawl is a curious magical creature, mentioned in *Fantastic Beasts,* which is noteworthy because it is known to Muggles under another name — the Dodo. Folklore about the Dodo is recent and restricted; probably the largest share of it is about the stuffed Dodo kept at Oxford University. Charles Dodgson visited it with the Liddell Sisters, and it became a character in *Alice in Wonderland* (where it is thought to have represented Dodgson himself).[282]

The fact that the bird has different Muggle and Wizarding names is noteworthy as a sign of the increasing split between the magical and non-magical worlds. (And the name may hint at this, because *diri-* is a Latin root meaning something like *separate, categorize, align.*) The ignorance wizards display toward Muggles is in many ways more shocking than the Muggle ignorance of wizarding — after all, no one is going around applying memory charms to wizards to make them forget Muggles! In such separate cultures, we would frankly expect more linguistic separation than we see. There is no obvious explanation for this phenomenon of intermittent linguistic distinction. Language is, however, an important element in genre fantasy; Tolkien's whole universe arose primarily out of his linguistic work.

Divination: see under **PROPHECIES FULFILLED ONLY BECAUSE SOMEONE TRIES TO PREVENT THEM.**

DOBBY

Is the name "Dobby" significant? Dobby is, of course, one of the HOUSE ELVES. House elves are a minor variation on brownies, and brownies are closely associated with hobgoblins. And hobgoblins are often called "hob," and the names "Hob," "Dob," and "Robin" are all Middle English nicknames of Robert. "Dobbs, dobby, dobie: These are regional nicknames for various supernatural beings, probably short for 'Robin.' Dobbs was used for a brownie in Sussex, dobby in Yorkshire and Lancashire, and dobie in Northumberland."[283] "Dobbs, or Master Dobbs. The Sussex Brownie, supposed to be specially kind to old men, like the Highland Bodachan Sabhaill.... In Yorkshire the same character was called Dobby.... He is very like a Brownie, but perhaps more likely to play mischievous pranks. In fact he is much like Robin Goodfellow."[284] Thus Dobby the House Elf is the same as Hob the Hobgoblin — and even, arguably, Shakespeare's Puck! This same sort of argument makes Dobby the House Elf the same as Hobbe the Robber — which, to a few crazed folklorists, would make him the same as Robin Hood. (This equation is certainly false. The one with Robin Goodfellow is at least possible. On the other hand, Robin Hood and Dobby do have something in common: Liberation. Robin Hood was not a displaced earl or anything like that; in the early legend, he was a yeoman,[285] or what we would now call a free citizen. But he managed, in feudal England, to define himself rather than having his place defined by the hierarchy. Similarly Dobby the Elf, born to a specific social position, managed to escape it.)

The brownies known by the name Dobbs or Dobby were supposed to have unusually strong links to particular families, and to guard their treasures,[286] just as house elves seem to have done in the Potterverse.

The DOOR OF DEATH

This gateway isn't given an actual name in the books, but we find it in the *Order of the Phoenix*. It is the old, old arch through which Sirius Black falls — and dies.

The symbol of a doorway of death is probably most familiar from Dante — the gate of Hell is famously marked, "All hope abandon, ye who enter here."[287] In the *Aeneid,* "night and day the door of gloomy Dis stands open" "noctes atque dies patet atria ianua Ditis;" VirgilLoeb, pp. 514–515. Dis is both the place of the afterlife and its ruler. Dis was probably originally distinct from Pluto, but they were soon identified as one god, the equivalent of Greek Hades — which meant that Dis the place was identified with Hades the place as well, or, as it is often rendered, "the gates of Dis are open day and night" — and Aeneas must have a special token (a golden branch) to enter and be able to return. Also, there is a Road to the Underworld in the *Odyssey;* "up out of Erebus they came, flocking toward me now, the ghosts of the dead and gone... Brides and unwed youths and old men who had suffered much."[288] Orpheus travels the road to try to rescue Euridice (Thompson F81.1).[289] Norse myth has something vaguely similar, the gateway Grindr (Tom Shippey speculates that this name gave rise to the name "Grindwall" in the poem "Bombadil Goes Boating" in *The Tolkien Reader*).[290] This entrance to Hel's dominion is very impressive: "she shar[es] her provision with those who were sent to her, namely men who die from disease or old age. She has a great homestead there with extraordinarily high walls and huge gates."[291] Even the New Testament says (metaphorically), "Broad is the road that leads to destruction" (Matthew 7:13, etc.).

Compare also the idiomatic expression "to go beyond the veil" for those who have died. There *is* a veil hanging on the door in the Department of Mysteries. Is it significant? According to the synoptic gospels, at the moment Jesus died, "the curtain of the temple was torn in two, from top to bottom" (Matthew 27:51; similarly Mark 15:38, Luke 23:45). This torn curtain is presumably the one that separated the Holy of Holies from the outside world, into which "only the high priest goes... and he but once a year, and not without taking the blood that he offers for himself and for the sins committed unintentionally by the people" (Hebrews 9:7, based on Leviticus 16:2, 12–15). It is said that, when the future Emperor Titus captured Jerusalem in 70 and cut the Temple curtain, it shed blood[292] — an obvious reminder of a curtain between the living and dead. But the analogy here is uncertain — the curtain in the Department of Mysteries seems to be intact.

The idea of a gate that doesn't really lead anywhere is rarer, although we see it at least twice in C. S. Lewis, in the door that takes the Telmarines back to earth in *Prince Caspian* and in the stable door (stable door. Hmph) in *The Last Battle*. The latter, like the door in the Department of Mysteries, was a door of death, but with different effects. The door in the Department of Mysteries sounds like a cross between the gate of hell and the cross of Jesus, traditionally located in isolation at the top of a hill, although Rowling may have been riffing on Lewis as well.

It is interesting that Harry never sees the Door of Death during his brief period of non-life.

See also Meeting DEATH ON THE ROAD.

DOPPELGÄNGER

German for "double-goer," i.e. a second copy of a person who moves independently of the original. The idea does not seem to occur very often in English folktales, but compare the "Fetch" or "Co-Walker" mentioned under the GRIM, as well as the mention under (Harry's) SCAR of the "false Guinevere" who had the same father as Guinevere and was conceived (by rape) on the same night — and looked almost exactly like her half sister, and in an evil way caused Arthur to love her. In the more numerous German accounts, the doppelgänger normally appears only to the close friends or relatives of the person being "doubled."[293] In the *Deathly Hallows,* Rowling has a rather impish twist on this: Not only do the doppelgänger *appear to* Harry's friends, they *are* Harry's friends! ("Friends identical in appearance" are Thompson item F577.1; "two friends exchange forms" is D45.3; "identical persons" includes F239.2 and H1381.3.5.)

One of the most widespread instances of "Friends Identical in Appearance" is the legend of Amys and Amelis, which gave rise to the popular Middle English romance of *Amys and Amiloun.*[294] Amys and Amelis are sworn friends, so close that they even look alike. When Amelis is charged with improper behavior and forced into a trial by combat, Amys comes forward and fights the duel on his behalf — and becomes a leper as a result of the deceit. Years later, Amelis learns of Amys's leprosy and that he can cure it only by killing his sons and bathing Amys in their blood — which he does, only to have the children come back to life, so everything ends happily.[295] This may sound gruesome, but the true significance of the Amys and Amelis legend is that it demonstrates the extreme power and importance of true friendship.

The unrelated double is also a key element of Charles Dickens's *A Tale of Two Cities,* a book which had a profound influence on Rowling.[296]

It ends with the hero Sydney Carton going to the guillotine to save the life of his double, Charles Darnay.

The problem of telling identical people apart is known in folklore; "Recognition of transformed person among identical companions" is Thompson H161. This idea also inspired one of the most widely respected science fiction stories of all time, John W. Campbell's "Who Goes There," which became the basis for the much lesser movie "The Thing.") The danger is that to see a doppelgänger is to risk imminent death[297] — and, indeed, the flight from the Dursleys' does bring death, although to Mad-Eye Moody, not to Harry.

The polyjuice potion, which produces doppelgängers, raises other interesting questions, some of them discussed under ANIMAGUS and TRANSFIGURATION. There are other variants on the idea of "becoming another person." For example, in *The Mabinogion,* the tale of "Pwyll Lord of Dyved" shows Pwyll swapping places with Arawn king of Annuvin for a year, so that each can rule the others' kingdom.

One does wonder if there were any instances of (say) husband and wife *both* taking polyjuice potion so as to take on the others' role, as identical twins are sometimes said to played each other in school or the like.

The whole "gimmick" of Ovid's *Metamorphoses* is of people or things (mostly people) changed into something else. Most of the changes are involuntary and permanent and involve only one person (or at least one group of people all undergoing the same change), but some sound rather "polyjuice-ish."

Doxy

The doxy, according to the *Order of the Phoenix,* has "shiny beetlelike wings," "tiny needle-sharp teeth," and a "fairylike body covered thick black hair," with four hands.[298] This is one of Rowling's stranger creatures, because "doxy" is an English word, and it doesn't refer to anything like this. Most English words involving the syllables "doxy" (e.g. "orthodoxy," "heterodoxy") are derived from the Greek root δοξα, *doxa, thought, notion, opinion, expectation.*[299] But "doxy" itself is an English word, although not commonly used today; it probably came into use around 1550 for a female beggar or a beggar's wife, and from there it came to mean a prostitute, and (much later) a foul old woman. It is perhaps this meaning which Rowling meant, but the sense "prostitute" is much more common. The root of the word is probably Dutch "docke," "doll,"[300] which can also mean a prostitute.

DRAGONS

In one sense, not much needs to be said about dragons, since almost every modern fantasy has them in some form or another; Gordon Dickson's *The Dragon and the George* is probably the most original modern treatment. They're Thompson Type B11. Dragons guarding treasure (as in the *Goblet of Fire*, or in Tolkien's *The Hobbit*, or in *Beowulf*, where the final third of the book tells of Beowulf having to fight a dragon which was aroused when someone stole one of its treasures*)* are B.11.6.2.

One of the most interesting things about dragons is their universality. Is a Norwegian Troll the same sort of being as an English Goblin? Hard to answer. But there is little doubt that a Chinese *lung* is the same sort of thing as a Croatian *zmaj* or a Finnish *lohikaarme* or a Turkish *ejderha* or a Cherokee *unktena*.[301] "The dragon or 'winged serpent'… is probably the most complex, widespread and ambivalent of mythical monsters, appearing in the mythology and symbolism of all nations."[302] It's as if some part of us just naturally imagines these reptilian fire-breathers. And yet, dragons aren't common in traditional Germanic folklore. Tolkien thought there were only two in northwest European tradition: Beowulf slays one that was apparently not sentient (but which, like the dragons in the Potter books, could be counted on to defend a treasure); Sigurð killed Fafnir that was sentient (indeed, in Norse myth, Fafnir had originally been a human who became a dragon because of greed,[303] an idea which C. S. Lewis adopted in *The Voyage of the Dawn Treader*); Tolkien also noted, but did not count, the Midgard Serpent of the Norse myths.[304]

Based on the geographic data in *Fantastic Beasts*, Beowulf's Dragon should have been a Swedish Short-Snout. The description does not fit well, however; Beowulf's Dragon, in addition to breathing fire, is poisonous — it is the poison that is ultimately fatal to Beowulf.[305]

The origins of the dragon legends have some interest, to scientists as well as folklorists; one Muggle scientist came up with an hypothesis based on the behavior of vervet monkeys. Their three great fears are leopards, snakes, and eagles. Combine the body of a leopard, the skin of a snake, and the wings of an eagle and you get something very like a dragon.[306] So perhaps the dragon is a combination of three instinctive primate fears. But this seems almost as much folklore as dragons themselves.

Muggle anthropologists have suggested that most dragon-slaying legends, including the Sigurð story and the legend of St. George and even sea monster stories such as the tale of Perseus and Andromeda, go back to the Mesopotamian story of the slaying of Tiamat and the creation of the world out of his body (which has also been claimed as the source of one of the Biblical tales of creation),[307] but even if this is accepted (and there are a lot of missing links in there), there doesn't seem to be much emphasis on dragon-*slayers* in the Potter books.

The Greek word δρακων, *drakon* (a word which the Greeks thought was derived from a verb meaning "to see clearly") gave us our word *dragon*, which "means 'serpent,' esp[ecially] 'dragon' or 'sea-monster.'"[308] The association of dragons with Satan is said to be widespread, found "in Persian, Babylonian and Assyrian, Egyptian and Greek mythology, and in essence this role is always the same; it is a power of chaos which opposes God either in the beginning of at the end of things."[309] The linkage with serpents is very strong; some would probably render the Greek word as *worm* or *wyrm* rather than *dragon*. Thus a Biblical dragon is actually more like Voldemort — an intelligent, evil serpent — than Rowling's flying fire-breathers!

Dragons are mentioned in the New Testament, in the Apocalypse (Revelation to John), where the Dragon represents the Devil. Note in particular Revelation 20:2, which refers to "the dragon, that ancient serpent, who is the Devil [διαβολος, *diabolos,* a native Greek word] and Satan" [a transliteration of the Hebrew word for *adversary* or *accusor*]. There are also many possible references in the Hebrew Bible (see also SEA SERPENT); it is likely that the Biblical mentions are responsible for putting the idea of dragons into European folklore (this would explain why they are so rare in non-Christian legends in Europe; they aren't "native").

On the other hand, the dragon in the Apocalypse is seen in a dream-vision, and it isn't clear what the dragon is actually like. Similarly with the mentions in the Hebrew Bible; it has been strongly suggested that some of the mentions of "dragons" in the King James Bible should refer to Sea Serpents.[310]

Although most Muggle cultures have some idea of dragons, their versions do not entirely agree. Is this an indication that they were observing different species of dragons? Possible, of course, but some of their dragon versions aren't much like any sort of real dragon. Perhaps they heard, from wizards, that there were different types of dragons, and then each made up their own version. After all, although we know that there are many types of dragons, the Muggles don't seem to be aware of it. By their standards, indeed, multiple species of dragons don't make sense. How much evolutionary pressure can there be on a species that can both fly and breathe fire?

Muggles did sometimes add something to the dragon legend. In China and Japan, for instance, old pine trees sometimes turn into dragons,[311] which would make it even harder to track them than it already is!

It should be pointed out that some of the information about dragons in *Fantastic Beasts* is inaccurate. For instance, Hebridean Blacks are said to require a territory of 100 square miles, or roughly 25,000 hectares. However, the inhabited isles of the Outer Hebrides have a combined area of less than 1200 square miles, and the smaller rocks add only about fifty more. The inhabited isles of the Inner Hebrides total about 1600 square miles. Thus the grand total of all the Hebrides is only about 3000 square miles, or enough land for thirty dragons. This is not enough for a sustainable population; genetic drift would eliminate them very quickly. Thus Hebridean Blacks must either have smaller territories or must have another region beyond the Hebrides which they inhabit.

Note that the name "Draco," as in "Draco Malfoy," is Latin for "dragon." Dumbledore's preface to *Fantastic Beasts* even uses the Latin name to this in his tag "Draco dormiens numquam titillandus" — "Never tickle sleeping dragons."

Dragon's Blood

Dragon's blood is a common potion ingredient in the Potter books; Dumbledore is said to have discovered twelve uses for it. (Compare Thompson D1355.3.8, "Dragonsblood as love charm.") Is this twelve uses for *all* dragon's blood, or uses for twelve kinds of dragon's blood? — we know there are multiple species of dragons in the Potter universe, which makes it likely that the different species would have different blood chemistries.

And is it actually the blood of a dragon? *Dragon's blood* is an actual chemical known to medieval scholars. Only it wasn't made from dragons — it was based on resin, although the exact recipe is a little unclear; it was imported to the west from Arabia and beyond. The color was a purplish-red, which gave rise to the name "dragon's blood."[312] (Cinnabar, or Mercury sulfate, HgS, was also sometimes called "dragon's blood," but this seems to have been the result of sloppy nomenclature.)

It is not clear if the organic sort of dragon's blood was an ingredient in Muggle alchemy (alchemical texts use very strange nomenclature, and tended to use it in mysterious ways anyway, so it's hard to tell) — but it was used in writing manuscripts, as an ink and a dye, employed for writing in red. It is almost as rare as "real" dragon's blood; it is no longer sold.

Dudley Dursley's Tail: see TAIL.

DUMBLEDORE, ALBUS

Although used as a given name in Rowling, "Dumbledore" is in fact an English noun, of relatively recent vintage (not recorded before 1787), used in some dialects for a bumblebee.[313] Thomas Hardy used the word in *The Mayor of Casterbridge,* and J. R. R. Tolkien's poem *Errantry* includes the lines

> He battled with the Dumbledors,
> The Hummerhorns, and Honeybees,
> And won the Golden Honeycomb.

Thus Tolkien was aware of the connection with bees. And so, it turns out, is Rowling, although she called it the "Old English" word for bumblebee (which it is not, since the word goes back only to 1787); she used the name for Dumbledore because he is benign, constantly moving, and hums quietly.[314]

Dumbledore's first name, Albus, is also interesting, since "albus" is the Latin word for "white," and there are many derivatives including "Albion," a name for Britain, the "White Island" (thought to be so named after the White Cliffs of Dover[315]). Thus Dumbledore is probably the White Wizard (as in, the one who fights on the side of "good" or "white" magic; see GOOD AND EVIL); he might also be the Wizard of Britain. This makes it interesting that Dumbledore's full name is "Albus Percival Wulfric Brian Dumbledore," because Perceval was the knight who, in the earliest versions of the Arthurian romances, achieved the Holy Grail;[316] perhaps the name hints at Dumbledore's quest for the DEATHLY HALLOWS. (Could this questing be a family trait? According to the biographies in the *Deathly Hallows,* Dumbledore's father was also named Perceval.) There are no really important Wulfrics in history or folklore, but it is a good Anglo-Saxon name, again suggesting Dumbledore's English-ness. "Brian" suggests such Celtic names as Brian Boru, the famous High King of Ireland who defeated the Norse invaders at the Battle of Clontarf, and Bran the Blessed, the semi-divine hero-king of Britain.[317] The mythological Brian, because of a murder he and his brothers committed, was condemned to seek various treasures[318] — a quest rather like Dumbledore's own for the Deathly Hallows. Thus all of Dumbledore's names at least hint at his very, very deep British-ness, dating back before the Norman Conquest, and even before the Anglo-Saxon Invasions.

DWARF

This is a conundrum. In the *Chamber of Secrets,* chapter 13, Gilderoy LOCKHART brings in a crew of dwarfs for Valentine's Day to cheer up the students, with Harry of course being subjected to Ginny Weasley's poem "His eyes are as green as a fresh pickled toad...."

But what are these dwarfs? The problem is, there are two meanings for the word "dwarf." One is simply a small human. The other is a creature of folklore, mentioned frequently in Norse myth; several sources assume that this is the type of dwarf involved in the *Chamber of Secrets.*[319]

In neither case is LOCKHART being very appropriate. In the Middle Ages, it was not uncommon for the nobility to hire small humans as jesters, or simply to put them in freak shows. For Lockhart to hire small humans to deliver singing telegrams is a dreadful reminiscence of this practice. On the other hand, for him to impose this role on another sentient species, and one with an ancient and noble history, is terrible. Of course, this *is* LOCKHART we're talking about....

So are they small humans, or something else? There are several indirect clues. First is the plural we see used. It is "dwarfs," not "dwarves" or "dwarrows." "Dwarfs" is the proper Modern English plural for a short person. By contrast, the creatures of Norse folklore are now generally assigned the plural "dwarves," the name given by J. R. R. Tolkien to these creatures based on his linguistic studies,[320] which were a substantial part of his mythology. Second, dwarfs are rarely mentioned in the Potter books — an odd thing if they were a separate sentient species. Finally, and probably most decisively, the Potterverse has a set of creatures equivalent to the Norse and Tolkien dwarves. They're called GOBLINS. As the entry for them shows, they are in many ways almost identical to Tolkien dwarves. It is not impossible for there to be two sets of creatures in the same ecological niche — but neither is it likely. Much more likely that the dwarfs of the Potterverse are just that: small people, not a separate species.

Edifices: see HOGWARTS: THE EDIFICE.

Golden Egg

In the *Goblet of Fire,* one of Harry's tasks is to steal a golden egg from a dragon.

Eggs in general have a very rich folklore, often as a symbol of life — after all, a living creature comes out of a seemingly-dead egg! This is part of why eggs are a symbol of Easter and resurrection, for example.[321] They are also used for divination, and eggs are sometimes said to be used as sailing vessels by witches — which caused many peoples to crush empty eggshells.[322]

The golden egg is a much more specific item, and seems always to be associated with geese. There is one tale of a man killing the golden goose to try to get all the gold at once,[323] but the usual tale of the goose that laid the golden eggs (Thompson D876) is in the story of "Jack and the Beanstalk" (Thompson motif 328, "The Boy Steals the Giant's Treasure"), in which a giant in the clouds has a golden goose (and a golden harp that plays itself), and Jack steals both and kills the giant.[324] The only significance of the golden eggs in this case seems to be the fact that they are golden and hence valuable; they have no magic powers.

I know of no folk tales of stealing eggs from a dragon, but stealing eggs from a bird is part of Thompson K305.1.

Isaac Asimov once wrote a science fiction story, "Pâté de Foie Gras," about what would happen if a group of scientists were confronted with an actual goose that laid golden eggs.

See also OCCAMY.

The Elder Wand: see under The DEATHLY HALLOWS.

Elf, Elves: see HOUSE ELVES.

The Elixir Of Life: see under The PHILOSOPHER'S STONE.

The Enchanted Lake: see The LAKE.

ERKLING

Is this a typo in *Fantastic Beasts?* The "erkling" is said there to be a murderous creature from Germany's Black Forest area. There is such a creature in folklore, but it is called the "erlking" or "erlkönig." ("König" is German for "king." The creature is sometimes said to be the King of the Dwarves.[325]) "In German legend, a malevolent goblin who haunts forests and lures people, especially children, to destruction."[326] The creature became famous largely because of a poem, "Der Erlkönig," by Goethe (translated by Walter Scott[327]), "in which a father riding home with a delirious and dying child in his arms is pursued by the goblin."[328] The poem ends with the father carrying the dead child in his arms; he had not been able to outrun the soul-stealer.

ETHNIC PURITY

"Do not marry a girl from abroad" is Thompson J21.4. This is a topic carrying a very heavy political burden right now, and I really don't want to get into that! But Rowling clearly supports the liberal view that marriages between magic users and Muggles are proper and fair, and does not accept the view that the Muggle-born should be treated as "mud-bloods" (although even the term "Muggle" is rather pejorative). Nonetheless, the separatist view is very ancient, and marks one of the places where Rowling rather goes against Biblical tradition: both Nehemiah and Ezra attempted to ban marriages between Jews and non-Jews (Ezra 10:9–17; Nehemiah 9:2, etc.). And Solomon is condemned for his marriages to foreign women (1 Kings 11:1–11, etc.), and foreign women are several times condemned in the Pentateuch (Numbers 25:1–9, the Baal of Peor affair, is a typical example). The Bible is not the only instance of this sort of ethnic purity. Brother-sister marriages were common among the Egyptian Pharaohs because Pharaohs were supposed to be semi-divine and didn't want too much mortal blood. The Persian monarchs also tended to marry into a very small circle — the seven noble families who had put Darius I on the throne. The Greek gods were very inbred — Hera, e.g., was her husband Zeus's sister.[329]

On the other hand, the Biblical book of Ruth clearly praises a foreign woman and even says that the great King David was descended from one (Ruth 4:13–22). The New Testament shows Jesus's followers including both Greeks (Philip and Andrew are definitely Greek names) and Jews (Simon, James, John, Judas, and most of the rest of the Twelve Disciples have Hebrew names) — indeed, Simon/Cephas has a Hebrew name, and Andrew a Greek, yet they are brothers (Mark 1:16, etc.), raising a strong possibility that they were born of a "mixed marriage." Thus, although there are many places in the Bible which stress genetic exclusiveness, Rowling's inclusiveness is also an old and well-attested tradition.

Rowling's world also bears an interesting twist on the techniques of modern fantasy. Many fantasies are dynastic[330] — few more so than Tolkien's, where the line of Aragorn can trace its ancestry for more than six thousand years, including a thousand years as wanderers without a nation of their own. And the most magically powerful elves are the ones with the best bloodlines. Shakespeare's history plays are also dynastic fantasy (emphasis on the fantasy, since they contain very little history, but they're certainly about the dynasty of the Plantagenets and which ones deserved to be kings).

In the Potterverse, on the other hand, the purebloods — those who can most explicitly trace their ancestry far back — are mostly the bad guys. There are, of course, purebloods who are good people (the Weasleys, Sirius Black), but the impression we gain is that Voldemort's forces are almost entirely purebloods. Or, as we might say it, racists.

This makes it interesting to note that the Malfoys, those staunch purebloods, have the yellow hair of the Nazi/"Teutonic" ideal.[331] To be sure, many other Death Eaters are darker-haired, but the Malfoys are the most visible of the type.

It is worth asking if the pure-bloods could actually survive without Muggle-born. We know that there are eight Gryffindors in Harry's class. If all houses had the same number of students, that would mean only thirty-two students per year at Hogwarts. The total may be a little more than that (it is likely that Hufflepuff, the non-selective house, would have a larger population), but it seems unlikely that there were more than fifty students per year. Assume an average lifetime of eighty years and we find that there are a mere four thousand wizards in all of Britain and Ireland. Perhaps fifteen hundred of them are of breeding age. What fraction of them are purebloods? We don't really know, but if Slytherin House is half pureblood and the rest a quarter pureblood, then perhaps a third of wizards are pureblood. Five hundred purebloods of breeding age. In such a small group, genetic drift will have major effects, including a high chance of abnormalities such as low intelligence. Which might explain Crabbe and Goyle....

Fairy, Fairies

Fairies play little role in the Harry Potter story, but they are mentioned in *Fantastic Beasts* as being small, attractive, and not very bright.

The great problem with discussing the folklore idea of "fairies" is that there is no real definition of a fairy, and the word is used to translate a wide variety of non-English words: "Since the term 'fairy' has come to be applied so widely to all diminutive sprites, mischievous or friendly, visible or not, it is difficult to define it with any precision."[332] Michael Denham listed some 170 different types of "fairy" just in English folklore.[333]

J. R. R. Tolkien remarked tartly that not even the *Oxford English Dictionary* could make much sense of fairies.[334] The word "fairy" is thought to derive from "fey" or "fay," which might be translated as "fairy-struck" — a person who is not insane, necessarily, but who sees things in a different way or from an unusual perspective. Often those who are fey cease to value their lives as ordinary folk do; those who are manic and those who are in despair may both become fey.

"The basic European repertoire of beliefs and tales about fairies is less fully preserved in England than in the Celtic areas of Wales, Ireland, and Highland Scotland.... Unfortunately it has been overshadowed by literary portrayals, medieval, Shakespearean, or modern":[335] Shakespeare's contribution probably began with Titania, Oberon, and Puck in *A Midsummer Night's Dream*. Fairy rings, the rings of trampled grass (or of mushrooms) in which fairies danced, seem to be first mentioned in *The Tempest*.[336] Pigwiggen (i.e. Pigwidgeon) was also a fairy. From this already dumbed-down concept, we proceed to the Tooth Fairy and Tinkerbell, small, attractive, generally voiceless creatures not far removed from the concept in the Potterverse.

For an example of the Celtic version of fairies, try online resources for "Sidhe," the Irish version — the very word "sidhe" properly means "mound," where the fairies used to dwell.[337] In Scotland, they were divided into the "Seelie" and the "Unseelie" Court, depending on whether they were good (safe, sociable) or not.[338]

The major recent attempt to reclaim "fairies" was probably by Tolkien, for whom a fairy was an inhabitant of "Faërie," the perilous realm, and not necessarily small. "Faërie" is the land to which (e.g.) Heurodis was carried in the romance of "Sir Orfeo"; here, the Fairies are a numerous people, "all... on snow-white steeds, their clothes white as milk.... The king had a crown on his head that was not of silver or red gold, but it was all of a precious stone; as bright as the sun it shone."[339] Their land is underground, accessed through a rock, it is "a fair country, as bright as the sun on a summer's day, smooth and level and covered with green"; it made Orfeo think of paradise.[340] Faërie, or Elfland, is the middle way, leading neither to heaven nor hell; The Queen of Elfland, after showing Thomas of Ercildoune the roads to Heaven and Hell, points out

> And see not ye that bonny road
> That winds about the fernie bray?
> That is the road to fair Elfland,
> Where thou and I this night maun gae.[341] *[must go]*

Tolkien died when J. K. Rowling was still a child, but his distinction probably stands: The Potter books are not about fairies, but they are, in the highest sense, a Fairy-Story.

FAMILIAR

In the *Philosopher's Stone,* beginning students are advised that they may bring one animal — owl or cat or toad — to Hogwarts. Nowhere are we told that these animals are the students' familiars, but the idea of a witch or wizard having an animal companion — or at least something that *looks* like an animal companion — is well-known: "Familiars. Minor demons who, at Satan's command, become the servants of a human wizard wizard or witch. It is one of the distinctive features of English witchcraft that these spirits were very often thought to take the form of small animals, such as would be found around farms and homes...."[342] These creatures did not have to be mammals, or even vertebrates; one story involves a man who had bumblebees as familiars! Other animals claimed as familiars include CATS, dogs, toads, mice, rabbits, black birds and even flies;[343] also, some were creatures not found in nature. Today, we think of black cats as the "standard" familiar, but supposedly mice and toads were once the most popular in Britain, so that the phrase "I'll toad 'ee!" was used as a warning and threat,[344] since one of the tasks of familiars was to go after the enemies of the witch.

The Potterverse alters the idea of the familiar quite significantly. There is no real conversation between the animals in the Potter books and their owners; certainly the creatures are not demonic, and they aren't sentient, either (at least, they don't speak; Crookshanks is obviously very bright indeed, and Hedwig is also much brighter than any real owl). And owls and toads are not animals found at home, so they would not be a likely candidate for a true witch's familiar. But by using them for delivering mail, Rowling has taken the idea of a familiar and made it something that a witch could usefully employ *without* needing to employ an evil spirit — a clever twist. Indeed, the animal which acts most like a traditional familiar is Mrs. Norris, Filch's cat — but Mrs. Norris cannot really be a familiar, because Filch is a squib!

In a way, the real familiar of the Potterverse is not the wizards' pets but their patronuses — which are a genuine aid, and which can be made to speak. This would also explain why they are always animals; why, if you think about it, shouldn't a patronus be human, or a robot, or even a self-guided bicycle?

Fate: see FELIX FELICIS.

FELIX FELICIS

Felix is the Latin word for "luck" or "lucky" — the conqueror Roman Lucius Cornelius Sulla, for instance, took the surname "Felix" because he had been so successful.[345] So the name *felix felicis* amounts to "lucky luck" — and Hermione's description of the potion as "liquid luck"[346] is pretty close to dead-on.

The idea of luck as an actual physical item is by no means original to Rowling. The Romans felt that luck was a commodity that some people had and others didn't — hence that tendency to call people "Felix." Luck often came from a *genius*, which to the Romans was a sort of guardian spirit.

The Romans weren't the only ones; "Whether good or bad, 'luck' is an idea basic to folk belief, ancient and widespread."[347] This is related, in a way, to the idea of "fate" — a destiny attached to a person whether looked-for or not. The notion of a sort of personified destiny is a widespread idea — note the Three Fates of Greek mythology, or the Three Norns. In Anglo-Saxon, we have the word *wyrd,* which means something like fate, or destiny, but isn't quite as deterministic as that sounds: "*Wyrd* can be an oppressive force, then, for no one can change the past; but it is perhaps not as oppressive as 'fate' or even 'fortune,' which extend into the future.... '*Wyrd* often spares the man who is not doomed,' says Beowulf, but he adds 'as long as his courage holds.'"[348] How reminiscent of the battle in the *Half-Blood Prince* in which Hermione, Ron, and Ginny survive by fighting but trusting their (artificially enhanced) luck!

Filch, Argus: see under **HERMIONE.**

FINGAL THE FEARLESS

Quidditch refers briefly to this "legendary" Irish wizard, who "is alleged" to have been a champion of the broomstick-riding game of Aingingein. This raises the question: Is Fingal the Fearless the inspiration for the Celtic hero Fingal? The name "Fingal" is artificial, a Scottish version of the name Fionn mac Cumhaill (anglicized as "Finn MacCool"[349]), but it is well-known because of its use by James MacPherson ("Ossian") and by Felix Mendelsohn.[350] Mac Cumhaill is "the most celebrated hero in Irish literature and folklore. Stories about him are continuous in the literature for well over 1,000 years."[351] He was both a warrior and a seer.

Interestingly, mac Cumhaill seems almost like a graft into an existing literature; "already in the seventh century, the Leinster genealogists were at work finding a place for Fionn in the tracts."[352] This is exactly what we would expect if mac Cumhaill were a real person who had to be amalgamated into a legendary framework (and some of his exploits are also told of others, including King Arthur and Taliesin: Ellis, p. 99, who mentions the idea that Fionn, like Arthur, is sleeping in a cave, and that Fionn — like Taliesin, although Ellis does not point this up — accidentally consumes the potion of wisdom meant for another and is forced to flee). He is said to have been able to outrun deer,[353] which makes some sense for someone who participated in a sport where the point was to fly through burning hoops at the greatest possible speed!

These parallels are interesting, but since so little is known of Fingal the Fearless, we probably have to leave the matter there.

Lost/Missing Fingers: see PETER PETTIGREW'S FINGER.

Flamel, Nicholas: see The PHILOSOPHER'S STONE.

FLUFFY

Fluffy, the three-headed sort-of dog who guards the way to the PHILOSOPHER'S STONE, is obviously a riff on Cerberus, the dog which guarded the underworld in Greek myth (note that Hagrid got Fluffy from a "Greek chappie"). Cerberus was normally said to have three heads, although Hesiod credited him with fifty.[354] Music could be used to tame it, just as in the Harry Potter books — although, in Greek myth, it took the music of Orpheus to do the trick.[355]

Chaining Cerberus was one of the Twelve Labors of Hercules.[356]

Hercules defeating Cerberus, woodcut from an edition of Ovid's Metamorphoses *published by Janson and Tempesta, 1606. From Los Angeles County Museum of Art via Wikimedia.*

Fluffy isn't nearly as deadly as Cerberus; some tales say that the latter's glance could turn one to stone (see PETRIFICATION), and his spittle was said to have been the source of the poison aconite.[357] Aconite is found in the plant known as monkshood or wolfsbane, which Snape asks Harry about in his very first potions lesson in chapter eight of the *Philosopher's Stone.*

"Dog as Guardian of Treasure" is Thompson B292.8.

FLYING CARPETS

According to the *Goblet of Fire,* flying carpets are forbidden in Britain but are manufactured somewhere in the Middle East (where their popularity is said to have reduced the interest in Quidditch, a sport which cannot be played on carpets). Flying carpets seem like a good idea as a family means of transport; although there are many ways for wizards to travel, there doesn't seem to be a good way for a family of British wizards to all travel together.

"Magical carpets" are Thompson D1155, but they are rare in western folklore. Jewish folklore claims that Solomon had a carpet that could travel magically,[358] but there is absolutely no hint of this in the Bible — the word "carpet" does not even occur in the King James Bible. Western knowledge of flying carpets probably comes primarily from the *Thousand and One Nights;* in the tale of "The Story of Prince Ahmed and the Fairy Paribanou,"[359] Prince Houssain (the eldest son of a sultan, who is competing with his younger brothers for the hand of his cousin, a princess) has one. The merchant who sold it to him said of it, "whoever sits on this piece of tapestry may be transported in an instant wherever he desires to be, without being stopped by any obstacle."[360]

E. Nesbit's *The Phoenix and the Carpet,* part of the "Psammead" series which was one of Rowling's major influences, was titled after the two primary magical objects it featured, a phoenix and a flying carpet.

The FORBIDDEN FOREST

Although the adventures of Our Heroes in the Forbidden Forest are unique, the concept known as "Into the Woods" is old.[361] And so are haunted forests. Dante opens the *Inferno* "alone in a dark wood,"[362] which we usually call "the wood of error." Shakespeare's *A Midsummer Night's Dream* takes us "Into the Woods" as well. The forest is the usual scene of "Little Red Riding Hood" and many other tales; Hansel and Gretl get lost there, and Sleeping Beauty's castle is usually surrounded by thick woods. Tolkien loved forests, whether basically good (Fangorn) or wicked (The Old Forest) or capable of being influenced either way (Mirkwood, which was made dark by the presence of Sauron in Dul Guldur). He also mythologized on the "Woodwos[es]" of *Sir Gawain and the Green Knight* (line 721, "Somwhyle with wodwos, þat woned in þe knarres";[363] Tolkien's and Davis's edition of the poem explains wodwos as "satyrs, trolls of the forest,"[364] and Tolkien translates the word as "wood-trolls" in his modernization[365]; he would later re-imagine *wodwos* as a false form, with the original being *woodwose,* woodman, who became his *woses*[366]). LeGuin was so fascinated by treescapes that she wrote a long story, "The Word for World is Forest." *The Wind in the Willows,* one of the most beloved of English children's tales, is set largely in the Wild Wood. Even Winnie-the-Pooh lived in the Hundred Acre Wood. Little wonder, then, that the Forbidden Forest is unsafe, and that uncanny things are found there.

The Fountain of Fair Fortune

Beedle's tale is about a magical well — or, rather, the quest to reach one. Magical fountains and wells are a commonplace — there are said to be two hundred holy wells in England alone.[367] A famous example in folklore is the Fountain of Youth (the quest for which is Thompson H1321.3). Wishing wells, too, date back very far.[368] There is also at least one Cursing Well, at Llanelian-yn-Rhos.[369] (A cursing well lets you drop in an offering and offer a curse, as you offer a wish at a wishing well.) As between wells and fountains, the latter seem to inspire more stories — "Fountain as lovers' rendezvous" (Thompson T35.1), "Hero finds maiden at fountain" (Thompson N715.1), "Location of fountain revealed in dream" (Thompson K1816.1), "Magic fountain" (Thompson D925), and many more. Probably the seemingly-living nature of the water in a fountain gave rise to the thought that it was somehow magical.

An early instance of a magical fountain is in the Bible, at the beginning of chapter 5 of John, regarding the pool of Beth-zatha/Bethesda/Bethsaida, where folklore says that the pool sometimes foamed up, and that the first person to enter it when it did so would be healed of whatever disease afflicted him. (This explanation, in fact, is found in the King James Bible, but it is not part of the original text of John's gospel.) Observe that, just as in "The Fountain of Fair Fortune," only one person had the chance to gain the benefit of the pool.

The ROMANCE of *Owein, or The Countess of the Fountain,* in the *Mabinogion,* involves a fountain with mysterious powers. There are many other fountain stories in Arthurian legend.

Many of the penalties in the Beedle's story also have their place in folklore. When Sir Luckless attempts to pay with his only coin, we are reminded of the many tales of people sharing the only meal they have. There is also the New Testament tale of the Widow's Mite, in which Jesus sees a poor widow put two coins in the collection basket and declares to his disciples, "this poor widow has put in more than all those who are contributing to the treasury. For all of them have contributed out of their abundance; but she out of her poverty has put in everything she had, all she had to live on."[370]

The idea of a river that causes one to forget all one's ills goes back at least to the Greek Lethe (Λη θη), the river of the underworld; the dead forgot their earthly lives upon drinking from it.[371]

The idea of a place that is magic not in itself but because of what is learned to get there is the basis of Alexander's *Taran Wanderer,* where the Mirror of Llunet corresponds to the Fountain of Fair Fortune.

Free Will: see under WHICH SIDE ARE YOU ON?

The Gates of Hell: see under **The Door of Death.**

Ghosts: see under **The Soul.**

Ghouls

Fantastic Beasts describes ghouls as ugly but mostly harmless. This seems to fit the most important ghoul we encounter, the creature in the Weasley attic which, in the *Deathly Hallows,* is disguised so that it appears to be Ron; prior to that time, it had done little except occasionally create noise.

These minor "haunts" do not match the traditional description of the ghoul, which is a lesser demon of Arabic origin, sometimes written as *ghūl.* The females were sometimes called *ghulah;*[372] these were to be distinguished from male *qutrub.*[373] They were said to haunt graveyards and consume corpses, turning to living creatures when that did not supply a sufficient diet. They might also appear in deserts. In the *Thousand and One Nights,* the fifteenth night features "The Tale of the King's Son and the She-Ghoul," in which a female ghoul tries to lure a prince into her home in a ruin, so that she can feed him to their children. This seems to involve the ghoul taking on human form.[374] But thought they are said to be able to change shapes, they must always retain their hooved feet.[375]

This shape-shifting ability might explain why Hermione in the *Chamber of Secrets* mentions "chameleon ghouls." There also seems to be some uncertainty about just how deadly they are (an indication that they were more common in the Middle East than in England, perhaps?). The Weasley ghoul is mostly noisy, but Gilderoy Lockhart wrote a book, *Gadding with Ghouls,* which would seem to imply that they were more nasty, and a "murderous old ghoul" turns up in a bathroom in Sirius Black's house in the *Order of the Phoenix*. Harry in the *Deathly Hallows* is "sure that ghouls were generally rather slimy and bald,"[376] but we aren't told why he feels this way; at least some traditional ghouls are said to have been hairy, while others looked like a one-eyed ostrich.[377]

GIANTS

Thompson Type F531.

As Katharine Briggs tartly remarks, "About the only trait that [folk-loric] giants have in common is their enormous size and strength."[378]

The pseudo-historian Geoffrey of Monmouth, writing in the twelfth century, claimed that giants were the only inhabitants of Britain until Brutus came there after the Trojan War. Brutus and his followers drove the giants to hide in the mountains[379] — a situation that sounds much like Rowling's history of giants in England.

A giant called Gogmagog was well-known in medieval England; the name being based probably on the Gog and Magog of Ezekiel chapters 38–39.[380] Geoffrey describes him as fighting Corineus, for whom Cornwall was named, in the period after the arrival of Brutus.[381]

Legends of giants are much older, of course. There are giants mentioned in the Bible — the Rephaim and Anakim;[382] probably also the Nephilim, mentioned in the entry on HAGRID AND THE HALF-GIANTS. We have several measures of these creatures' sizes, notable the bed of King Og of Bashan, one of the Rephaim. This was nine cubits long (Deut. 3:11) — meaning that he was presumably shorter than this thirteen foot height. This is shorter than Rowling's giants. But then, Og wasn't magical. Even the Potterverse' giants pale in comparison to the forty foot monster in the ROMANCE of the *Lybaeus Desconus*.[383] This is pretty typical of Arthurian ROMANCES — "all Arthurian heroes at some time or another" are confronted with giants,[384] their usual technique being to cut off the giant at the knees so they were the same height. This also occurs in Child ballad #59, Sir Aldingar.

The Norse gods were the enemies of the giants — and the giants were the stronger. And, on the whole, the smarter. They were able to deceive Thor and Loki, and Vafthrúdnir was able to play knowledge games even with Odin, who had made tremendous sacrifices to gain wisdom.[385] In the end, Odin in effect cheated to win the contest with Vafthrúdnir, asking not a riddle but a piece of hidden knowledge — much as Bilbo Baggins asked what he had in his pockets in Tolkien's *The Hobbit*: "What did Odin say in the ear of his son before he mounted the pyre,"[386] i.e. "what did Odin whisper to the body of Baldr before burning the corpse" — something that no one but Odin could know. (Vafthrúdnir *does* get the last word; until that time, he had treated Odin as an unknown traveller, but once Odin cheats, Vafthrúdnir calls him out as the chief god.) The Norse giants also have a high culture — nothing like Rowling's uncivilized brutes.

The Irish tale of *Bricriu's Feast* features a giant who fights with three different Irish heroes; the same tale goes on to tell of the Beheading Game that was also the chief component of the famous *Sir Gawain and the Green Knight*.[387]

The Titans of Greek myth were giants, the fathers of the later normal-sized Gods.[388] This idea that giants preceded ordinary humans is surprisingly common. Even in the Bible, they seem to exist primarily before the Flood. In Norse myth, Ymir the giant preceded the Gods. And in Aztec tales, "The first men created by the gods were giants; they neither sowed grain nor tilled the soil, but lived by eating acorns and other fruits and wild roots."[389]

Of the modern writers, only Alexander and Lewis mentions giants, and we never actually encounter them in Alexander — he simply refers to the story in the *Mabinogion* of *How Culhwch Won Olwen*, in which Olwen is the daughter of the chief giant (but herself seemingly human). Tolkien's name "Ents" is supposedly based on an old word for "giants," but Tolkien recorded that Ents were not based on any folklore he knew.

Since Ysbaddaden father of Olwen was the "chief giant"[390] in *How Culhwych Won Olwen*, the Welsh obviously believed that there were many more giants. In addition, the god Brân is said to have been so tall that no house could ever cover him.[391] It has been suggested that, in Welsh, "giant" was simply a word for an important person,[392] as we might refer to a "big man" — but there seems to be no direct evidence for this.

The Potterverse's giants seem rather more reminiscent of C. S. Lewis's than those in the *Mabinogion* — foolish, violent, and mostly wicked although they can sometimes be brought around.

See also HAGRID AND THE HALF-GIANTS.

It's interesting to ask why the wizarding world tries to hide giants. Are giants in fact magical creatures? The answer is probably "yes" — because it takes magic to keep their bodies working. The fact that giants are big affects their bodies in many ways. There is a mathematical rule called the square-cube law which says that, as the length of an object increases, the surface area increases as the square of the length, and the volume increases as the cube of the length.

In practical terms, that means that the Biblical giant Og was almost too heavy to walk on human-type legs; the Potterverse's seemingly human-but-scaled-up giants aren't really possible under the laws of Muggle physics. Something that tall needs to build thicker legs — think about how thick an elephant's legs are. So giants are definitely magical.

The square-cube rule applies to giants in more ways than one. They need big legs to hold up all that extra weight — but the increase in size gives them much bigger brains. Proportionally, giants would have more brains per height than humans. So why aren't they smarter? Possibly it's because much thinking seems to happen on the surface of the brain, and that doesn't increase as fast as the volume of the brain. More likely, though, it's just that no fantasy writer worried about it much....

GILLYWEED

There is, of course, no such plant as Gillyweed, which in the *Goblet of Fire* allows Harry to breathe through gills. This is similar to Thompson D170, Human to Fish. The name, although not the activity, of the plant may have been suggested by the Gillyflower, which is another name for the carnation and similar plants. The gillyflower is said to be associated with heaven in folklore.[393] It is mentioned by Shakespeare ("The fairest flow'rs o' th' season Are our carnations and streak'd gillyvors,"[394] and possibly by Chaucer ("and many a clowe-gylofre";[395] glossed as a "clove"). In the old flower symbolism (in which Rosemary, as Ophelia says, is for remembrance, and so forth), we learn that

> *Gillyflowers* is for gentleness,
> Which in me shall remain,
> Hoping that no sedition shall
> Depart our hearts in twain.[396]

One rhyme that you may know in another form also mentions the gillyflower:

The rose is red, the violet blue,
The gillyflower sweet, and so are you.
These are the words you bade me say
For a pair of new gloves on Easter day.[397]

The plant is also associated with women who die in childbirth who are taken to heaven:

"Their beds are made in the heavens high,
Down at the foot of our good Lord's knee,
Well set about wi gilly-flowers...."[398]

Several other ballads involve gillyflowers: "Babylon" (Child #14 C); "The Gardner" (Child #219 A, B); "Young Peggy" (Child #198).[399]

There are instances in balladry of herbs transfiguring a person into an animal; also of people being turned into fish, although not via herbs.[400]

It seems pretty unlikely that Rowling connected gillyflower with gillyweed, but it is interesting that the gillyflower serves to bring lovers together, and that Harry uses gillyweed to be reunited with what he treasures most.

The idea of a non-technological way for humans to live underwater occurs several times in folklore; the Irish, for instance, imagine the *Cothulin Druith,* a headpiece which allowed an underwater existence.[401] Compare also the tales of Selkies, under ANIMAGUS.

Even to Muggles, the idea of humans growing gills is not as absurd as it sounds. Embryological and genetic studies show that we retain at least some of the genes used in fish to create gills; the trick the gillyweed would have to perform would be to activate them — and hope that the genes still work after long being unused. There is no real possibility that the genes would be unchanged — but there might be enough gill genes left that gillyweed would perhaps have to override only a few.

There is a second problem, though, and that is the availability of oxygen. Water does not hold as much oxygen as air. Cold water holds more oxygen than warm, but not enough. A warm-blooded animal, especially one with a large brain, cannot function on the amount of oxygen in water. (This is why dolphins and whales, the smartest creatures in the ocean, are air-breathers; they need the extra oxygen.) So gillyweed, in addition to activating the gills, would have to somehow make up for oxygen deficiency. Perhaps this is why it wears off so soon; it can cover up hypoxia for only so long....

GINEVRA

Why did the Weasleys name their one and only daughter "Ginevra"? Talk about a name of ill omen!

Ginevra (full name, Ginevra dei Benci[402]) was a character in the poem "Italy" by Samuel Rogers (1763–1855); her story is often split off as a separate poem, "Ginevra." "Italy" was published 1822–1828. The first and last lines of "Ginevra" are as follows:

> If thou shouldest ever come by chance or choice
> To Modena, where still religiously
> Among the ancient trophies is still preserved
> Bologna's bucket....
> Stop at a palace near the Reggio-gate,
> Dwelt in of old by one of the Orsini.
> Its noble gardens, terrace above terrace,
> And rich in fountains, statues, cypresses,
> Will long detain thee; but, ere thou go,
> Enter the house — prithee, forget it not —
> And look awhile upon a picture there.
>
>   * * *
>
> Full fifty years were past, and all forgot,
> When, on an idle day, a day of search
> 'Mid the old lumber in the Gallery,
> That mouldering chest was noticed; and 'twas said
> By one as young, as thoughtless as Ginevra,
> "Why not remove it from its lurking-place?"
> 'Twas done as soon as said; but on the way
> It burst, it fell; and lo! a skeleton,
> With here and there a pearl, an emerald-stone,
> A golden clasp, clasping a shred of gold.
> All else had perished, — save a nuptial ring,
> And a small seal, her mother's legacy,
> Engraven with a name, the name of both,
> "GINEVRA."
> There, then, she had found a grave.
> Within that chest she had concealed herself,
> Fluttering with joy, the happiest of the happy;
> When a spring lock, that lay in ambush there,
> Fastened her down for ever![403]

This is the long form of the story of "The Mistletoe Bride," in which a girl, laughing, tells her newly-wedded husband that she will hide and he must find her. She hides in a chest — which locks her in and muffles her cries. She dies in the chest and is not found until long after. This legend also became the basis of "The Mistletoe Bough," a song by Thomas Haynes Bayly:

> An oak chest that had long lay hid
> Was found in the castle, they raised the lid,
> And a skeleton form lay mouldering there,
> In the bridal wreath of a lady fair....

This has been found in tradition in both England and the U. S.; it seems particularly popular in the American Midwest.

It is just barely possible that the story is true; stories of a bride who married on Christmas Eve and vanished, to be found dead much later, are recorded from Maxwell Hall, Owslebury, Hampshire; Brockdish Hall, Norfolk; Minster Lovell Hall, Oxfordshire; and Bramshill House near Basingstoke, Hampshire.[404]

To be sure, there are other Ginevras in history and myth. Sir Edward Bulwer-Lytton (the "It was a dark and stormy night" author) in his poem "The Fairy Bride" (an adaption of the romance of *Sir Landval*) calls King Arthur's wife "Ginevra" rather than "Guinevere."[405] Perhaps of slightly greater relevance is the character Ginevra in *Orlando Furioso*, who is falsely accused and condemned to die until a champion, Rinoldo, "proves" her innocence in a trial by battle.[406] This is vaguely similar to how Ginny Weasley was taken over by the diary and rescued by Harry. Also, Ginevra degli Amieri, known from Shelley's *Story of Ginevra*, becomes ill and is buried alive before escaping, which also has some similarities to the story of the *Chamber of Secrets*. But the similarity in both cases is faint, and how could the Weasleys have known Ginny's fate? The poem "Ginevra" seems to be far better known in any case.

GNOMES

We first meet gnomes in the *Chamber of Secrets*, where they are a semi-intelligent speaking species of lawn pests. The small size fits the classic Muggle idea of the gnome, but the rest does not; they were creatures found in treasure mines. In their more benevolent moments, they might guard miners or guide them to treasure.[407] In the Middle Ages, when philosophers thought that the universe was composed of four elements, Earth, Air, Fire, and Water, gnomes were a sort of earth elemental. The physician Paracelsus, who was important enough to have a Chocolate Frog card, is sometimes credited with inventing the word "gnome";[408] he thought they could swim through earth the way a fish swims through water. It has been suggested that the name is Greek, from γηνομος, ge-nomos, earth-home, earth-dweller,[409] although this word is not actually attested in Classical or New Testament Greek, and others have argued for New Latin gnomus, although this isn't any better attested. Alexander Pope helped popularize the word in *The Rape of the Lock:* "The four elements are inhabited by spirits called sylphs, gnomes, nymphs [otherwise called undines], and salamanders. The gnomes, or demons of the earth, delight in mischief."[410] The standard garden gnome statue was a German invention imported into England in the 1860s.[411] J. R. R. Tolkien initially called his Noldorin Elves "gnomes," thinking the name implied wisdom (it is similar to the Greek word γνωσις, *gnosis, knowledge*), but eventually abandoning the idea when he realized that most people though of the word in terms of garden gnomes.[412]

Xenophilus Lovegood has various comments about gnomes — that they are "wise," that their saliva is beneficial, and that their scientific name is *Gernumbli gardensi.* This all has about as much scientific value as anything else Lovegood says, though — e.g. the "scientific" name is just Latinized English (the Latin root for "garden" is *hortus,* whence *horticulture,* and there is of course no classical Latin name for gnomes).

Because gnomes did not become part of folklore until relatively recently, we sometimes see other creatures described by the name.

The gnome has one other interesting feature: it is one of the few creatures, if not the *only* creature, in *Fantastic Beasts* to have a natural predator (the Jarvey). Yet it is evident that there must be other magical predators, or else there wouldn't be anything to control the dragons, chimaerae, and manticora that proliferate in the Potterverse. Perhaps it's time a few wizards went to Muggle schools to study ecology, biology, and biological statistics. It might have made Magizoology a much safer topic. Also, a creature that could see through (for instance) demiguise hair could be very useful for security services....

The Goblet of Fire: see under AMULETS.

GOBLINS

"Goblin" is one of those words that has no particular meaning — notice that Tolkien called his evil creatures "Goblins" in *The Hobbit* but later took to calling them Orcs; he felt the name "goblin" was too vague. The word is relatively recent; it cannot be traced before the sixteenth century.[413] The source may be from Greek κοβαλος, *kobalos, impudent rogue, arrogant knave, mischievous goblin;*[414] there may also have been a French intermediate.[415] The same Greek word probably gave rise to the Germanic "kobold," another sort of not-quite-human. "Goblins are usually portrayed as small, grotesque figures, much given to wreaking havoc in the house by night, breaking dishes and banging on walls."[416] They were, however, often kind to children.[417] Thus the goblins of the Potterverse have significantly increased intelligence and organization but perhaps less willfulness and malice. Rowling isn't the only one to have her way with the tradition; "goblins owe as much to literary invention as to true folklore."[418] George MacDonald in *The Princess and the Goblin* portrayed them as hard-headed, soft-footed, light-hating relatives of humanity. They are perhaps most often seen at Halloween.

In a very real sense, the "goblins" of the Potterverse are the dwarves of most folklore — goblins, in the Potter stories, are obsessed with treasure (Gringott's), are the great artificers of the world (goblin-made weapons and armor), are small, are secretive, are often found underground. This is very much like the people of Alberich in the *Volsunga Saga* and the *Nibelungenlied,* or those of Thorin in the *Dvergatal,* whom we now know best as Tolkien's dwarves.

Golden Egg: see Golden Egg.

Good and Evil

The notion of good and evil is at the heart of many religions — and I'm not going to touch it, because the questions about the nature of good and evil are just too tricky. The issue has exercised famous philosophers such as Plato, Aristotle, Augustine of Hippo, and Descartes. Perhaps the most important voice in this debate, however, is that of the Roman Senator Boethius, who wrote *The Consolation of Philosophy* while awaiting execution. It was Boethius's view that evil was a lack — not a real thing but an absence of good. For discussion of this view of evil, and an argument that Rowling adopts it, see Baggett & Klein, pp. 132–133. Rowling is not the only one influenced by Boethius; Tolkien's entire world view seems to have been Boethian, and C. S. Lewis also valued Boethius's ideas (Shippey-Author, pp. 130–136, etc.). But there is an important point to note. There are only three possibilities as to their relative strengths: Either good is stronger than evil, or evil is stronger than good, or the two are about equal. Equality is the opinion of Zoroastrianism, and C. S. Lewis talked a lot about this dualism.[419] In the old Norse myths, evil was stronger — the giants beat the Gods in the end.[420] But in Judeo-Christian theology, good is incomparably stronger and evil survives on sufferance. In the Potterverse, we note, Dumbledore (in his incarnation as the spirit of good) is stronger than Voldemort (the representation of evil), which, I repeat, is the Christian position. Dumbledore also dies before Voldemort, but triumphs from the grave — which is entirely the Christian position.

See also under Magic; also Which Side Are You On?.

One of the oddest aspects of the Potter books, philosophically, is the approach — or perhaps we should say the *lack* of an approach — to what defines good. In many fantasies, going back to such pre-Christian writings as Homer as well as to more recent writers such as Dante, the justification of what is "good" is religious; indeed, fantasy often falls into theodicy. Theodicy is the belief that the purpose of evil in a "good" universe is to allow the Gods to show what good is by revealing the inverse of good. On the tendency of fantasy toward this particular defect — which can, in Christian terms, approach heresy — see Clute/Grant, p. 939.

Rowling's universe admits the existence of "Dark Arts," and the teachers of Hogwarts explicitly refuse to teach them. It is even possible that they are not *able* teach them because they are too moral for that. "Religion in Harry Potter's world is not merely irrelevant; it literally doesn't exist. There is no divine being to pray to, no 'higher power' from which to seek guidance or strength."[421] Rowling's universe seems to have no religion and no gods, even though souls exist, and despite the fact that there is an afterlife (see The Soul.) An alternate approach to morality, sometimes used by science fiction writers, is to try to create an empirical morality ("do *this* for the good of the species"). There is no hint of this in Rowling, although we are never told how it is decided what is a "Dark Art." She seems simply to assume what is good. This even though, as many aspects of this dictionary reveal, there seems to be a strong Christian undercurrent to her work.

It is widely suggested that the reason we preserve folklore and my-thology is that they help give us a moral grounding. The "postmodern" world, which has lost these supports, is a world afflicted by moral rel-ativism — a relativism which, ironically, has given rise to such things as the rise of Wicca-style "witchcraft." The Potterverse largely rejects this view: "There is a very real evil in the stories — Lord Voldemort and his Death Eaters — and resisting them is a necessary and import-ant thing.... In this scheme, love is the central and greatest power, the core reality, and in it there is no constitutive 'other....' The only ones excluded are those who cannot love, and Dumbledore tells Harry flat out, 'Do not pity the dead, Harry. Pity the living, and, above all, those who live without love' (*Deathly Hallows,* chapter thirty-five).... Here's the problem with love as a core belief: There is no way to get there by argument or demonstration. You have to make a choice to believe in order to get there...."

See also LOVE CONQUERS ALL.

GREEN/GREEN EYES

Is it significant that Harry Potter has green eyes? Even more, is it significant that *Lily* Potter — who was Muggle-born — had them? Just possibly, because green was the fairy color, and a person in green cloth-ing risked abduction by fairies.[422] Thus her green eyes might have been a signal that she was a magical child.

GRIFFIN

Thompson B42. Described in *Fantastic Beasts* as having the head and shoulders of an eagle and the hindquarters of a lion, and as having origi-nated in Greece. This is straight out of classical and medieval mythology, which sometimes gives them the tail of a snake as well.[423] Its role as a guardian of treasure is also found in ancient legend; they warred with a Scythian people over possession of gold — a fact used by Milton in *Paradise Lost.*[424] They were sacred to Apollo.[425] Although there is no hint of this in the classical sources, medieval legend said that Alexander the Great was carried in a coach drawn by griffins;[426] there is even a mosaic of this in Otranto Cathedral.[427]

The griffin became famous as a heraldic beast because it combined the bodies of lions and eagles, both considered noble animals (the one the king of beasts, the other at least a contender for the king of birds) and both individually popular in heraldry.⁴²⁸ The church sometimes used it as a symbol for Jesus because Christ "was like a lion because he reigned as a king and like an eagle because of his resurrection";⁴²⁹ in Dante, a griffin pulled the chariot of the church.⁴³⁰

The spelling "griffin" is common today, but it really ought to be spelled "griphon" or "gryphon"; the original is Greek γρυφων, *gruphon/gryphon.* Note that "Gryphon" is the spelling used in *Alice in Wonderland,* which is probably the place where most moderns meet gryphons. The creatures were very familiar to Oxford students; it was the emblem of Trinity College there.⁴³¹

The name Gryffindor is probably French, *Gryffin d'or,* "Golden/Gilded Griffin." Although how an English wizard of the tenth century (*before* the Norman Conquest) came to have such a French name is hard to imagine.

Because they were so popular in heraldry, griffins came to have a lot of folklore about them. "Griffin as guardian of treasure" is Thompson N575. "Griffin disdains to go on ark: drowned, hence extinct" is Thompson A2232.4. "Transportation to fairyland on back of griffin" is Thompson B542.21.

The Grim

The Grim, mentioned in the *Prisoner of Azkaban,* is a death portent (Thompson E723.2, "Seeing one's own wraith"). Listing all the death portents in folklore is pretty close to an impossible task; a few British omens include the sound of knocking as Death comes to the door, or the howling of dogs who detect Death;⁴³² the appearance of black creatures, such as crows (a flight of four crows being particularly ominous);⁴³³ the hooting of an owl (see Owls); a "Fetch" (an image which appears to relatives when someone dies, occasionally called a co-walker or waff);⁴³⁴ the "Bean Nighe" (a fairy washerwoman, perhaps with only one nostril or with webbed feet,⁴³⁵ who washed the perhaps-bloody clothes of the one about to die,⁴³⁶ and known in other Celtic cycles simply as the "Washer at the Ford";⁴³⁷ she had many other powers including one of answering and asking questions,⁴³⁸ and two of them were said to have appeared before the death of Cuchulain⁴³⁹); the Irish Bean Sí or Banshee, whose cry portends a death;⁴⁴⁰ and Gabriel's Hounds, a pack of spectral dogs (perhaps with human heads) that ride with the wild hunt and which can only be seen and heard by those about to die.[441]

It was also said that one could keep watch on St. Mark's Eve (April 24/25) to see the wraiths of those who would die in the coming year.[442]

"The Yorkshire 'church grim' lurked inside the building, but would 'maraud abroad' in stormy weather; it might toll the death-knell at midnight, and peer from a window during funerals.... It also sometimes showed itself as a death warning, in the form of a black dog."[443]

The idea may have been originally Swedish, with one account claiming the *kyrkogrim* or *church grim* were souls of animals sacrificed at the founding of churches.[444] The Swedish *kyrkogrim* and the Danish *kirkegrim* were both said to guard the dead who were buried in the church.[445]

In general, these hounds are part of the "Wild Hunt," a "general term for any ghostly or demonic huntsman or group of huntsmen, accompanied by phantom hounds, seen — or, more often, simply heard — galloping across the sky by night."[446] Encountering them was a token of disaster. There is at least one record of them in sober history, although it is a hearsay telling: when Peterborough Abbey selected a bad abbot, "afterward many men saw and heard many huntsmen hunting. The huntsmen were black and huge and loathsome, and their hounds all black and wide-eyed and loathsome, and they rode on black horses and black billy-goats. This was seen in the very deer-park of the town of Peterborough, and in all the woods there were from that same town to Stamford; and the monks heard the horns blow that they blew in the night."[447]

GRINDYLOW

"Like JENNY GREENTEETH, this is a Yorkshire water-demon who lurks in deep stagnant pools to drag down children who come too near the water."[448] The Welsh had a similar creature called the Afanc, although it seems to have been much larger and able to cause floods when upset.[449] The grindylow is one of the "Malevolent Water Spirits" included in Thompson F420.5.2.

Grunnion, Alberic: see ALBERIC GRUNNION.

Hag

Mentioned only briefly in the main Potter sequence, we read in *Fantastic Beasts* of a fourteenth century meeting at which "hags glided about the place in search of children to eat." It is not really clear, however, whether these were true hags or whether this was a canard against certain old women; when a hag is mentioned briefly in the *Goblet of Fire,* it is simply an unfortunate being who had a hard time disguising herself among humans. And hags really were unfortunate in their looks: "Supernaturally ugly, withered old woman, generally considered an evil witch in European folklore."[450] Sometimes they were reported to take on a beautiful appearance in order to seduce men.[451] Some have claimed that they are vague memories of fertility goddesses, and equated them with Irish *cailleach:*[452] "The name Cailleach is alternately translated hag, crone, or wise old woman. Yet it is clear from the accounts of Cailleach's ability to move mountains, and to have carried massive stones of the sacred circles and cairns in Her apron, that She was viewed as far more than a mortal woman."[453] One famous Irish hag, the Cailleach Bhéarra or Hag of Beara, was the subject of a poem thought to have been written in the ninth century. One of the stories about her says that she lived for many generations until a saint placed a holy veil upon her, causing her to instantly turn old.[454] This motif of very long life seems to be common in the Irish versions of hag legends. This might explain legends that they built very permanent constructions such as cromlechs and even islands. Hags are also said to have imposed impossible tasks upon those who gambled with them.[455] Few fantasists really use hags, but C. S. Lewis has a few mentions of them in the Narnia books; they are followers of the White Witch.

Modern Muggles may not know much about hags, but they probably know the word "hag-ridden" — which means literally that: being ridden, or controlled, by a hag. It refers specifically to the feeling of being unable to move when awakened from sleep — a genuine phenomenon, properly known as "sleep paralysis,"[456] which comes about because nervous signals to the body are generally shut down during sleep to keep us from thrashing around. Sometimes the paralysis continues after the sleeper wakes up, resulting in the feeling of being hag-ridden.

HAGRID AND THE HALF-GIANTS

Hagrid, we know, is the child of a giant woman and a human man. This is an interesting and physiologically difficult problem. But it is attested, at least by appearance. In *Sir Gawain and the Green Knight* we read of the Green Knight that:

> Half etayn in erde I hope þat he were[457]
> *Half ettin in earth I think that he was.*

An ettin is a TROLL or a giant, the name being derived from the Old English *eotan, giant*;[458] if you've read your *Blue Fairy Book,* you may know the Scottish legend of "The Red Etin." C. S. Lewis listed Ettins among the White Witch's followers in *The Lion, the Witch, and the Wardrobe* and referred to the land of the northern giants as "Ettinsmoor" in *The Silver Chair.* The map in Tolkien refers to a region in the north, reported to be troll country, as "Ettenmoors." Ettins were often said to be two-headed (note that Tolkien in *The Hobbit* makes the remark "I am afraid trolls do behave like that, even those with only one head each"), but the Gawain story obviously implies that they could interbreed with humans.

In Greek myth, the giant Titans gave rise to the normal-sized Olympian gods,[459] so obviously giants and non-giants were the same species.

This also seems to be the implication of *How Culhwch Won Olwen,* in which Olwen is the daughter of the chief giant but is a desirable mate for the human Culhwch.[460] Is her mother human? Or is there extreme sexual dimorphism in the giant race? Biologically, sexual dimorphism, or extreme difference in male and female body types, seems very likely in this species; given how violent giants are in the Potterverse, we would expect the males to be much larger than the females, as gorilla males are much larger than gorilla females and elephant seal males are tremendously larger than the females. We could have lots of other fun with giant biology — e.g. they should have a lot of foot problems — but I doubt that's what you want....

The Norse myths do not describe interbreedings between the giants and normal creatures, but the man Agnar does breed with "an ogress in a cave."[461] Freyr falls in love with Gerd, a giant's daughter,[462] and the giant Thrym tries to gain permission to wed the goddess Freya after stealing Thor's hammer.[463]

The earliest tales of giant/human interbreedings may go back to the Bible. The entry on GIANTS mentions the Rephaim and Anakim. And then there is the cryptic reference in Genesis 6:1–4 to the "sons of God" taking human wives and having children by the "Nephilim." The meaning of this is disputed — it is often suggested that they were cross-breeds between humans and pagan gods[464] — but it probably involves giants somehow; the other use of the word, in Numbers 13:33, says that the Anakim, who were certainly giants, were descended from the Nephilim. The King James Bible translates "Nephilim" as "giants." The post-Biblical *Book of Enoch,* which featured prominently among the Dead Sea Scrolls, had much to say about these interbreedings: the "mingling of angel and human was actually the idea of Shemihaza, the leader of the evil angels, who lured 200 others to cohabit with women. The offspring of these unnatural unions were giants 450 feet high. The wicked angels and the giants began to oppress the human population and to teach them to do evil."[465] The Dead Sea Scrolls also contain five copies of *The Book of Giants,* which adds details to parts of the story in Enoch;[466] clearly, they were a popular idea among the residents of the Qumran community.

Hagrid does, however, seem rather exceptional in that he is one of the "good guys." The Biblical half-giants are regarded as wicked, and the ettins certainly were. Olwen was, at best, neutral. I know of no positive images of half-giants.

HAND OF GLORY

"Luminous Ghosts" are Thomson Type E421.3; the Hand of Glory is specifically D1162.2.1 and K437. Hands of glory are real — sort of. There is, for instance, a Hand of Glory in the Walsall Museum in Britain.[467] It is the arm of a dead felon treated (don't ask how...) so that it could hold a candle.[468] The magic of the Hand of Glory was that it cast a sleep over a household as robbers carrying the hand robbed the house by the light of the candle.[469] This idea goes back to 1440,[470] although the phrase "Hand of Glory" is not attested until 1707.

The source for that 1440 reference is, however, pretty dubious. The person involved was a criminal named Robert Goodgroom, who also called himself Robert Green and Robert Bewer. In 1439, he was charged with breaking into two churches and stealing items made of precious metal. In 1440, upon conviction, he became an "approver" — that is, he tried to offer what we would call King's Evidence. (It didn't work; the accusations he made were not accepted, and as a result, Goodgroom's sentence was made harsher — he was drawn and quartered.) Goodgroom's evidence consisted of a tale in which he described being hired as a mole-catcher. Being brought to the work site, he snuck a look into a building where he saw a dead man's arm and hand. The proprietor for some reason told him how this was made into a tool for criminal acts.[471] Although it is likely that Goodgroom was describing a method he had heard of somewhere, it should be kept in mind that he was a known thief and a liar, and gave his story in an attempt either to lessen his sentence or gain revenge on others.

The Ingoldsby Legends (nineteenth century fakelore) made hands of glory a popular motif among the Victorians.

Incidentally, if by some chance you run into someone with a Hand of Glory, water will not put out the flame, but milk will.[472]

Hands of glory weren't the only body parts that cast light. In one version of the ballad "Lamkin" (Child #93), the murdered woman's head gives off a light which shows up the murderer. There are many instances of this in Faroese and Icelandic tales.[473] And there are other ways in which a body part can reveal guilt; in the well-known murder ballad "The Twa Sisters," the body of the dead woman is made into a fiddle or harp which sings out the tale of her murder. This motif is known as "The Singing Bone" after the Grimm tale of the same name and is Thompson motif E632, tale 780. Belief in the the magical power of murder is widespread (as attested by the phrase "murder will out"); see also under BLOOD.

In the age of electric light, we are apt to forget how hard it was to obtain light in the Middle Ages. Light is easy in the Potterverse, too, where anyone mageborn can use the "Lumos" spell. But light was much respected and sought for in the pre-industrial era — an artifact that gave light was highly desirable. Magical objects attested as giving light include swords, garments, rings, and of course body parts.[474] This ties in closely with flaming swords, a motif first met in the Bible (Genesis 3:24 speaks of a flaming sword guarding the way to the Garden of Eden) and common in myth; Alexander's Dyrnwyn is a flaming sword, and so are many blades in Tolkien; see under The DEATHLY HALLOWS.

Hallowe'en: see under BONFIRE, PUMPKINS.

Happily Ever After: see AND THEY ALL LIVED HAPPILY EVER AFTER.

The HEADLESS HUNT

"Headless revenants" are Thompson Type E422. Ichabod Crane of course met one of these in *The Legend of Sleepy Hollow* (1820). T. Crofton Croker printed an Irish tale of "The Headless Horseman" in *Fairy Legends and Traditions of the South of Ireland* in 1825. Anne Boleyn, the second wife of Henry VIII, is sometimes said to haunt the Tower of London, with her head still separated from her body (Thompson F511.0.4, "man carries his head under his arm"). This gave rise to the song "Anne Boleyn" ("With Her Head Tucked Underneath Her Arm") by R. P. Weston and Bert Lee.

The idea of headless monsters goes back at least to Herodotus, who refers to the ακεφαλος, *a-kephalos, no-head, headless,* called *acephalos* in English; they are supposed to be known in Egyptian legend also.[475] The trolls in the Norwegian story of "Butterball" seem to have a fetish about wandering around with their heads under their arms.[476]

The most interesting aspect of the Headless Hunt may be the games they play — "Horseback Head-Juggling" and "Head Polo." This is very similar to the outcome of the "Beheading Game" in *Sir Gawain and the Green Knight.* The Green Knight invites Sir Gawain (or anyone in Arthur's court) to try to strike off his head with the axe he supplies. Gawain takes up the challenge and lops off the Knight's head at one blow. (Not a trivial feat, and one reason why being a headsman took training and skill — Nearly Headless Nick took forty-five stokes to the neck and still didn't have it entirely severed.) When Gawain had beheaded the Green Knight,

> The blood burst from the body, bright on the greenness,
> And yet neither faltered nor fell the fierce man at all...
> Caught up his comely head and quickly upraised it,
> And then hastened to his horse, laid hold of the bridle...
> His head by the hair in his hand holding;
> And he settled himself then in the saddle as firmly
> As if unharmed by mishap....[477]

This aspect of the Beheading Game is not so evident in the likely source, the Middle Irish tale of *Fled Bricrend* or *Bricriu's Feast,* in which the beheaded man simply puts his head back on his shoulders;[478] most of the other parallels are similar.[479]

Actually playing with the head of a beheaded person occurs, e.g., in the tale of "The Tale of a Youth Who Set Out to Learn What Fear Was" (Thompson 326, H1376.2) where a crew of monsters plays ninepins with human legs as pins and skulls as balls.[480]

The name also reminds us of "The Headless Haunt," which is an American folktale, said to be of African-American origin. A couple find themselves in the home of a headless ghost who was beheaded for money. If they can reunite his head and body, he will grant them the home and possessions. They dig up the corpse and live happily ever after in his home.[481]

The HEALER-KING

"The hands of the King are the hands of a healer." The words are J. R. R. Tolkien's, but the idea is ancient. Jesus himself was a healer-king — indeed, the *ultimate* healer-king, being in the Christian view the King of All as well as one who can even heal the dead (see the resurrection of Lazarus in John 11). Rogers, p. 76, points out that Tolkien was clearly making Jesus and Aragorn, the one who had the "hands of a healer," parallel.

In many early myths, the King was identified with the health of the land — and, if a sufficient disaster came upon it, might be sacrificed to purify it. In more recent times, there are a number of instances of a doctor coming to visit a king, and healing him — and, as a result, being granted his daughter's hand and succeeding him. George MacDonald used this as the underlying theme of *The Princess and Curdie.*

A legend in the ROMANCES said that, during a plague, Charlemagne had a dream in which he was told how to treat the disease, and used the herb he discovered to treat the sick.[482]

The kings of England were long considered to have the healing touch; "touching" for the "King's Evil" (scrofula) is sometimes said to have originated in the reign of Edward the Confessor (reigned 1042–1066), although this may simply be a reference to his (overblown) saintliness. We known that the Capetian kings of France at times "touched" (no doubt a follow-on to Charlemagne's healings); it appears that Henry I of England (reigned 1100–1135) took up the practice. Eventually it became a formal ceremony. Several of the Stuart kings opposed it, but Charles II and Anne practiced it, meaning that "touching" continued until 1714. In France, Charles X kept on "touching" until he was deposed in 1830.[483]

Rowling takes this myth and turns it on its head. Voldemort calls himself king, or at least some sort of overlord — and he does have restorative powers, as he shows with his healing of Peter Pettigrew. This fits with his serpent nature; serpents were associated with healing and the caduceus of Hermes.[484] And yet, Voldemort's healing comes with a sting: It is not a perfect healing (Pettigrew does not regrow a flesh arm) — and, when Pettigrew fails to obey Voldemort's exact will, the magical arm kills him. Voldemort, the anti-king, is for the most part also an anti-healer.

Replacement hands like Pettrigrew's are attested in folklore; Thompson F1002 is "Silver hand used as if flesh."

HEDWIG

There were multiple saints named "Hedwig" (Jadwiga).[485]

1. Hedwig of Silesia, 1174?–1243, was married to Henry of Silesia, by whom she had seven children. She founded hospitals and monasteries, then retired to a convent after her husband's death; she became a teacher and, supposedly, a miracle-worker.

2. Hedwig of Buda, 1374–1399, was a member of the Polish royal family who became queen in 1384. Noted for piety and promotion of a Byzantine liturgy, she was married into the Lithuanian royal fami-

ly, resulting in a union of the crowns (this despite intrigues by the Habsburgs). But she died in 1399 four days after the birth of a premature daughter who also died.

Although it seems likely that Harry's owl was ultimately named after one or the other saint, it is hard to see any connection between either woman and Hedwig the owl; it has been suggested that the reason for the name is that the nuns of Hedwig of Silesia's convent helped educate orphans.

Hengist of Woodcroft

One of the famous wizards whose chocolate frog card Harry collects on the Hogwarts Express in the *Philosopher's Stone.* Sources outside the books say that he was the founder of Hogsmeade, and that his statue is found in *Prisoner of Azkaban;* the exit Harry uses to reach Hogsmeade is located by it.

There does not ever seem to have been an historical person by this name. The name "Hengist" is reminiscent of Hengist and Horsa, the two brothers who invaded England supposedly in the time of King Vortigern. They are considered to have founded the kingdom of Kent,[486] one of the seven ancient kingdoms that eventually became England. Hengist supposedly died in 488.[487]

All our surviving sources about Hengist and Horsa were written much later, and the fact that the two brothers were given names that mean "Stallion" and "Horse" has caused some to suspect that they were entirely fictional. Certainly we have few details about them — which raises the faint possibility that Hengist could be "our" Hengist, particularly as some experts have linked the two with horse gods or horse rituals,[488] implying that they had unusual abilities. But the designation "of Woodcroft" seems to argue against that; although "Woodcroft" is the name of several actual places around the world, there is no reason to think any of these are meant. The name probably means "the shack in the woods" (an unlikely place for horses), although it could mean "the small plot of land in the woods set aside for the devil" (a more fitting meaning in the Potterverse). Or we could read "wood" as "wud," an old word for madness, so "wudcroft" would be the madhouse. Or, just possibly, "Woodcroft" might be a distortion of "Wodenscroft," meaning "Woden's croft," "the shed used by (W)oden" — a genuinely fascinating name, since there *are* tales of the Norse god Odin visiting small crofts. Some Christians thought that pagan gods like Woden/Odin were historical figures whose exploits were magnified until they were regarded as gods. Could Hengist of Woodcroft in fact be the archetype of Odin? This probably files under "just barely possible but requiring an absurd list of assumptions."

Geoffrey of Monmouth, who was responsible for creating most of the "King Arthur" legend, had a little bit about Hengist, too, saying that he married his daughter Renwein to Vortigern king of the Britons.[489]

HEREWARD

Xenophilus Lovegood, in describing the Deathly Hallows, tells "of how Godelot died in his own cellar after his son, Hereward, took the wand from him...."[490] In *Beedle*, Dumbledore also mentions Hereward, whom he calls mad, locking away his father.

This has fascinating parallels to the story of a semi-historical character, Hereward the Wake. This Hereward was not the son of Godelot but, supposedly, of one Leofric of Bourne,[491] but this was before the Norman Conquest, so all the records are very hazy. Hereward the Wake was such a troublesome youth that his own father drove him away from his estates — causing Hereward to attack the estates repeatedly.[492] His father went so far as to petition King Edward the Confessor to exile Hereward; he was only eighteen years old when he was driven from England.[493] After the Norman Conquest, Hereward became one of the leaders of the resistance, commanding a garrison on the almost-inaccessible Isle of Ely.[494] Supposedly William the Conqueror himself had to lead the army that attacked Hereward.[495] His saga was sufficiently well-known that the famous novelist Charles Kingsley retold it in the nineteenth century as *Hereward the Wake: "Last of the English."*[496]

Considering his poverty of resources, Hereward's success against the Normans (assuming it actually happened and isn't just some minstrel's tale) was amazing. Some of the incidents sound rather magical. Could the Elder Wand have been what gave him the power to accomplish these feats?

HERMIONE

Character names in the Potterverse are often significant. It's not clear if this is true of Hermione Granger, but Hermione in Greek myth was the daughter of Menelaus and Helen of Sparta (later Helen of Troy). Despite Helen's having three husbands, (Seyffert, pp. 272–273, lists Menelaus, Paris, and Deiphobus, on whom everyone agrees, as husbands of Helen; Grimal, p. 176, observes that some claimed she had as many as five husbands). Hermione was probably her only child:[497] "To Helen the gods had granted no more offspring once she had borne her first child, the breathtaking Hermione, a luminous beauty gold as Aphrodite."[498] One account says Hermione was nine when Helen was swept away by Paris.[499] A tradition says that Hermione was betrothed to Orestes the son of Agamemnon. But the *Odyssey* says Menelaus betrothed her to Neoptolemus the son of Achilles.[500] Apparently there was a dispute between Orestes and Neoptolemus over this. (Shades of Ron and Viktor Krumm?) The marriage with Neoptolemus was childless, and after Neoptolemus was killed at Delphi (it's not clear whether a mob killed him, or Orestes),[501] Hermione married Orestes; their child was Tisamenus king of Sparta (whose life, however, was anything but happy).[502]

There are other Potter characters with names from classical myth — *Minerva* (i.e. Athena) McGonagle, *Penelope* Clearwater — but it seems even less likely that these names are intended to mean something. (Although it is interesting that Penelope Clearwater, like Penelope the wife of Odysseus, had to wait for some time for her boyfriend Percy Weasley to come around....) See also REMUS.

Argus Filch is a more interesting case. The classical legends about Argus are somewhat confused, but the typical story makes him a creature with many eyes (perhaps a hundred), which made him an ideal guardian for Io, since some of his eyes always stayed open.[503] Hermes slew Argus, perhaps by lulling him to sleep with the pipes; his eyes were then set in the peacock's tail.[504] This is an interesting match for Argus Filch, since Filch is always seeking to catch students misbehaving. But Argus's abilities were greater than a normal creature's; Filch's are *sub*-natural, since he is a squib.

HINKEYPUNK

"Hinky-Punk. One of the many names for the will o' the wisp. It occurs on the Somerset-Devon borders.... It was described... as having one leg and a light, and led you into bogs.'"[505] As such it is an example of Thompson tale 491.1, "Will-o'-the-Wisp leads people astray." Another name for this sort of creature is the "Jack-O'-Lantern;" for this, see under PUMPKINS.

HIPPOCAMPUS

This is another instance where a creature thought to be mythical in the Muggle universe is known in the wizarding world to be real. *Hippocampus* is a Greek word, ιπποκαμπος, *(h)ippo-campos, horse-(sea) monster.* Hippocampi were creatures with the forequarters of a horse (sometimes rather "fishified") and the hindquarters of a fish or a dolphin — something like a seahorse. (Indeed, the part of the brain known as the hippocampus is so-called because it looks like a seahorse.) In Roman legend, they were said to draw the chariot of Neptune/Poseidon.[506] The Greek bestiary known as the *Physiologus,* usually dated to the second century although dated by some as late as the fourth and translated into Latin in the fifth century or later,[507] claims that some called it the king of fishes.[508]

HIPPOGRIFF

Thompson B42.1. This is, one might say, a doubly fantastic creature, since it is supposedly the result of the fantastic mating of a Griffin (itself a fantastic creature) with a horse, producing a creature with a griffin's wings, head, and weaponry, but the torso and feet of a horse.[509] It is not a mythological creature; Ariosto invented it for *Orlando Furioso,* perhaps based loosely on a comment of Virgil's. In *Orlando Furioso* it "carries Rogerio away from his beloved Bradamant and into many strange adventures."[510]

Although there are no traditional tales of hippogriffs to the rescue, "Escape on flying horse" is Thompson B542.2.

The Hog's Head

It's not easy to tell if it is significant, but the phrase "Hog's Head" has at least three meanings relevant to the pub kept by Aberforth Dumbledore. One is a "hogshead" — a barrel containing at least 62 gallons or 225 liters, implying the possibility of drinking to excess. A second possibility, the head of an actual hog, also implies consuming in abundance. And then there is the boar's head, which — because boars were so hard to catch and kill — was considered a rare delicacy. This was shown by the "Boar's Head Carol" (from the Richard Hill MS, Balliol College 354, c. 1500):

> The bores hed in hondes I brynge,
> With garlondes gay and byrdes syngynge,
> I pray you all, helpe me to synge,
> Qui estis in convivio
> Caput apri refero,
> Resonens laudes Domino.[511]

> *The boar's head in hands I bring,*
> *With garlands gay and birds singing,*
> *I pray you all, help me to sing,*
> *Who are joined in company.*
> *The boar's head I carry,*
> *Singing praises to the Lord.*

Folklore has been busy with this song; I read, somewhere, that it was the earliest English carol to see print, and that it originated when an Oxford student named Copcot was on his way to mass when attacked by a boar. He allegedly killed it by stuffing a volume of Aristotle down his throat, then took the head to the cooks.

The boar's head came to be associated with high holidays and extravagant celebration, as well as mystical power — desirable associations for a pub, surely.

HOGWARTS: THE EDIFICE

Hogwarts, as the name of a place, is unique to the Potterverse. But the idea of a wizarding school is not (LeGuin's Roke is a college of wizardry, developed as LeGuin thought about where all those grey-bearded, staff-carrying Wizards came from;[512] Hogwarts, by contrast, is really an elementary school) — indeed, there were rumors of schools of magic in medieval Europe. Reagin, p. 98, mentions one in Auvergne (which might be Beauxbatons), one in Turku, Finland (which it is suggested might be Durmstrang, although we do not encounter any Durmstrang students with Finnish names), and others in Cracow (a better Durmstrang candidate), Padova, and Venice. And Hogwarts, although it seems to be based mostly on the settings of Boarding School novels such as the famous *Tom Brown's Schooldays,* also bears a strong resemblance to a common fantasy motif known as the "Edifice." (Compare Thompson type D6, "Enchanted Building.") Clute and Grant list a number of characteristics of these places exhibited by Hogwarts, including a (famous and ancient) name, the fact of being larger inside than out (Rowling doesn't state this, but doesn't Hogwarts seem as big as a city? This even though it is occupied by only about 300 students, perhaps two dozen teachers and staff, and a lot of house elves), it is labyrinthine (the Chamber of Secrets alone proves that!), and it stores much hidden and lost lore.[513] Other common characteristics of these places include being alive and having connections to past and future. Rowling reportedly has said that Hogwarts could not stand in the mundane world; much of it is held together by magic.

Clute and Grant mention the Tower of Babel (Genesis 11:1–9) as a possible Edifice, but I'd be more inclined to look at the Cretan Labyrinth. Hans Christian Anderson's Snow Queen's palace was an Edifice; so is the castle in George MacDonald's *The Princess and the Goblin* (although not, I would say, the castle in the sequel *The Princess and Curdie*). Elrond's house in Tolkien also seems edifice-like.

Hogwarts as a whole is only mildly like these parallels — but consider the Room of Requirement. It is actually sentient — it not only meets the user's needs (not a rare thing; there are many wish-fulfilling objects in folklore) but it meets them *intelligently*, supplying what is needed to truly meet the user's wish, not merely what is casually asked for. Also, in the *Philosopher's Stone,* we are told that the various parts of Hogwarts "seemed to move around a lot."

We do not have an exact date for the founding of Hogwarts. It is generally believed that it was around the tenth century; in the *Chamber of Secrets,* Professor Binns said that the date was uncertain but it was more than a thousand years before 1992. This would make it probably the oldest castle — and among the oldest structures of any kind — surviving in England. Castle-building was an idea brought to England by the Normans in 1066; any castles older than that would have to have been built under foreign influence. Arguing against such an early date are the names of the four founders, Godric Gryffindor, Helena Hufflepuff, Rowena Ravenclaw, and Salazar Slytherin. Note that all four have surnames — something Englishmen didn't really start to develop until the late Middle Ages. (This apart from the fact that those names mostly aren't Old English. Maybe they have been modernized.) On the basis of the surnames, a date in the fifteenth century for the founding of Hogwarts

would seem more likely. On the other hand, wizards were ahead of their
time — and the names are all alliterative, and Old English poetry was
based on alliteration, such as was used much later by Langland in *Piers
Plowman:*

> In a somer seson, whan softe was the sonne,
> I shoop me into shroudes as I a sheep were....
>
> *In a summer season, when soft was the sun,*
> *I wrapped me in shrouds [cloaks], as I a shepherd were....*

A date in the Old English period would also raise questions about
the *meaning* of the name "Hogwarts," because "hog" is not an Old English word (in that language, the word is rare; it is usually spelled *hogg,*
and is said to be from Celtic roots). Of course, the pronunciation of
the name might well have changed over the years. I rather like the idea
that "Hogwarts" is a much damaged form of *hyge-word, "heart/mind/
thoughts-word,"* or perhaps *hyge-wyrd, heart's/mind's-fate.* But this is speculation in the absence of evidence.

Alternately, Hogwarts might be derived from the plant "hogwart,"
properly *Croton capitatus* — but this is a strong laxative,[514] which makes
it a strange name for a school (particularly one that was built before
flush toilets were well known in Britain!), plus there is again the problem
of that anachronistic spelling "*hog*wart." If this is the actual source of the
name, we can only speculate that learning at Hogwarts involves purging
one's self of false opinions, which is a very "alchemical" thing to do.[515]

(The name "Hogwarts" is surprising in light of the other wizarding
schools. *Beauxbatons* is straightforward French, *beautiful-sticks,* hence in
effect "Good-wands." *Durmstrang* is typically explained as a variation on
the German cant phrase "Sturm und Drang," "Storm and Desire," i.e.
tumultuous feelings — but *Strang* is properly a *rope,* and *dur(ch)* means
(coming) through; I rather suspect *Durmstrang* really is intended to imply
a school that keeps students on a very tight leash. Which, to be sure,
could cause them to feel sturm und drang.... But the students whose
names we know are Slavs, not Germans.)

The Edifice is a sort of general-purpose version of the relatively common enchanted castle (as an example of the latter, consider the home of
"Sleeping Beauty").

The Hopping Pot: see the Hopping Pot.

HORCRUXES

The horcrux, as explained in the *Half-Blood Prince* and the *Deathly Hallows,* is an object containing a part of a person's soul, created by murder; its purpose is to keep the soul alive even if the body is slain. The idea of a soul not found in a body is extremely common, and gives rise to several folklore elements: Thompson Motif E710, "External Soul," and Tale-Type 302, "The Monster with His Heart in the Egg;" also G229.1, "soul of witch leaves the body." In this tale-type, which in Britain is best known in the Highlands of Scotland,[516] a monster has transferred his soul into an external object, and cannot be killed while the object (such as an egg) exists.

The Potterverse has two variations on the external soul, one the horcruxes themselves; the other, in which a man cannot *love* while his heart is outside his body, is in Beedle the Bard's tale "The Warlock's Hairy Heart." In a way, Beedle's change simplifies the story, because in folklore the external heart (Thompson D2062.1, "Heart removed by magic") is usually a sign of one clinging fast to life — and, therefore, one who has little love for others.

The idea of the literally heartless person is common: Tolkien in effect used it for Sauron, who could not exist if the One Ring were destroyed. Tolkien, in fact, gave a short list of folktales of this sort: "The Giant That Had No Heart," "The Sea-Maiden," "Die Kristallkugel," and the early Egyptian "Tale of the Two Brothers," in which the enchanted heart is used to revive a dead man[517] (very like the revival of Voldemort, although the folklore method is simpler; this story also has some resemblance Beedle's tale). There are also some Germanic folk-tales in which a person's soul appears in the form of a mouse, which might leave his sleeping body by means of the mouth.[518] But the mouse had to return to the body for the person to revive.

Other versions are reported from Thailand or Cambodia, Malaysia, Indonesia, Nigeria, Greece, Russia, the Roma, Transylvania, Scandinavia, the Celtic countries, Mongolia, some American Indian tribes, and the Islamic world;[519] only a few examples are given below.

"[T]he story of the external soul is told, in various forms, by all Aryan people from [Hindu India] to the Hebrides. A very common form of it is this: A warlock, giant, or other fairyland being is invulnerable and immortal because he keeps his soul hidden far away in some secret place;

but a fair princess, whom he holds enthralled in his enchanted castle, wiles his secret from him and reveals it to the hero," who then seeks it out and kills the evil being.[520] The Biblical version is the story of Samson and his hair (Judges 13–16, especially chapter 16) — although, in that instance, it is not Samson's life but his strength that is contained in the fetish object, and it can regrow.

Peter Buchan had a Scottish folktale, "The Widow's Son and an Old Man," which features a number of "transfigurations" — a man becomes a fish, a snake, a magpie. Charlotte Sophia Burne called this the "Punchkin" type.[521] In the case of Punchkin, the magician's soul is transferred into a parrot, and the hero destroys the magician by tearing the parrot to pieces.[522]

There is also a very faint hint of this in the folk song "Tam Lin"[523] where the Queen of Elfland/Faërie must every year "pay a tithe to hell" at Halloween — i.e. sacrifice a living human to extend her own life or that of her followers. In that song, she wishes she had replaced Tam Lin's living heart with a heart of stone or wood.

Thus, although the making of horcruxes is not directly attested in Muggle folklore, all the component motifs are found elsewhere. The power of murder is widely accepted in folktale — indeed, the phrase "murder will out" (Thompson N271) derives from the belief that murder produces enough magical power to reveal the truth. For a few minor examples, see BLOOD and HAND OF GLORY. There does not seem to be a traditional English example of one person living by feeding off the life force of another, but consider "The Picture of Dorian Gray."

Observe that a horcrux is dangerous to destroy (dealing with the Resurrection Stone cost Dumbledore his hand and eventually his life) and dangerous to keep (as the diary took over Ginny Weasley and the locket proved a great burden on Harry, Ron, and Hermione). This somewhat resembles the traits of Tolkien's One Ring, which had to be destroyed in a particular way and which would eventually turn any user to evil.

The One Ring is like an expanded horcrux in another sense: Sauron invested much of his native power in making it. In practical terms, it was like an external heart/soul, since its destruction destroyed him. But it had the added dimension that it conferred a power which others could use (although at great peril to their sanity and morality). Thus the One

Ring was a sort of ultimate horcrux. But then, it was the horcrux of a demonic power, not just a human being.

Folklore has an interesting twist on the almost-undestroyable horcrux: Thompson D1651.10, "Container for soul can be split only by man's own sword." We see this in the *Deathly Hallows*: Voldemort, and only Voldemort, can apparently destroy the part of his soul that lives in Harry.

This raises an interesting question about Horcruxes, which probably never came up until Voldemort tried to split his soul in seven: are all the horcruxes equal?

Consider this: When Voldemort made his *first* horcrux, presumably half his soul went into the horcrux and half stayed with Voldemort. Now imagine when he makes horcrux #2: the Voldemort who actually makes this horcrux has, in his own body, only half a soul. Half of half is a quarter. So when he splits his soul again, does he end up with a horcrux containing only a quarter of a soul, and only a quarter of his soul left in his own body, while horcrux #1 retains half his soul? Or does part of the soul somehow come back from horcrux #1, so that each portion has a third of his soul? If the latter does not happen, then by the time Voldemort gets to horcrux #6, he's dealing with only one-sixty-fourth of a soul. Probably no loss if it's lost; it's horcrux #1, with half his soul, that matters. But if the horcruxes "rebalance" his soul, the question becomes, *how?* Do souls travel? Is there a way to block them? This sounds, oddly enough, very like the "entanglement" aspects of advanced quantum mechanics. We have no answers, but those with mathematical training may wish to speculate.

See also RITUAL OF DESECRATION, THE SOUL, SEVEN.

Horse, Flying/Winged: see WINGED HORSE.

HOUSE ELVES

The House Elf seems to be a Rowling invention, but based loosely on the old Scottish creature the Brownie (Thompson F482). Brownies, for whatever reason, happily served around the house[524] in exchange for no reward except a saucer of milk[525] — but would abandon a home if given clothing,[526] or perhaps any reward at all.[527]

The name of these creatures varied. There was a twelfth century Yorkshire being called "the hob-thrush, a benevolent naked creature who works with supernatural speed and power, and disappears offended if offered clothing."[528] Other regions originally called similar creatures names such as "hobs" or "pucks,"[529] but "brownie" seems to have become the standard title. Thus the house elf is, in essence, a brownie which is in involuntary rather than voluntary servitude.

Quite a few "big names," including King James VI and I[530] and Sir Walter Scott, wrote about brownies; Scott said that they were "a class of beings distinct in habit and disposition from the freakish and mischievous elves."[531] They worked primarily at night.

Brownies did like to be appreciated; supposedly one was called lazy by a householder and responded by turning into (or at least acting like) a boggart.[532] But they would not take direct rewards for service.

The house elf, as a family servant with magical abilities, also bears some very faint resemblance to the "Billy Blin'," a household spirit in a handful of ballads[533] (e.g. in Willie's Lady, Child #6, the Billy sometimes helps release a woman in labor from her mother-in-law's curse). But the Billy Blin' seems much more a spirit and less a creature under an enchantment.

One does wonder a little about the name *house* elf. Is there some other sort of elf we don't know about in the Potterverse?

One possibility is that the name derives from German. The *heinzelmännchen* is one word for a brownie; the *hausmädchen*, housemaid, house-girl, house-damsel, is properly the name for a domestic servant (and has come as a result to be used for some rather unsavory things), but it seems also to have been used for a creature very like a brownie — but female:

"In the house of the farmer Lederer in Tirschenreuth there used to appear a tiny being on the stove whom they called 'house damsel.' [When a new servant spotted it]… The mistress entreated her by no means do the house damsel any harm and not even to talk to her.

"Whatever was removed from the table was placed on the stove, and very often the leftovers were completely eaten up, and the dishes and plates were cleaned and placed in the platerack. [On Saturday, the servants were allowed to leave the washing for a day, but all was cleared up anyway....] The house damsel had performed this kind act for the tired servants.

"Once the servants forgot to place the leftovers on the stove. Thereupon the house damsel left and never came back."[534]

A similar German story tells of a pair of tiny people cleaning a home, but appearing naked, so a servant decided to help. "The charitable woman decided to do them a good turn and put down two full sets of clothes in the following night. When they came and saw the clothes, they started crying very loudly and the goblin said to his companion, 'Now we are being paid here, too, and cannot go on working any more. Where shall we find another decent family?'

"Lamenting, they took their presents, left without doing any work, and never returned again."[535]

Perhaps Rowling liked the German sort of brownie, but didn't like the name *housemaid*, and so converted it to *house elf*.

See also DOBBY.

HUNTING THE SNIDGET

This form of outdoor recreation, which we are assured by *Quidditch* was one of the sports which eventually combined to form the sport of Quidditch, sounds very much as if it might be related to the behavior known as Hunting the Wren. "The usual time for the custom is St Stephen's Day (26 December), when groups of young men hunted and killed wrens and then paraded them about the neighbourhood with much singing and music."[536] They also tried to trade the bird for rewards, just as we are told Quidditch players were offered cash for catching the Snidget in 1269. Wrenning has given rise to at least two widely-known folk songs, "Hunt the Wren" and "The Wren (The King)," and is likely responsible for a third, "The Cutty Wren," as well. One version of "The Wren (The King)" begins

> The wran, the wran, the king of all birds,
> Saint Stephen's Day, he was caught in the firs;
> Drolin, drolin, where is your nest?
> It's in a place that I love best.
> Between the holly and ivy tree
> Were all the birds come singing to me,
> Sing holly, sing ivy,
> To keep next Christmas, it will be holly.[537]

No really convincing explanation for hunting the wren has ever been offered; perhaps the custom arose in imitation of the wizarding practice.

HYBRIDS, HYBRID ANIMALS

Creatures of mixed ancestry or parts (anything which Dolores Umbridge hates, be it Centaurs or Hagrid and the Half-Giants or Hippogriffs or Mermaids/Men or WEREWOLVES) are collectively Thompson B1114.

IMMORTALITY

The motivating force of the Harry Potter cycle is the quest for immortality: Voldemort wishes to live forever, and will take any course required to achieve that end.

It is curious to note that Voldemort chooses to use HORCRUXES when at least three other methods are available. The gallery of Hogwarts headmasters shows that the intelligence, at least, can be preserved after death. Any magic-user who wishes to can become a ghost. And one could at least hope to recreate the PHILOSOPHER'S STONE — what one man can discover, another can rediscover! Voldemort tried to steal it, but he didn't try to *make* one.

For that matter, the whole theory of HORCRUXES is that they divide the SOUL, which means that the soul must exist. Which inherently implies some form of immortality. Voldemort's whole quest seems, on its face, somewhat peculiar. He is not really after eternal *existence* but the survival of his body. This reminds us a bit of Tithonus, who (at the request of Eos, who loved him) was granted immortality — but not freedom from aging. He grew so old and feeble that eventually Eos turned him into an insect to be rid of him[538] (Thompson M416.2, "eternal life without eternal youth as curse").

The quest for immortality in the sense of eternal youth is an ancient folk theme. The tale of Gilgamesh's quest to live forever is thought by some to have been composed four thousand years ago.[539] Greek and Roman legends of humans becoming gods date back several thousand years also. Juan Ponce de León sought the Fountain of Youth in the sixteenth century.[540] There have been innumerable other quests in the years between and since. And most of them end badly.

"Postponing Death" is Thompson D1855. See also OLD AGE.

IMP

Described in *Fantastic Beasts* as creatures found only in the British Isles, small, and having a low sense of humor, but not really dangerous. This contrasts to the "correct" folklore usage: "Imps were often sent by the Devil to serve the whims of the witches and wizards who swore allegiance to him ["Imp as witch's familiar," (Thompson G225.8.] They were reputed to be responsible for many malicious acts, from the harming of livestock to child murder."[541] It is not always easy to tell a malicious spirit from one that is merely "tricksy," however. "'Imp' properly means a small devil, an off-shoot of Satan, but the distinction between Goblins or Bogles and imps from hell is hard to make."[542] The name "imp" is thought to be connected with Middle English "ympe" (or "impe"), probably a graft or a joining-place; the is perhaps most evident in "Sir Orfeo," where the King of Faërie was able to abduct Heurodis because she rested beneath a "ympe tree," a grafted tree, which gave him access to our world.[543] Thus an "imp" is a graft from somewhere — probably from the demonic regions, but possibly merely from Faërie or some other enchanted realm.

INFERI

Inferi are defined as "Dead bodies that have been bewitched to do a dark wizard's bidding."[544] In other words, the walking dead. Inferi under that title aren't common in folklore — the word "inferi" (singular "inferius") is Latin for "the dead" or "the inhabitants of the land of the dead"; it is related to the word *inferior* (in the sense of "lower," i.e. "the lower world, the underworld"); *inferus* means *below*. But if the word is rare, tales of the walking dead — "revenants" — are extremely widespread. Most often it is the spirit that walks, not the body, but some accounts make VAMPIRES the spirits of the dead, and we find ZOMBIES in Voodoo mythology.

In English legend, the dead do sometimes walk, usually for a reason. For example, in the ballad "The Unquiet Grave," a dead man comes back to his lover to tell her that she has grieved for more than "a twelvemonth and a day;" it is time for her to stop mourning so that he can rest. When she asked for a kiss, he tells her bluntly, "My cheek is as cold as the clay, true-love, My breath is earthy and strong; And if I should kiss your lips, true-love, your life would not be long."[545]

The concept of The Dead is so large that Thompson devoted his entire letter "E" to it. The cave scene in the *Half-Blood Prince* is particularly reminiscent of Thompson G299.1, "Witch calls up dead, makes them walk on water;" also G263.5, "Witch revives dead."

Thus the inferi are a very common idea and simply given a very suitable Latin name.

The INNER CIRCLE

There is an interesting tendency, in modern adventure fiction, to create what Google would probably call "circles." Harry Potter has an "inner circle" of friends in Hermione and Ron, who are his constant companions, and an "outer circle" of faithful followers which includes Ginny, Neville, and Luna, plus Dobby. In Tolkien Sam constitutes Frodo's inner circle; the rest of the Fellowship is his outer circle. Alexander has an inner circle of four Companions, Taran, Gurgi, Fflewdur, and Eilonwy, with others such as Doli, Gwydion, and Coll as an outer circle. Gordon Dickson's *The Dragon and the George* features an inner circle of Jim Eckert, Sir Brian, Daffyd, and Aragh (and if you think that's a pretty strange-sounding list — yep....)

Crossley-Holland doesn't have an inner circle as such, but it is clear from the start that Gatty is Arthur's special friend and vice versa.

Members of the Inner Circle seem to be just about guaranteed to survive whatever happens. (If you exclude Lewis's Narnia, anyway, where the all end up dead but that's a happy ending.) They don't always stay together (note that both Tolkien and Alexander eventually split their inner circles), but they're still around at the conclusion.

This is an interesting new twist. In the *Odyssey*, Odysseus comes back alone — and doesn't seem to have had any particular special friends even before that. Robin Hood in the "Gest of Robyn Hode" has a core gang of Little John, Much the Miller's Son, and Will Scathelock (Scarlock, Scadlock, Scarlett), but they don't seem to be his particular friends, and, with the possible exception of John, they aren't with him when he dies. In the *Gest* the tale of Robin's death is in stanzas 451–455, and no one other than Robin is mentioned; Waltz-Gest, pp. 105–106. In "Robin Hood's Death," Child #120, volume III, pp. 102–107, John is with him at the end, but he is the only one, and only after Robin has been betrayed and is already dying. King Arthur has trouble with almost everybody close to him.

On the other hand, Jesus had an inner circle of Peter, James, and John, and an outer circle of the rest of the Twelve. Thus the modern fantasy idea largely revives a very old motif.

As a theme of genre fantasy, the "band of companions" seems to go back to Tolkien. Usually he calls his group the "Fellowship," but occasionally they are the "Company of the Ring." In Alexander, the term "the Companions" is used almost to monotony, and "Companions" seems to be the standard term for this sort of thing.

These companions are often of multiple species[546] (human/elf, hobbit, and dwarf in Tolkien; human, Fair Folk, and Gurgi in Alexander; human, dragon, and wolf in Dickson). Rowling's troupe is mostly human, but Dobby gives them one non-human companion. It has been suggested that Companions are usually assembled in one of two ways: A collected group of specialists, such as a bunch of expert warriors (these are referred to as a "Dirty Dozen," and are popular in military fiction);[547] or a group which assembled voluntarily, which is filed as a case of "Seven Samurai."[548]

Power, indeed, seems to define most inner rings — "the purpose of power is power." And this is why most of them are so evil. The difference between an Inner Ring and an Inner Circle is that the point of the Inner Ring is simply to be part of the ring; the purpose of an Inner Circle is to be with one's friends.

C. S. Lewis's thoughts on friendship are very relevant here. "*Friendship* is the least instinctive, biological, and necessary of our loves. Today it is hardly considered a love" [which is interesting, since the Greek word for friend is φιλος, *philos*, from the same root as *love*, as in, for instance, "philosophy," "love of wisdom"].... "The ideal climate for friendship is when a few people are absorbed in some common, and not necessary, interest. Lovers are usually imagined face to face; friends are best imagined side by side, their eyes ahead on their common interest.... Friendship, reckoned C. S. Lewis, made good people better and bad people worse."

The Invisibility Cloak: see under The Deathly Hallows.

Janus: see Two-Faced Figures.

Jarvey: see under Gnomes.

Kappas

We encounter these minor malefic creatures in the *Prisoner of Azkaban* and in *Fantastic Beasts.* The description in the latter is almost verbatim from Japanese folklore sources: "A river demon with the body of a tortoise, the limbs of a frog, and the head of a monkey. His head has a hollow at the top containing a strength-giving fluid. He lives in the water and comes out in the evening to eat. He sucks the blood of horses and cows.... He also drags humans into the water and sucks out their blood through their anuses. Humans can outwit him by being civil to him and bowing."[549]

The reason that bowing works is because the kappa must respond to a bow by bowing itself — which causes the fluid it carries on its head to leak out, causing it to become weak.[550]

Kelpie

In the *Half-Blood Prince,* as Harry and Dumbledore circle the lake where Voldemort has hidden the HORCRUX, Harry fears that there might be kelpies guarding it. This does not seem to have been the case, but *Fantastic Beasts* says that the Loch Ness Monster is the largest kelpie known to wizard-kind. Some Muggle observers had also said that "Nessie" is a kelpie,[551] although the descriptions of Scottish monster usually involve a serpent-like creature and, in Muggle reports, kelpies are horse-like.

A kelpie is a Scots demon, living in water, which sometimes appears as a fine horse. (The Gaelic name is *each uisge,* which means "water horse."[552]) It tries to lure riders on its back so it can drown them[553] — it is said that, once a person touches it, he cannot let go.[554] It might also crush a human to death with its unnaturally strong arms.[555] Still other accounts say it could thrash its tail to produce thunder and lightning, and that that might kill its victims.[556] Kelpies are associated with rivers more than with still water, and are sometimes said to help mills keep turning at night.[557] The Welsh Ceffyl-Dŵr (another name meaning "water horse") is very like a kelpie.[558]

Some accounts claim kelpies live only in salt water (which, since Loch Ness is fresh, argues against "Nessie" being a kelpie). The fresh water equivalent of a kelpie, which is smaller, is the glashan.[559]

In some accounts, a kelpie could be tamed by putting a bridle on it, but this was an almost impossible task.[560]

A few stories of kelpies describe them as shape-shifters, and in these accounts, they may come and seduce humans. The kelpie may betray itself by neighing like a horse rather than laughing like a human.[561]

KILLED HIS FATHER AND MARRIED HIS MOTHER

The prophecy guided it all. He killed his own father. Voldemort? No, Oedipus (Thompson type 931). A prophecy said that he would kill his father (Thompson motif M343)[562] and marry his mother (M344), so his parents had him exposed (Thompson M371.0.1, "abandonment to avoid fulfillment of prophecy"), with his ankles pierced (hence the name Oedipus, which refers to his damaged feet; Thompson S333 is "Ankles of exposed child pierced")[563] — and, yes, like Harry, he grew up an orphan, raised by others than his parents,[564] and then headed for Thebes. Grant & Hazel, p. 252; Grimal, p. 307. Some sources say that he had learned from the Delphic oracle that he would kill his father and marry his mother, and thinking his adoptive parents were his real parents, he set out for Thebes to prevent it. See PROPHECIES FULFILLED ONLY BECAUSE SOMEONE TRIES TO PREVENT THEM. Along his way there, he killed his father Laius without knowing who he was.[565] Then he solved the riddle of the SPHINX (H541.1.1),[566] and became king of Thebes in return for marrying the old queen, Jocasta, who was his mother.

When the truth came out — as a result of Oedipus's own investigation of a plague that had overcome Thebes[567] — Jocasta killed herself, while Oedipus blinded himself[568] and went into exile, but the curse continued to work itself out in the lives of his sons Eteocles and Polynices and his daughter Antigone.[569]

Nor was this the only case of kin-murder in Greek myth; Orestes murdered his mother Clytaemnestra to avenge his father Agamemnon,[570] and some accounts say Telegonus killed his father Odysseus (see the description under CIRCE).

The Greek gods also got into the act. Ouranos (Uranus) mated with his mother Gaia, and their son Cronos (Saturn) castrated and overthrew Ouranos;[571] later Zeus son of Cronos overthrew (but did not mutilate) his father.[572]

Even Judas Iscariot is said, in one legend, to have had this sort of history. His mother, warned by a prophecy that her son would cause the ruin of his people, casts him out to sea. Raised by a childless queen, he murders his brother, flees, kills his father, marries his mother, seeks help from Jesus, then betrays him.[573] The Oedipus legend surely influenced that story, which, of course, is not Biblical.

Nor is Judas the only "bad guy" cast adrift; Malory's version of the King Arthur legend has Mordred abandoned to the sea when Arthur learns that the boy is his child by his half-sister.[574]

The parallels to Voldemort are not close. Tom Riddle grew up as a genuine orphan, whereas Oedipus at least had adoptive parents, and Orestes had two available parents for part of his childhood and one (even if the one was Clytaemnestra) for all his youth. And the two Greek cases had much more mixed messages — Oedipus was cursed, but he was mostly a good king for Thebes, and various towns competed to be his last resting place.[575] Orestes went mad, but was eventually acquitted by Athena of the guilt for his murder and probably married his cousin Hermione of Sparta (see the entry on the True/Taboo NAME).[576] Whereas Voldemort becomes the Dark Lord, and apparently gains no release even in the happy-ever-after world of Rowling's afterlife. Oedipus and Orestes certainly were not direct sources of the Potter universe. But still.... killed his father and lived his life in response to prophecy: The motifs are closely linked.

The King: see The HEALER-KING.

LABYRINTH

The final task in the *Goblet of Fire* consists of navigating through a labyrinth, with, as it turns out, a monster at the end. This is vaguely reminiscent of the tale of Theseus, the Minotaur, and Ariadne (Benet, p. 1113; Grimal, pp. 431–433. "Thread of Ariadne given as a clue out of the Labyrinth" is Thompson Type R121.5: Theseus had volunteered to rid Greece of the scourge of Minos, which meant slaying the Minotaur in the labyrinth, where Theseus risked being surprised — and where he would be lost even if he killed the Minotaur. But Ariadne gave him a ball of thread to show him the way out, so Theseus not only killed the beast, he also escaped), although Rowling's treatment is very different.

The (Enchanted, Merpeople's) LAKE

The enchanted lake of Hogwarts is mentioned many times, but becomes a major plot device only in the *Goblet of Fire,* when it becomes the scene of the Second Task.

This task has a certain resemblance to the second part of *Beowulf,* where the hero goes under a lake to dispose of Grendel's mother.[577] It also reminds me of the tale of Orpheus, who goes under the earth to rescue Euridice, or, rather, to *fail* to rescue Euridice.[578] However, the myth of Orpheus gave rise to the ROMANCE *Sir Orfeo,* in which Orfeo goes to Faërie to rescue his wife Heurodis — and, because it's a ROMANCE, manages to pull it off.[579] The Second Task is thus a sort of combination of Beowulf, Orpheus, and Sir Orfeo.

We also see a hint of an "underwater adventure" in a version of the ballad "The Queen of Elfan's Nourice," where we read of the nurse being called to care for an elf child "Down 'neath the sea" — but this occurs in only one version and is not followed up.[580]

The LAST BATTLE

The idea of the Final Battle between mighty forces at the end of the universe is so widespread that the phrase has entered our language. The concept is indeed common — we see it in the Christian apocalypse ("And there was war in heaven"; Revelation 12:7). The Norse gods will die at Ragnarok.[581] Zoroastrianism is the story of a battle between Ahura Mazda and Ahriman, and the idea tempted even C. S. Lewis (who wrote a book called *The Last Battle,* although it was the Christian version).

The interesting thing about the Last Battle is the question of who wins. At Ragnarok, the Good Guys lose. In Zoroastrianism, the question may not yet be settled; it will be a close call. In Christianity, the victory of God is preordained; see under GOOD AND EVIL.

It would be hard to sell a fantasy series as big as Rowling's with an unhappy ending, so it is no surprise that the stories turn out well. But given the prophecies, and the strings Dumbledore pulls, one gets the impression of an inevitable win for the Good Guys. Rowling's Last Battle model seems more Christian than Zoroastrian; there is no hint at all of a Ragnarok-style defeat.

Latin, and Magic Words spoken in: see Wizards.

LEPRECHAUNS

Although the Potterverse's leprechauns seem almost to be based on a cereal commercial, they are a genuine part of Irish legend — although not always under the name "leprechaun." It has been suggested that the original word was "luchorpán," "little body," which became "luprachán" (i.e. "leprechaun") in northwest Leinster, "luchramán" in Ulster, "loimreachán" in east Leinster, "lúrachán" in Connaught, and other variations in the rest of Ireland. The other designation for them in the Potterverse, "Clauricorn," appears to derive from "Clúracán," a name known from Munster.[582] The earliest tales of them seem to date to the eighth century. There aren't all that many stories about them in Irish legend, but they do seem to emphasize that leprechaun gold will turn to dust if misused[583] — not too unlike the way it vanishes in the *Goblet of Fire.* If leprechauns have an occupation, it is as a shoemaker[584] — an activity possibly derived from *leith bhrogan,* one-shoemaker.[585] According to *Fantastic Beasts,* leprechauns are no more than six inches tall, which accords with the name "little body."

LETHIFOLD

This murderous, suffocating cloak, mentioned in *Fantastic Beasts,* does not seem to have been documented in the Muggle world, although some of its characteristics sound rather like some versions of VAMPIRE legends. But the name is interesting, since "Lethe" is a river of the underworld; drinking of its water causes forgetfulness;[586] see under THE FOUNTAIN OF FAIR FORTUNE. Thus "Lethifold" is a "folding [cloak] that causes the forgetfulness [of death]" — a very fitting name.

LOCKHART, GILDEROY

Gilderoy Lockhart's surname is an obvious example of Rowling's use of meaningful NAMES; he latches onto the hearts of women. But Rowling's use of the first name "Gilderoy" is also interesting. She has said that she found the name "Gilderoy" in the *Dictionary of Phrase and Fable,* which says that Gilderoy was a "handsome Scottish highwayman."[587] The reference is presumably to one or another of the hundreds of editions of *Brewer's Dictionary of Phrase & Fable.* The edition I have gives this entry for Gilderoy: "(3 syl., *g* hard). A famous robber, who robbed Cardinal Richelieu and Oliver Cromwell. There was a Scottish robber of the same name in the reign of Queen Mary. Both were noted for their handsome persons, and both were hanged."

Information about this allegedly-historic Gilderoy is quite thin. The name probably is from Scots Gaelic "Giolla Ruadh" ("Gillie Roi"), meaning "Red-haired boy."[588] The one who supposedly went after Richelieu and Cromwell was said to have been hanged in 1636, giving rise to the phrase "hanged higher than Gilderoy's kite."[589] "It is curious that this wretched miscreant, who robbed the poor and outraged all women who came his way, should have become popular in the south of Britain. His adventures are related in Captain Alexander Smith's *History of the Highwaymen,* &c., 1719, and in Johnson's *Lives and Exploits of Highwaymen,* 1734."[590]

Gilderoy seems to have become a fixture in folklore very soon after his demise, but the main reason for his fame is a well-known song, "Gilderoy," which has a fascinating and unusual tune, a minor-key hornpipe. The words seem to have first been published in the *Orpheus Caledonius* of 1733, already somewhat corrupt,[591] and may go back to 1650 or earlier. Thomas Percy made the words of the song famous; his version (with some corrections to the spelling) began

> Gilderoy was a bonnie boy, Had roses till his shoon,
> His stockings were of silken soy, Wi' garters hanging doon;
> It was, I ween, a comely sight, To see sae trim a boy;
> He was my jo and heart's delight, My handsome Gilderoy.

Which we might translate

> *Gilderoy was a bonnie boy, had roses in his shoes,*
> *His stockings were of silks so fine, with garters hanging down.*
> *It was, I know, a comely sight, to see so fine a boy,*
> *He was my love and heart's delight, my handsome Gilderoy.*

Much of the song is devoted to the singer's delight in her handsome love. The Gilderoy of the song really does seem to enchant women, as Gilderoy Lockhart enchanted Mrs. Weasley and Hermione and others.

This sort of exaltation of highwaymen is by no means unusual. Dick Turpin was a robber who became known as a later-day Robin Hood. Jesse James was a flat-out terrorist who became a folk hero. Gilderoy lived in a rough era; it is perhaps no surprise that the oppressed common folk would root for anyone who got in trouble with the authorities and ended up dead.

LOVE CONQUERS ALL

In 1 Corinthians 13, the Apostle Paul wrote the greatest ode to love ever penned — it is one of the most-quoted sections of the New Testament. And yet — he did not actually say "Love conquers all." That phrase comes from Vergil: *Omnia amor vincit,* "All [does] love conquer" (*Eclogues* X.69).[592] That phrase caught on enough that Chaucer's Prioress — who should surely be wearing a scriptural message if anything — has the slogan *amor vincit omnia* on her brooch (*The Canterbury Tales,* General Prologue, line 162).[593]

Except that Paul... didn't exactly refer to love. As a matter of fact, the word the Vulgate Latin Bible uses in 1 Corinthians 13 isn't even *amor*; it's *caritas*, usually rendered *charity* in English. The situation in the original Greek is somewhat similar. The noun Paul uses is αγαπη, *agape*, as well as the related verb αγαπαω, *agapao*. But *agape* is not what sweethearts feel toward each other. Greek has a word for that, and for the love between friends; that word is φιλια, *philia*. Greek also has a word for the love between family members; that is στοργη, *storge*. It has a word for sexual love, too; that's ερος, *eros*. So what is this *agape* thing? It is, roughly, *to be affectionate, to treat as a good neighbor, to respect, to honor.* It is a *disinterested* love — you love your children or your spouse because they support you, and carry on your genes; you have *reason* to love them. *Agape* is what you feel for people who don't have those ties to you. It is the love of the Good Samaritan.

The New Testament quote that perhaps sums up this idea best is John 15:13, "Greater love [*agape*] has no one than this, to lay down his life for his friends [*philoi,* from the same root as *philia*]," which is what Harry did in the *Deathly Hallows*.

So how did this *omnia amor vincit* idea get to be so well-known? Don't look to the Bible, certainly, nor the Church, nor classical nor northern mythology. If the popularity derives from any one thing, it is the French ROMANCES, which originated in the early part of the second millenium of the Christian era.

The classical story of Orpheus is a typical example. In the original form of the tale (known from Ovid and Vergil), Orpheus's love Euridice is killed, and he follows her to Hades to win her back.[594] His music earns her release — but on condition. He fails the condition, and Euridice is lost forever. But in the ROMANCE of *Sir Orfeo*, Orfeo finds Euridice (in the court of Faërie, not Hades), and wins her back unconditionally — and returns to regain the throne of his kingdom.[595] Here, love really does conquer all.

The French tale of *Amys and Amelis* (for which see DOPPELGÄNGER) ends with Amelis sacrificing his sons to cure Amys's leprosy — and having the boys come back to life because his motives were so good. Here, the empowering emotion is love *between friends*.

Marie de France, who is largely responsible for the ROMANCE genre of the Breton Lay, in her tale of Guigemar tells of a girl who would commit suicide for love — but is prevented by the power of love.[596]

Contrary to a sort of modern myth, not all medieval ROMANCES are about romantic love — or, indeed, about love at all. But it was the single most important theme of the ROMANCES — so important that "romance" today means mostly "love story," not "questing adventure in a good cause." The Harry Potter books are a ROMANCE in the latter sense — but because it is Lily Potter's sacrifice, in a *family* sense, they are also a ROMANCE in the sense that *storge*, not *agape*, conquers all.

A quote from J. K. Rowling perhaps explains much: "I really don't believe in magic. I believe in some kinds — the magic of imagination and the magic of love."

See also Medieval ROMANCE.

LOVE POTIONS

Romilda Vane certainly wasn't the first to try a love potion. Not by centuries. The whole plot, and tragedy, of the Tristan legend is caused by a love potion (Thompson D1355, "love-producing magical objects"), which causes Tristan and Isuelt to fall in love rather than Isuelt and Mark.[597] This same sort of chemical, which causes the user to fall in love with the first person he sees rather than with a particular person, provides the basis for much of Shakespeare's *A Midsummer Night's Dream*. Nor is the idea confined to British, nor even European, folklore: "Love Magic. One of the most widespread forms of folk magic, consisting of a bewildering variety of charms, spells, potions, practice, superstitions, and taboos associated with winning and keeping of one's love. Love magic is found in almost every society, in more or less sophisticated forms. The basic principle of much love magic is the transference of an aspect of the lover to the beloved — nail parings, an item of clothing, hair, blood, etc."[598]

It will presumably be obvious that if any of these things actually worked, they would be selling faster than hotcakes — and would probably *stop* working, at least in some instances, because the rich men, movie stars, and royalty at whom they are mostly aimed would be exposed to so many of them that they would all cancel each other out. Or, as Don Nichols points out to me, celebrities might start appointing "tasters" to check for love potions — and wouldn't *that* get interesting.

Not all artificial sources of love are potions; Sir Bors is given a love-inducing ring in some Arthurian tales,[599] and sometimes some sort of Amulets will be used. But the love potion is clearly the most common mechanism.

In the notes to "The Warlock's Hairy Heart," Dumbledore remarks that love potions produce infatuation, not genuine love. This would seem to imply that love potions promote the emotion known as *eros,* not *agape* or *philia;* see the notes to Love Conquers All.

Even more common than love potions are "love divinations," that is, tricks to determine one's future love partner (the simplest being the old "He loves me... he loves me not" game; for another example, see under the Mirror of Erised), but these do not seem to appear in the Potter books.

There are two interesting notes about love potions in the Potterverse. One is that love is the only emotion for which there is a known potion — there are, e.g., no "Please-be-my-friend" or "Please-forgive-me" potions, both of which the current author could use. The other is that these emotion-inducers are *potions,* not spells. The other magical operations which involve emotions or the mind — the Imperius curse, memory charms — are *spells.* If we assume this isn't just a matter of inconsistency, it implies that love potions are probably very old, dating back to the period before magic was controlled by Wands; they were presumably discovered by alchemists, not wizards. Since love potions existed, there was little reason to try to develop love spells as well.

Also, the love potion used on Tristan and Isuelt seems to have worked on animals as well; in one version of the Tristan legend, a dog, Houdain (elsewhere Idonia or Usdent or Utant), drinks the same potion as the lovers and thereafter remains faithful to them.[600]

Love potions are one of the few potions in the Potterverse where we can actually speculate as to the contents. You may have heard reports of a real "love potion" called oxytocin. This is genuine science; oxytocin is a real hormone, and you won't fall in love without it.

Before you get any ideas, though, *you* can't make a love potion with it. For at least four reasons. First, it's not stable at room temperature; it has to be kept refrigerated. Second, like most hormones, it's complicated to synthesize; you aren't going to make it using the Real Home Chemistry Kit for Children Under Seven-type methods used by Snape and Slughorn. (Of course, they may have some special way of extracting it from living creatures — lots of animals use oxytocin in their bodies.) Third, you can't just swallow it; the best way to administer oxytocin is to spray it in your nose. And fourth and most important, you can't "aim" oxytocin; it doesn't tell you who to fall in love with. That has to be decided by other reasons; the oxytocin just says, "Oh, you like so-and-so?

Let's make you really love her." If the love potion Ron drank had been oxytocin, he wouldn't have fallen in love with Romilda Vane, he would have gotten even more misty-eyed over Hermione. It makes sense to assume that oxytocin (surely under some other name) is part of wizarding love potions — but they have to contain at least two other ingredients (a stabilizer for the oxytocin plus something to decide who you fall in love with), and the other two ingredients are the important ones.

There is another interesting thing about love potions: in the only case we know of where a love potion was the *only* reason for the relationship — the marriage of Tom Riddle Senior and Merope Gaunt — the child turned out to be the disastrously emotionally defective Tom Riddle Jr.[601] Coincidence? Not necessarily. One thing modern science has shown quite clearly is that exposing developing children to abnormal hormonal mixes results in all sorts of physical and psychological defects. Voldemort is a sociopath, unable to feel genuine love. It makes perfect sense to assume that this capability was destroyed in him because he grew up in an atmosphere of artificial love hormones.

Luck: see **FELIX FELICIS**.

Lupin, Remus: see **REMUS**.

Magic

This topic is so huge that Thompson's entire letter D is devoted to magical phenomena. Magic is, in a way, the essence of fantasy. If a book is predicated on "unnatural" phenomena, it is fantasy. "An event is magical, as I define it (according with anthropological definition), if it shows the marvelous *controlled by man*."[602] If the phenomena are explained, even somewhat loosely, it is science fiction, or just plain fiction. (The third possibility, that the marvelous is done by a god, has no universal genre; it may be fantasy, religious, or something else, depending on the author's purpose and whether we are expected to believe in the god involved.)

But magic has another dimension: *Good* magic or *bad* magic. (Tolkien played with this concept in several ways, even using different words: *magia* for the good people's magic and γοητια, *goeteia, sorcery, necromancy* for evil.) Or perhaps we might even have white, black, and grey magic. Or other divisions; it has been suggested that C. S. Lewis had three classes: *divine* or *creative* magic, the *magic of service,* and *occult* magic or *magic for profit* (the first two being "good" magic but of different types).[603]

The easiest of these classifications is good versus bad magic. Christian and Jewish doctrine argues strongly that magic is evil — "you shall not suffer a witch to live" is the way Exodus 22:18 is usually quoted. But the flip side is, this defines *magic* entirely in terms of particular acts. In this theology there are in fact two beings capable of acts of power: God and the Adversary. Calling on God for acts of power is acceptable; it's called "prayer." It's just that the results are anything but guaranteed! It's trying to exploit power without invoking God that causes the trouble.

This no-compromise doctrine (which has not always been followed by the Church) contrasts, to a significant degree, with (e.g.) Tolkien. There are good characters — Gandalf, Galadriel, Elrond — with substantial "magical" powers. But evil, at least in Middle-Earth if not in the wide universe, has a much greater power of magic — note that Sauron was able to make a ring stronger than any other ring of power, even though he had to invest much more of himself in the process. And we see far more sorcery on the evil side than the good. Similarly with Alexander; there is a small amount of good magic (Dallben; Eilonwy), and some neutral magic (Orddu, Orwen, and Orgoch) — but the main power of magic is purely evil (Arawn, Achren), and only Arawn builds his power around magic.

In the Potterverse, magic for the most part seems to be ethically neutral. The good and bad sides use the same spells. What matters is how one uses them: "It is a great strength of Rowling's work that she does not treat [issues of good and evil magic]... as unique to the situation of her characters, belonging to a social context entirely unlike our own. Her books would have much less appeal if they did not speak to circumstances in which we find ourselves. Rowling's characters worry about how to use their magical power because magical power is the primary medium of their existence."[604] But there are some interesting points:

> Dumbledore, not Voldemort, is the strongest wizard there is. He was stronger than Voldemort, and also stronger than Grindelwald even when Grindelwald held the Elder Wand (see GOOD AND EVIL).

> A loving act — Lily Potter's sacrifice for her son — has more power than even the strongest curse Voldemort could cast. (See "AND GIVE HIS LIFE AS A RANSOM FOR MANY").

It would be interesting to know if a muggle could perform such magic — in other words, if a muggle mother dying for a muggle baby could still protect the child. No data, of course.

Still, the bottom line in Rowling is clear: Although magic is mostly not ethically weighted, "good" is more powerful than "evil" even in dealing with magic.

Thompson, in his descriptions of magic in folktales, points out the curious fact that, although magic is common, magicians are not: "In

[some] tale[s]… the magic power is thought of as inherent in the hero. Much more common in folktales is the use of objects whose intrinsic magic power does not depend upon any special quality in the person who uses them"[605] — in other words, AMULETS. Rowling's wizarding community seems to be small — there seem to be only eight Gryffindors in Harry's class, for instance, implying that each year's Hogwarts class contains only about fifty students (perhaps fewer). This would seem to imply a total wizarding population in all of Britain of perhaps four thousand people. While not really large enough to form a proper society, it is still a large number of magicians compared to the typical folktale.

When the Death Eaters take over the Ministry of Magic in the *Deathly Hallows,* we see them make claims that the Muggle-born acquired magic skills by gift or theft rather than by being born with it. This is a fascinating development, because this was exactly what Muggles themselves believed in past centuries![606] The conviction of the "good guys" is that this is wrong — Muggle-borns can sometimes be magic users. Does this tell us anything?

The case of Kendra Dumbledore is highly informative. For whatever unknown reason, performing magic without a wand is extremely hazardous. Indeed, it seems to be pretty hazardous *with* a wand. Wizards (Dumbledore and Ron's Aunt Muriel aside) seem to die young. Consider: Harry's parents were barely out of their teens when Harry was born — and yet he had no living grandparents when he died at age one. In the Muggle world, his grandparents would likely have been fifty-ish and very much alive. Similarly, Neville Longbottom apparently has only one living grandparent. Dumbledore himself apparently had no living grandparents when Kendra Dumbledore died, or they would have been able to help take care of Ariana.

If we treat the Potterverse as science-fictional as opposed to fantastic — that is, as a world which can be explained by physical laws — this might explain magic's bad reputation. Until wands came along, the raw ability to perform magic was more dangerous than helpful to those who possessed it. So they would be regarded as cursed and dangerous — and some fools, seeing their tricks, would try to imitate them, and thus we would get the "magicians" condemned in the Old Testament. *Possessing* the power of magic is not evil; *seeking* it evidently is.

While we're making Harry Potter into science fiction, it's worth mentioning the strange way in which wizarding powers are transmitted. It is, frankly, impossible, genetically, if you assume that wizarding is enabled by a single gene — we know that there are children of Muggle parents who have wizarding powers. This means that it must be a recessive gene that can only be exhibited if a child has two copies. But almost all children of wizarding parents are themselves wizards. But if the gene is recessive, then there should never be squibs born of wizarding parents, because every wizard should have two copies of the magic gene and every child would inherit those genes.

This raises two other possibilities. Either wizarding is the result of an "epigenetic" factor (one which is not directly determined by the genes) or it is the result of many genes acting in concert — i.e. if you have *enough* magic-related genes, you will yourself be magic. There are other conditions like this: autism derives largely from having a sufficiently large number of autism-related genes, and tall people are tall not because of one "tall" gene but because many genes each make them a little bit bigger.

But the many-genes hypothesis is ruled out by the rarity and randomness of squibs. If magic is enabled by having a lot of semi-magic genes, then there should be far more squibs born to Muggle-born parents, or to parents who marry Muggles. And there aren't. Also, if many genes contribute to magic, then a phenomenon known as a "soft sweep" would probably be taking place, making magic much more common. That isn't happening either.

As for epigenetic factors, this is more promising. It allows the possibility that there is something in the cells of wizards, not directly determined by their genes, which makes them able to do magic. There might, e.g., be some chemical found in the eggs of wizarding women which causes their children to be magical. But here again we have a problem, because such abilities usually come from just one parent. This would mean that mothers would always transmit wizarding powers to their children, but fathers would not, or vice versa. Epigenetics has possibilities — it would even raise the chance that Muggles could be converted to wizards by giving them an appropriate dose of the right chemical — but the mechanism is tricky.

The best possible solution, then, is that the gene for wizarding power is a dominant gene but one that differs by only one codon (genetic letter) from a gene for non-wizarding. And this one codon is a "hot spot" — that is, a place where mutations are particularly likely. So some people, including Hermione (and Lily Potter, etc.), experienced this mutation and became wizards. In the past, before wands were developed, this was a dangerous mutation, which is why the number remained small. Now, it is a helpful mutation, but it has not yet had time to fully penetrate the population. Presumably, given time, it will.

As for how it works — this starts us back toward folklore, and the objects which have the power of magic. Various traditions have various suggestions: saints' relics, places where the gods performed certain acts, soil transported from magical lands. One might speculate that there is a molecule in the atmosphere (call it "mana;" this is a common name for such a thing) which can be caused to release energy when subjected to a certain sort of radiation, as certain chemical compounds can decompose when exposed to light of the right frequency. And the minds of wizards can emit this radiation. This is why wands are so important: they allow the radiation to be directed. This makes wizarding possible.

No, I don't believe it either.

It does raise a possibility that wizarding power could be depleted over time as the mana is used up. Larry Niven suggested this in his "Warlock" series of stories.

Magic Wands: see WANDS.

MANDRAKES

Mandrakes are a real plant, *mandragora afficinarum*.[607] Their forked root structure is such that many mandrakes, when pulled up, give the impression of resembling the trunk of a human body — often the male groin region, including the, um, generative organ.[608] This gave rise to a legend that they promoted fertility (hence Rachel's desire for Reuben's mandrakes in Genesis 30: Rachel was infertile, and she wanted a child, so when Reuben, Rachel's nephew, showed up with mandrakes, Rachel wanted them as a fertility drug). In fact mandrakes are poisonous and narcotic, but hey, it's folklore.

Mandrakes (also known as love apples[609]) do not grow well in Britain, which perhaps promoted even more absurd legends — e.g. that they only grew where men were executed[610] (Thompson A2611.5), or that they let forth deadly shrieks when plucked up. (Hard to see how that worked given that Reuben was able to pluck them!) In the absence of true mandrakes, bryony was therefore sold as mandrakes — or, if the root structure suggested it, womandrakes.[611] (This fact was the inspiration for John Donne's line "Get with child a mandrake root" in the song "Go and catch a falling star.") Rowling takes the theme to a whole new level: Not only do mandrakes *resemble* babies and give forth deadly calls, the roots actually *are* babies!

Real mandrakes don't cry out, but they can be deadly if eaten — especially if consumed before they are ripe. The plant contains several dangerous alkaloids, including atropine.[612] At one time, it was so strongly associated with witchcraft that simply possessing mandrake root was grounds for execution in Germany.[613]

MANTICORE

Briefly mentioned in the *Prisoner of Azkaban,* where one was allowed to live in 1296 because no one was up to disposing of it. In *Fantastic Beasts* we learn that they are "capable of intelligent speech but will attempt to devour any human that goes near them." Also, the blast-ended skrewts in the *Goblet of Fire* are said to be crosses between manticores and fire crabs — which means that the skrewts, for all their armament, are actually *less* dangerous than their ancestors (although it's hard to imagine how anyone could breed a manticore). The manticore is one of several fantastic beasts first mentioned by the Greek Ctesias in the fourth century B.C.E.;[614] it was said to have the head of a man, the body of a lion, a scorpion's poisonous tail, and perhaps the quills of a porcupine. Medieval Christians used it as a symbol for the Devil.[615] The name may be derived from an old Persian word for "man-slayer"[616] — the Persian word is said to be *mard-khora,* which gave rise to Greek μαρτιχωρας/μαρτιχωρος, *martichoras/martichoros* (not μαντιχωρος/ *mantichoros*), which produced Latin *manticora*[617]), and Ctesias seems to have gotten most of his wild ideas from a visit to Persia. Pliny's great encyclopedia mentions it and says that its sting was instantly fatal. The animal, despite being fictional, was often found in medieval "bestiaries," or catalogs of strange animals, but Rowling may have first encountered it in E. Nesbit's *Book of Dragons.*

The Mark of Cain

Thompson Q556.2. "And the LORD put a mark on Cain, so that no one who came upon him would kill him" (Genesis 4:15). Cain thus became the first of the "Accursed Wanderers,"[618] figures such as the Wandering Jew and the Flying Dutchman who can never die and seemingly never find rest. (Cain reportedly did eventually die; Jewish legend has it that he was shot, in ignorance, by his descendent Lamech. Lamech, in the legend, was blind, firing his shots by sound and with the help of others, and he shot Cain in ignorance, only realizing what he had done after he felt Cain's mark.[619] But that was seven generations later.)

Witches are also supposed to have borne a mark, often a birthmark, regarded as a place where the Devil had branded them.[620]

It has been suggested that C. S. Lewis envisioned a sort of Mark of this type in *The Magician's Nephew*: "Lewis referred to another ancient tradition at this point.... This is the 'mark of Cain' that appears to be in common to Jadis [the White Witch] and [Digory's] Uncle Andrew. It is apparently a look that all wicked magicians have, a look or mark that Jadis says she is unable to find in Digory's face."[621]

The evil traits of Cain seem to become more intense, not less, with the passage of years and generations; Grendel, the first adversary of Beowulf, was described as a descendent of Cain.

Harry of course has a scar. This might be the mark of a king (see Harry's SCAR) — but it might be a Mark of Cain. If so, this is an interesting twist: It is Harry who bears the mark, but it is Voldemort whose soul is damaged and who has at least one characteristic of the Accursed Wanderer: the inability to die. Harry bears the external Mark of Cain — but it is Voldemort whose soul has been marked.

Unwanted Marriages: see CRUEL PARENTS AND UNWANTED MARRIAGES.

Meeting Death on the Road: see Meeting DEATH ON THE ROAD.

MERLIN

One of the famous wizards whose chocolate frog card Harry collects on the Hogwarts Express in the *Philosopher's Stone*. Merlin is mentioned several more times in the Potter series, mostly without much detail. This is probably as it ought to be, for the history of the Merlin legend is very confused.

According to the records, Merlin wasn't even originally Merlin. He was Myrddyn. "Merlin (Myrddin), prophet and magician, was born of the fertile imagination of Geoffrey of Monmouth in his *Historia Regum Britanniae* (ca. 1135), with some inspiration from local traditions and the chronicler Nennius."[622] "Several Welsh poems allude to the tragic story of Myrddin, possibly a historical person whose lord Gwenddolau was killed in the battle of Arfderydd (*c.* 575) by his enemy Rhydderch. Consequently, Myrddin, maddened and uttering prophecies, leads a life of exile in the Caledonian woods."[623]

Alternately, it has been suggested that Myrddin was the god worshipped at Stonehenge,[624] but if true, very little of this has survived in extant legends.

Neither Merlin nor Myrddin is mentioned in *The Mabinogion*, the basic collection of Welsh myth which also contains most of our earliest references to King Arthur. Nonetheless Myrddin does seem to have originated in Welsh tradition; the Red Book of Hergist contains "A Dialog between Myrdin and his sister Gwendydd":

> I will address my twin-brother
> Myrdin, a wise man and a diviner....[625]

The Red Book also contains "A Fugitive Poem of Myrdin in his Grave," which calls him the son of Morvryn[626] and tells of his loss of influence while forecasting the future.[627]

The tale of Merlin as prophet (for which see the CHAMBER OF SECRETS) seems to be Geoffrey of Monmouths's graft on a different folktale (Thompson B11.3.4, "Dragons live beneath castle"). King Vortigern is trying to build a castle, and cannot, and calls upon Aurelius Ambrosianus to explain what is going on, which Ambrosianus does. But Geoffrey assigns this role to Myrddin, whom he renamed Merlin (probably in part because he was writing in Latin and that Welsh "dd" didn't work too well). Almost the whole of Arthurian legend was built upon Geoffrey (although, interestingly, Geoffrey does not make Merlin an advisor to Arthur[628]). But none of it is genuine folktale; it's all literary, derived from Geoffrey and his followers Wace and Laʒamon and the French romancers which started a tradition that runs all the way up through C. S. Lewis's *That Hideous Strength*.

It is also sometimes said that Merlin is the same as Taliesin, or Gwion Bach.[629] This would explain Merlin's great knowledge. The tale begins with the witch Ceridwen, whose son Morfran was so ugly that he made people afraid. She decided that she would make people respect him by brewing him a special potion that would supply all the world's wisdom. She picked the boy Gwion Bach to stir the cauldron. Just as she was about to gather the brew to give to Morfran, Gwion, whether by accident or on purpose, swallowed the three drops that contained the wisdom; the rest was worthless. Ceridwen, in a fury, chased him; he used transfigurations to try to escape, and she pursued, transfiguring herself also. At last he became a seed, and she swallowed him — but he was reborn, nine months later, as Taliesin the bard, still with his wisdom.[630]

MERMAIDS/MEN

For the most part, *Fantastic Beasts* simply talks *about* the creatures it covers. In the case of Merpeople, it (and the other Potter books) tells us a little more. We know that Merpeople live in the Hogwarts LAKE, and that they speak a language called Mermish, and that they have been offered the status of "beings" (which in effect refers to sentient creatures) rather than "beasts" (for dumb animals), but they have refused it.

This still leaves us with a number of curious questions, because *Fantastic Beasts* lumps merpeople with Selkies, Sirens, and Merrows. This is surprising — Selkies (for which see ANIMAGUS) are skin-changers, and cannot breathe under water. Sirens are more mermaid-like, but they engaged in a particular behavior, of singing and luring sailors onto rocks; in this, they were closer to VEELA than to the Merpeople of the Potter-verse. Besides, the descriptions of Sirens show them not as half woman, half fish but as as half woman, half *bird*.[631] The name "merrow" is more correct; it is a corruption of "murdhaucha" (pronounced "muroo-cha"), the Irish Gaelic name for a mermaid.[632]

Mentions of creatures half-human, half-fish are very ancient — often as divinities. "Atargatis was especially associated with the temple at Ascalon on the Mediterranean coast, about 50 miles west of Jerusalem [in what was then Philistia and is now Palestine]. This temple was famous for its dove cotes, and as a shrine of oracular prophesy, yet the primary image of Atargatis was as a Goddess of the Sea, sometimes depicted with the tail of a fish."[633] A goddess with this name (Ατεργατις; 2 Maccabees

12:26) was also worshipped by the Aramaeans of the Tigris-Euphrates region[634] — but this doesn't sound at all like a fish goddess; the equation is somewhat dubious.[635] It is claimed that she is the Roman Dea Suria, and she has been equated with Aphrodite.[636]

Also from Philistia, and attested even earlier, is the god Dagon (דָּגוֹן), mentioned in Judges 16:23, 1 Samuel 5:2–7, 1 Chronicles 10:10, as well as in some Canaanite records. Very little is really known about this god — the most important Biblical description, 1 Samuel. 5:4, is almost certainly corrupt but is thought to say that the statue of Dagon at Ashdod fell down and broke, with only its "trunk" being left. What this "trunk" was is unknown. The Hebrew scholar Jerome, living in the fourth century, thought Dagon should be associated with fish, and later Jewish legends support this, so it has been suggested that Dagon was similar to a merman.[637] Milton used this idea in *Paradise Lost*.[638] The best modern guess makes Dagon a grain deity[639] or perhaps a storm god.[640] Still, the Jewish legends shows that the mermaid idea existed in the Middle East by the year 1000.

The Sumerians, one of the oldest societies to leave written records, had a goddess Nanâ who was honored in Erech,[641] and there was a lunar goddess Nanna who was honored in Ur;[642] it has been suggested that these are all manifestations of an ocean-goddess, "Nina" or the like, who was another human/fish hybrid.[643] This is another case where the evidence is thin, but there do seem to have been human/fish hybrids in Sumerian literature.

Apart from the confusion over names, there is little to distinguish Merpeople in the Potterverse from Muggle Mermaids and Mermen. The sea folk are Thompson Types B81 and B82. Known as *muirgen, sea-children* in the Celtic languages,[644] mermaids are found in most accounts of Saint Brendan's voyage,[645] and are fairly often mentioned in British ballads (Wimberly, p. 124, mentions "Clerk Colvill" (Child #42), "Sir Patrick Spens" (Child #58), "The Mermaid" (Child #289), "Kemp Owyne" (Child #34), and "The Laily Worm and the Machrel of the Sea" (Child #36) as involving mermaids, although often the role is quite minor. Only "The Mermaid" is really *about* a mermaid[646] — and even there, all it really does is appear:

> One Friday morn as we'd set sail,
> And our ship not far from land,

> We there did espy a fair mermaid,
> With a comb and a glass in her hand, her hand, her hand.[647]

The legend is that seeing a mermaid means that a ship will sink, so the crew observes her and panics. (This idea is perhaps to be linked with the classical tales of Sirens, who like mermaids sat on rocks, sang, and lured sailors.[648] One wonders if this was because of their lack of an afterlife and their jealousy of those who had one — mermaids, in stories such as Hans Christian Andersen's "The Little Mermaid," were said not to have souls.) Mermaids, if trapped or if their mirrors were stolen, were sometimes credited with the ability to grant wishes.[649] They also had prophetic powers and great knowledge of herbs.[650] None of these themes appears in the Potterverse. It is interesting that merpeople live in a lake; although "Mermaid lives under lake" is Thompson B81.13.12, they normally dwell in salt water — the root *mer* is, after all, French for "sea"; compare Latin *mare*. (That might be why mermaids so often have combs — their hair, being exposed to so much salt water, needed extra care.[651]) Could there be two species of merpeople, saltwater and freshwater? A few sources refer to fresh water mermaids as "nixies," but the German term "nixie" refers to other sorts of fairies also. Perhaps the fresh water mermaids may be Welsh *gwragedd annwn,* who were "ladies of the lake" and had no tail.[652] Certainly the folklore seems to describe different sorts of creatures — there is a report of a mermaid fully 160 feet long.[653]

Mermen, oddly, did not behave much like mermaids: "generally wilder and uglier than Mermaids, mermen have less interest in mankind. They do not... court mortal women.... [One mermaid] said they were rough husbands and even capable of eating their own children if they were left hungry."[654] It has been suggested that merpeople marriages do not last because, while both live long, the women *appear* younger, so the marriages seem to be May-December pairings.[655] Some accounts also credit mermen with control over weather.[656]

Merpeople is one class of the "Malevolent Water Spirits" included in Thompson F420.5.2.

Much modern mermaid lore can ultimately be traced back to Andersen's "The Little Mermaid," but it is noteworthy that almost none of the tales which claim to be based on Andersen's work in fact include its whole range of motifs (e.g. the fact that the mermaid is forced to give up her voice).[657]

MEROPE GAUNT

Merope Gaunt, Voldemort's mother, was an unattractive witch whose powers seem to have been rather weak and who married a Muggle. In Greek mythology, Merope was one of the Pleiades (the "Seven Sisters," a constellation as well as a set of lesser goddesses). "Merope was the only Pleiad to marry a mortal [Sisyphus], and the star that she became in the constellation shines less brightly than those which represent her sisters."[658]

The Merpeople's Lake: see The LAKE.

The MIRROR OF ERISED

In the *Philosopher's Stone,* the so-called Mirror of Erised has the peculiar property of showing the onlooker his heart's desire rather than his reflection. Which makes it rather peculiar that it is even labelled a mirror.…

High-quality mirrors are a relatively modern invention; they required the ability to pour glass and coat it with metal, which is a recent thing. Ancient mirrors, such as they were, were made of polished bronze,[659] and neither very good nor particularly affordable. But there are natural mirrors, such as lakes. These probably seemed much more mysterious in the days when mirrors were not common. And there are tales of mirrors that show the onlooker what he wants to see — in a way: consider Narcissus looking at his reflection and falling in love.[660] "Snow White" involves a mirror that is supposed to reflect the wicked Queen's desire — but doesn't.[661] *Through the Looking Glass* involves a mirror that Alice wishes would grant certain desires, although it hardly works that way in practice

There is a Japanese tale, "Faces in the Mirror," which shows how mirrors might be seen in a society that wasn't used to them — and it reminds us a bit of the Mirror of Erised. A young man marries a wife at his father's urging. The father dies soon after. The boy's wife urges him to go to the city to relieve his sorrow. While there, he buys a mirror without knowing what it is — when he smiles and looks in the mirror, not knowing what he is seeing, he thinks he sees his father's face smiling back at him. So he spends much of his time looking at the mirror, wanting to see his father. His wife wonders why he is so interested in the mirror — and upon looking into it, sees a woman, and thinks her husband is in love with this other woman. They disagree over what the mirror means — and eventually give it away to a "wise woman," without ever figuring out what is going on.[662]

Mirrors are better known in the west, so we don't seem to have folk-tales about a person who doesn't understand what one is. Burton's 1660 *Anatomy of Abuses* is the first claim that gazing into a mirror in the right way will reveal a future spouse.[663]

Mirrors which can be enchanted to reflect a remote reality (scrying mirrors) or a false reality, go back to Lucian of Samosata, and are found also in Chaucer's "Squire's Tale" and in Spenser's *The Faerie Queen;* compare also Tolkien's Mirror of Galadriel (for this, see PROPHECIES FULFILLED ONLY BECAUSE SOMEONE TRIES TO PREVENT THEM). The tale of Reynard the Fox is said to involve a magic mirror.[664] Crystal balls are said to be based on scrying mirrors.[665] In Madame de Beaumont's French telling of "Beauty and the Beast," Beauty can see her family in the large mirror in her room.[666] Thus mirrors with special functions are commonplace. The interesting question, to which we do not know the answer, is *why* someone would want a mirror such as the Mirror of Erised. It would be one thing if the Mirror could make the desire come true — but it can't.

The Mirror of Erised reminds me a little of the mirror in Tennyson's poem "The Lady of Shalott. " The Lady, because of a curse, cannot look at the real world; she must observe it through her mirror as she weaves the images she sees. But when she views Sir Lancelot going by, she is unable to resist turning and seeing him in real life; the mirror breaks and she soon dies. Thus both the Mirror of Erised and the lady's mirror show a reality the watcher wishes to see — and when the onlooker turns to try to see this in the real world, she dies. The mirror theme is not present in Tennyson's source, the tale of Elaine of Astolat, although Elaine does see Lancelot and die.

See also AND LEAD US NOT INTO TEMPTATION.

The Mistletoe Bride: see GINEVRA.

The Monomyth: see The PRICE.

MORGANA

One of the famous witches whose chocolate frog card Harry collects on the Hogwarts Express in the *Philosopher's Stone*. Although we cannot be sure, the assumption is that this Morgana is the witch most often known as Morgan le Fay. (Morgana is the name used for her in *Orlando Furioso*;[667] other names include *Morgaine, Morgen, Fata Morgana*, and *Famurgan*.)

Unfortunately, identifying Morgana doesn't really tell us all that much, because Morgan is one of the important figures in the King Arthur complex of legends — and everything in the Arthurian legends was constantly rewritten as new authors tried their hands at it. "Although Morgan may be human or supernatural, ugly or beautiful, her talents are relatively consistent."[668] Her first appearance is in Geoffrey of Monmouth's *Life of Merlin*, from about 1148, but it is believed that she existed in Celtic legend before that. It is sometimes suggested that her name derives from the Irish goddess Morrigan (Mór-Ríoghain),[669] or from Breton tales about mermaids.[670] The best-known version of her story is from Malory's *Morte d'Arthur*, which says she was Arthur's half-sister, the daughter of Arthur's mother Ygraine by her first husband, Duke Gorlois of Cornwall. She tries several times to hurt Arthur, including swapping his sword Excalbur to her lover Accolon so that he can use it against Arthur. Yet she also is one of those who carried his body to Avalon.[671]

Other tales give her other roles. In *Orlando Furioso*, she lives at the bottom of a lake and gives gifts; in the romance of "Ogier the Dane," she restores an old man to youth.[672] One story makes her the wife of King Uriens (whom she tried to kill to marry Accolon) and mother of Ivain/Uwain.[673] She was responsible for the action in *Sir Gawain and the Green Knight*, where she cooked up the plot in order to upset Guinevere.[674] Geoffrey of Monmouth's tale makes her a shapeshifter and one of twelve sisters who ruled a magical Avalon[675] — an idea later picked up in part by Marion Zimmer Bradley.

The list above barely scratches the surface of the stories about Morgan. Because the tales are so diverse, we can hardly even hope to guess what was on Morgana's chocolate frog card. It was probably very interesting, though.

Mudbloods: see under Ethnic Purity.

Mungo: see under St. Mungo's.

Mummy

How is a mummy like a Horcrux? Answer: They're both attempts to stay alive after death, they both involve really nasty methods, and they don't really work.

A true mummy is the body of a dead Egyptian (usually a rich one, since mummification was a fairly expensive process). The parts of the body that rotted most easily, including the organs and the brain, were removed, often to be placed in jars with the corpse. The body was wrapped in cloths and parchments, and complex chemicals were poured on them, as well as being placed in the body cavity.[676]

An actual mummy is no threat (remember, it *doesn't have a brain,* so it isn't going to chase you even if it could be brought back to life). Indeed, it can be quite valuable — the people who prepared it had to get parchment from *somewhere* to wrap it up, and what they used might be a useful document which has not otherwise survived — including, e.g., fragments of the ancient Greek dramatist Menander: "Much of the rediscovered material came from scripts that had been used for covering mummies."[677] So if you really see a mummy coming at you, don't run, ask, "Do you have anything to read?"

Nonetheless, a mummy is Parvati Patil's great fear in the *Prisoner of Azkaban.* Why? Frankly, the likely answer is "Too many stupid Saturday morning cartoons." In the early Renaissance, mummies, or ground up parts of them, were actually considered a healing agent.[678] But Edgar Allen Poe wrote a story, "Conversations with a Mummy," about bringing a mummy back to life,[679] and it has all been downhill from there.

Of course, it would be very easy for ideas about mummies, which are dead bodies carefully treated but not brought back to life, to be confused with Inferi, which are dead bodies which have *not* been carefully treated but which *have* been reanimated.

Nagini

When Voldemort chose to name his snake "Nagini," it wasn't by chance. A *naga* in Hindi is a "snake, mostly the Cobra Capella."[680] The nagas were also mythical creatures with human heads on serpent bodies, but the simple meaning "snake" is considered the primary one. (Indeed, the cobra family is sometimes given the genus name *Naja*.[681]) In Burma (modern Myanmar), the snake is also known as a Naga; their version of the Beauty and the Beast/Cupid and Psyche story is called "The Snake Prince," and the Prince is called "Naga"[682] (Thompson B646.1, "Marriage to person in snake form"). Thus, since "-ini" is generally a diminutive ending, "Nagini" probably means "little snake" or "little cobra." Since Nagini was in fact quite large (typical of cobras; the King Cobra can be up to 18 feet long), the name is probably Voldemort's little joke.

There was actually a naga named "Nagini Besandi," who in Burmese folklore was said to be the wife of Duttabaung King of Besandi,[683] but it seems unlikely that Voldemort knew this.

Nagini seems special in more ways than just the name. Although snakes as large as Nagini exist, she herself seems unlike ordinary snakes. When Nagini kills Snape in the *Deathly Hallows,* he seems to die within two or three minutes. But snake venom is not that swiftly deadly. It usually takes at least ten minutes to be fatal, and the time can be days.[684] The situation where the snake attacks Mr. Weasley in the *Order of the Phoenix* is more typical: Although the poison posed some risk, a greater danger to him was dying of loss of blood, because many snake venoms are anticoagulants.[685]

The Taboo NAME/The True NAME

Speaking Voldemort's name is dangerous and can bring consequences.

He isn't the only one with a taboo name. The phrase "Speak of the devil..." arose because it was considered dangerous to name the Devil. Hence the rise of circumlocutions such as "Old/Auld Nick" or "The Clootie,"[686] (a name used in ballads of riddling with the Devil, such as Child #1), "the Prince of Darkness," or even "The Dark One." Alternately, naming the Devil could force him away: "As sune as she the fiend did name, He flew awa in a blazing flame"[687] (Thompson G303.16.19.9, "Devil becomes powerless when called by name").

The Greeks avoided naming the Erinyes (Furies), calling them instead the Eumenides (Thompson A486, C433), the "Good Ones" or "Kindly Ones,"[688] lest they take offense ("the name certainly represented a desire to appease as well as a desire to honour"[689]); hence Æschylus's play *The Eumenides,* the last play of the great *Oresteia,* in which the Erinyes clamor to punish Orestes for the killing of his mother but in which Athena eventually declares Orestes innocent because he did it on the orders of Apollo.[690]

The refusal to name an evil is a weak version of "The Name Is the Thing" ("Guessing name of a supernatural creature gives power over it," Thompson C432.1), a belief held by some Australian aborigines.[691]

In Jewish lore, the name of God (YHWH, or "Yahweh," mis-transliterated as "Jehovah" in the King James Bible) was considered unspeakable; the Jews came to say *adonai, Lord,* instead, and this came into the New Testament as Greek κυριος, *kyrios, Lord*; the divine name YHWH is never used in the New Testament.

It is not clear whether the true name has power in the Bible. There is a fascinating incident during the arrest of Jesus in the Gospel of John (18:4–8). The soldiers come upon Jesus. He asks who they are looking for. They say, "Jesus the Nazorean." Jesus answers, "I am" — and they fall to the ground. Those words "I am" (ἐγώ εἰμι, *ego eimi*) are usually translated "I am he," but the Greek does not have an object, and the verb *does* have a pronoun as subject, which is a most unusual Greek formation (usually the verb implies the subject pronoun). This statement is strongly reminiscent of Exodus 3:14, where God offers the name "I am who I am" — the Greek translation of these lines begins with that same

"I am" phrasing used in John. Thus it appears that in these verses, Jesus claims the divine name and that name causes the soldiers to fall down.

Elsewhere in the New Testament, we are told that "at the name of Jesus every knee shall bow" (Philippians 2:10). Jesus at one point declares that he will do whatever the disciples ask in his name (John 14:13–14). And he says that "no one who does a deed of power in my name will be able soon afterward to speak evil of me" (Mark 9:39).

When Moses and Aaron demand in the name of YHWH that the Israelites be released, Pharaoh is unimpressed ("Who is YHWH that I should heed him?") and refuses (Exodus 5:1–2) — but although the name doesn't cause any response in him, the plagues that follow certainly do! But when exorcists who are not Christians invoke Jesus's name to expel a demon, the demon successfully attacks them in return (Acts 19:13–16).

Names as a key to power lie at the heart of LeGuin's Earthsea books, where knowing a person's name gives one extra control over the person. Similarly, Alexander's Gwydion defeats the Horned King by learning his name, although this particular aspect of the books is not followed up elsewhere. Tolkien's dwarves never used their true names in public, for fear they would be magically misused; they adopted names in local languages instead.

Note how Harry calls Voldemort by a variant on his true name, Tom Riddle, at the end.

There is another application of True Names in the Harry Potter books, and that is the Meaningful Name. This too has a long history — the hero of the play *Everyman* is called "Everyman" because his experiences are supposed to apply to everyone; the lead character of Bunyan's *The Pilgrim's Progress* is called "Christian," and so forth.

Most names are, in a sense, meaningful — someone named Smith had, some time in his or her past, an ancestor who was a blacksmith; someone named Parker had an ancestor who maintained parks, and so forth. But we see many names in the Potter universe which *still* have that sort meaning — instances where Rowling is using names to give hints. Maria Tatar has said that the name "Tom Riddle" itself is meaningful — because one of the mysteries of the series is to understand what motivates Voldemort; his personality is itself a riddle. And several of the books are devoted to riddles Voldemort has created — e.g. locating the horcruxes. More significant still may be the element *mort,* meaning *death,* in the name Voldemort; Lord Voldemort clearly regards himself, and wants to be regarded, as the Lord of, or over, Death.

See also Sirius Black; Hermione; Gilderoy Lockhart; Merope Gaunt.

Nearly Headless Nick: see **The Headless Hunt;** also the discussion of ghosts under **The Soul.**

Necromancy

In the remarks on the "Tale of the Three Brothers" in *Beedle,* Rowling in her own person comments on Dumbledore's comment to say that necromancy never worked. This even though necromancy (from Greek νεκρωμανεια, *nekro-manteia, dead-prophecy*), the art of raising the dead to ask their advice about the future, is a very old tradition. According to Liddell & Scott, p. 938, the word *necromanteia* was used by Cicero in the first century B.C.E. and by Hesychius; *necromancer* was used by Lycophron in the third century B.C.E. The act is repeatedly condemned in the Bible (see the notes on Wizards) — and yet, the Bible also said it actually *worked.* In chapter 28 of the First Book of Samuel, King Saul, on the night before his death, finds a medium (one translation calls her a "ghostwife"[692]). She calls up the spirit of the prophet Samuel for him (Thompson E387.3, "Ghost summoned for necromancy"), and Samuel correctly predicts Saul's defeat and death. Thus, even though the so-called "Witch of En-Dor" is a pagan, she is able to call up a spirit, and that spirit is able to make a correct prophecy.

At least, when dealing with the Witch of En-Dor, no one died. (Saul would die the next day, but the circumstances were such that he would almost certainly have died anyway.) One common form of divination was hepatomancy or hepatoscopy (prophecy by inspecting the livers of victims; Thompson D1812.5.0.5, "Divination by condition of animal's liver")[693] — and, in extreme cases, the liver examined might be human, and its owner might not have been done using it.

This, clearly was among the darkest of dark arts — even making Horcruxes didn't inherently involve torture — so let's leave that and turn to the form of necromancy to which Dumbledore actually refers: not *divination* using the spirits of the dead but *raising* the spirits of the dead

— for which the proper Greek word is not *necromanteia* but αναστασις, *ana-stasis,* again-standing, resurrection. This idea too is attested in the Bible, and not just in connection with the feats of Jesus; in the Hebrew Bible, contact with the dead bones of the prophet Elisha is enough to bring a dead man back to life (2 Kings 13:21). We see the dead come back to life, or nearly, in other mythologies as well; in Greek myth, Euridice would have come back to life had not Orpheus looked back too soon,[694] and in Norse legend, Balder fell only one "vote" short of being restored to life.[695] In Egyptian myth, Isis was able to restore Osiris to life.[696] But restoring the dead to life is extremely rare and difficult in most myth systems.

See also Prophecies Fulfilled only because someone tries to prevent them and the instances of prophecy by someone dead under the Resurrected Hero.

Neither Can Live While the Other Survives

The prophecy about Harry and Voldemort says that they cannot both exist forever.

There is also a similarity to the Jungian concept of one's Shadow, which was so important to LeGuin; see the opening chapter on Folklore. But there, the idea is often to unite the two halves, in a yin-and-yang sort of way; in the case of Harry and Voldemort, only one will be around at the end.

Nunda

This dangerous feline, described in *Fantastic Beasts,* bears some similarity to the "Mngwa" or "Nunda," a creature said to haunt southeastern Africa, but there are few English-language accounts of this creature.

OCCAMY

This birdlike predator is described in *Fantastic Beasts* as laying silver-coated eggs — an interesting trick, given that silver, unlike gold, tends to accumulate in the body, causing a condition known as argyria, which is disfiguring although it doesn't seem to be very dangerous.[697] There does not seem to be a widespread tradition of animals laying silver eggs, but silver animals are Thompson B102 and following.

More familiar, of course, is The Goose that Laid the *Golden* Eggs, Thompson D876. Presumably this fowl is a folklore "improvement" on the genuine Occamy, less aggressive but more valuable. For this, see Golden EGG.

Oedipus: see KILLED HIS FATHER AND MARRIED HIS MOTHER.

OGRE

In the *Prisoner of Azkaban,* Ron and Hermione tell Harry they believe they saw an ogre in Hogsmeade, although no other details are given. The ogre is thought to be a made-up creature, with the name invented by Charles Perrault in his *Tales of Mother Goose.*[698] (There is an Italian term, "Orcus," which predates Perrault — it's used for a monster as early as 1634 — but it is certainly not the direct source of the English word, although its Latin root might be.) The name is "adopted from the French, and more literary than colloquial, for a man-eating giant like the ones in Jack and the Beanstalk and Jack the Giant-Killer."[699] They were not considered very smart, so that most of the stories about them show them being tricked by potential victims (e.g. the wicked woman in Hansel and Gretl is sometimes called an ogre),[700] but some stories say they could change into animal shape.[701] We see this, for instance, in the tale of "Puss in Boots," where the cat finds an ogre in its castle, convinces it to become a mouse, and eats it. Interestingly, in the Norwegian version of the tale, "Squire Per," the creature is a TROLL instead.[702] That the name "ogre" is late and literary is perhaps supported by Thompson's treatment of them; although his whole letter G is devoted to ogres and other monsters, there is no specific motif for ogres.

OLD AGE

In the *Order of the Phoenix,* there is a disturbing scene in which one of the Death Eaters falls into a sort of bottle which causes his head to grow old, then back to a baby, and so forth. It seems that age is an actual *material,* not just a condition one suffers. This would also explain the aging potion that Fred and George Weasley try to use in the *Goblet of Fire.* (Which is, if you think of it, an inverse to the Elixir of Life created by the PHILOSOPHER'S STONE — odd that the one is so much easier to produce than the other.)

There is a hint of the idea of age as a substance in Greek mythology, in the story of Tithonus, who (at the request of Eos, who loved him) was granted endless life — but not freedom from aging. He aged so dramatically that Eos turned him into an insect to be rid of him[703] (Thompson M416.2, "eternal life without eternal youth as curse").

A Japanese folktale, "Urashima, the Fisherman," makes it even more explicit. Urashima, a kind man, rescues a tortoise from abuse by children, and it responds by offering to take him to the King of the Realm Under the Sea. Urashima decides to go — and is met by the King's beautiful daughter, who says she will make him immortal if he will marry her. He agrees, and they are happily married — but, after what seems like a few days, he misses his parents and wishes to go for a visit. His wife at last consents, but gives him a box which he must not open. When he arrives at his home, he learns they are hundreds of years dead; time flowed differently in the immortal realm. Bitterly he weeps on the shore. And he has no way to return to the Realm Under the Sea, so he decides to open his wife's box, thinking it might help. Instead, opening it releases all the years of aging he has been spared. He instantly grows old and dies[704] (Thompson D56, "magic change in age"). To this compare the Irish tale of "King Bran and the Land of Manannán Mac Lir," in which Bran and his shipmates sail away to the Land of Joy and the Land of Women, and return to find that centuries have passed; one who tries to leap to shore crumbled to dust from all the years that had passed.[705]

The idea of "deflecting" age is common in literature, as we see, e.g., in Oscar Wilde's *The Picture of Dorian Gray.* LeGuin used it as a motivating element in *Tehanu.* Most of these version of the tale have an element of a scapegoat — one person or thing bearing another's failures or weaknesses, and suffering in place of the person who actually has earned the fate.

See also IMMORTALITY, and the discussion of wizarding longevity under MAGIC.

Orphans: see THE UNWANTED CHILD.

OWLS

Owls have a long, but very mixed, history in folklore. Owls are mentioned about sixteen times in the King James Bible, all in the Old Testament, (Leviticus 11:16–17, Deuteronomy 14:15–16, Job 30:29, Psalm 102:6, Isaiah 13:21, 34:11–15, 43:20, Jeremiah 50:39, Micah 1:8.) but this represents several different Hebrew words, and although it is clear that the references are to a raptor (and probably to an owl of some type), it is rarely clear which species. They are definitely unclean birds, however (it appears all birds of prey were considered unclean, that is, ritually defiling).

Isaiah 34:14 is particularly interesting, because the word is *Lilith* (תילית), and Lilith is also the name of a Jewish demon who devoured children;[706] she was supposed to be Adam's first wife, but wasn't willing to submit to his conditions, and having left him, she turned evil.[707] The New Revised Standard Version uses the name "Lilith" in that verse in Isaiah.

There is a legend that, when Jesus asked a baker's wife for a cake, her daughter insisted on using too little dough. Since the cake was for Jesus, the dough miraculously expanded — and the daughter, after crying out "Oo, ooo, oooo," was transformed into an owl a a result[708] (Thompson A1958.0.1, "Owl is baker's daughter punished for stinginess to Jesus"). This is believed to be the origin of Ophelia's statement that "the owl was a baker's daughter."[709] Another Christian legend makes it a symbol of the Jews who rejected Christianity.[710]

In France, if an owl hooted by a pregnant woman, it was said she would give birth to a girl.[711] In Wales, an owl's call was supposed to mean that a girl was about to lose her virginity.[712] Other Celtic legends make the owl an attribute of the god of the underworld. It also served as a messenger of Yama, the Hindu death-god.[713]

In Hmong legend, the owl originally had been like other birds, but one day, it let out a shriek which caused a series of accidents which caused a chicken's two babies to be killed. The chicken then twisted the owl neck until the latter could turn its head all the way around; this also resulted in it being able to see only at night.[714]

To the Egyptians, the hieroglyph of an owl meant death, and it was also a bird of death in many American Indian myths.[715] The Chinese considered it a portent of disaster — perhaps because of its large eyes, because demons were also said to have large eyes.[716]

On the other hand, the owl "was the emblem of Athena and hence a symbol of wisdom (Athens was renowned for its profusion of owls)."[717] Greek legend as told by Plutarch has it that, before the battle of Salamis, an owl was seen perching on the mast of the ship of Themistocles. The Greeks therefore accepted his plan — and defeated the invading Persians, keeping Greece free. Without the owl, they might have adopted another plan.[718] This presumably gave us the image of the "wise old owl," even though the Romans regarded the hoot of an owl as an ill omen. This legend was also found in England, where the screech of the barn owl in particular was regarded as dangerous, and to see an owl by daylight is even worse.[719] Chaucer wrote, "the oule ek, that of deth the bode bryngeth"[720] — "the owl also, that of death the warning brings" (Thompson B147.2.2.4, "Owl as bird of ill-omen").

Owls were also sometimes associated with courage; soldiers might carry their hearts into battle to make them brave.[721]

While there is no widespread legend of owls as message-carriers, birds in general were known for bearing messages (note the common remark "a little bird told me," based on Ecclesiastes 10:20; "Bird as messenger" is Thompson Type B291.1; "Bird as devil's messenger" is G303.10.7), and it would make sense for the wizarding world to give this role to owls, which had a reputation for wisdom and unnatural powers. And Rowling's owls aren't much like real owls anyway — they can be tamed (which real owls cannot), and Hedwig drinks orange juice and eats vegetables (which real owls do not).

Padma Patil: see PADMA AND PARVATI PATIL.

PARACELSUS

One of the famous wizards whose chocolate frog card Harry collects on the Hogwarts Express in the *Philosopher's Stone.* In the *Order of the Phoenix,* we learn that there is a bust of him in one of the corridors. Unlike most of the other famous wizards, Paracelsus perhaps does not belong in this guide, because he was a real person, born in Zürich probably in 1493 and died 1541.[722]

Properly Philippus Aurelius Theophrastus von Hohenheim (he took the name "Paracelsus" while studying at Basel, in honor of the famous Roman physician Celsius[723]), Paracelsus was an alchemist — but an alchemist with a difference. Up to his time, alchemists had concentrated their attention on finding the Philosopher's Stone primarily for purposes of making money,[724] and had been determined to keep their methods secret. Paracelsus insisted that the object of alchemy was "not to make gold but to prepare medicines."[725] He was a genuine radical, burning the books of his predecessors.[726] He also travelled the universities of Europe, from Basel to Bologna and Padua and even Constantinople and Egypt, learning as many techniques as he could.[727] At a time when Martin Luther was also burning books (the two apparently knew each other[728]), this might have gotten him in trouble with the church, but he was supported by the famous printer Frobenius — whose leg Paracelsus had supposedly saved from amputation.[729]

Paracelsus, because he questioned the ancients (and because he was a cranky character who was good at getting in trouble[730]), spent many years in enforced migration.[731] He apparently was a crusader on behalf of experimentation[732] — meaning that he possessed the spirit of a true scientist. His works had little long-term significance (unless you count his creation of laudanum as a pain-reliever), but they indicated a change in the tone of "natural philosophy," away from the ancients and toward a genuine sort of science. He died young and rather poor, far from home, from a fall that may have resulted from drinking too much. "He seized medicine by the scruff of it neck, so to speak, and if it wasn't entirely sense he shook into it, the shaking was beneficial just the same."[733] In the Potterverse, he may well have been one of the first great potion-masters. Severus Snape, with his dark arts obsession, would probably have liked him; another famous Paracelsus quote is "All substances are poisons; there is none that is not a poison. The right dose differentiates a poison from a remedy."[734]

Parents: see CRUEL PARENTS AND UNWANTED MARRIAGES and The UNWANTED CHILD.

PARSELMOUTHS

The theme of knowing the speech of animals is common in folklore, and we see small instances of it in Tolkien (in *The Hobbit* Bard of Dale can understand thrushes) and Alexander (Gwydion learns some animal speech at the end of *The Book of Three*). The classical prophet Tiresias was able to understand the language of birds.[735] We also see animals talking like humans in Lewis and others. The talking beasts usually come from species more popular than snakes — but folklore says that snakes have a special affinity for languages. Sigfried (Germanic)[736] and Melampus (Greek)[737] both learned animal speech from a serpent or dragon (Thompson B217.6, "Animal languages learned from dragon"); so also in the Grimm tale "The White Serpent" (also known as "The White Snake"), where eating a snake's body gives the gift of understanding[738] — similar to the way Sigurth learned of animal speech in the Eddic version of the Sigfried story.[739] Thompson also mentions a tale, without giving details, of learning the language of animals when one's ears are licked by a snake; Thompson B165.1.1. The Bulgarian folktale "The Language of Animals" says that the King of the Serpents could give the ability to learn the language of animals by spitting three times into the mouth of a man.[740] "Serpent language" is Thompson B215.5. And, of course, the serpent was able to talk to Eve in the legend of the Garden of Eden.

Much of the speculation about snakes in the Potterverse, especially in the *Chamber of Secrets,* is about the Heir of Slytherin. When Harry speaks to a snake, there is speculation that he is descended from Salazar Slytherin, who also spoke to snakes and chose a snake as the emblem of Slytherin House. We eventually learn that Harry is a parselmouth because he gained the ability from Voldemort — but this does not mean that Harry is not a descendent of Slytherin. If Slytherin had descendants at all, there is a good chance Harry is one of them. Why? Because most of the people of England are his descendants. Mathematical biology has shown that, after enough time, you will either have *all* the population descended from you, or *none* of it. Of course, it takes thousands of years (maybe more) for that to happen, but it has been a thousand or more years since Slytherin's time. If we estimate the average generation to be thirty years, there have been thirty-three generations between Slytherin's time and Harry's. If we assume that each descendant of Slytherin left just one and a three-quarters descendants (a pretty low rate of offspring, actually, since it is below the "replenishment rate"), then after thirty-three generations, Slytherin would have 104,774,502 descendents, or just about twice the population of Great Britain in Harry's time. Of course, some of those people married other descendants of Slytherin. But odds are that every member of a wizarding family is descended from Slytherin — whether they could speak to snakes or not.

Parvati Patil: see **Padma and Parvati Patil.**

Jesus's/Harry's Passion: see **"And Give His Life as a Ransom for Many";** also **The Resurrected Hero.**

Padfoot: see **The Grim.**

Padma and Parvati Patil

In Hindi, "Padma" is the lotus flower. In Hindu mythology, Brahma, the creator, was first seen as a lotus; the blossom is also associated with Vishnu, the preserver.[741] Parvati is the "daughter of the mountains" (Himalayas). She was the wife of Shiva, the Destroyer, but also (after a fight with him) was sent to earth, and became a girl who grew up to be extremely beautiful, once again winning Shiva's love.[742] Thus Padma and Parvati are, between them, associated with all three of the Hindu trinity of Brahma, Shiva, and Vishnu — but there is no direct link between the two of them. Certainly they are not twins! I do not believe that Rowling intended any mythological significance for the pair.

PEACOCKS

Malfoy Manor is patrolled by peacocks. The other characters regard this as a token of their great wealth. (It might also indicate why the Malfoys are so evil. Peacocks have a shrill, obnoxious cry — maybe the Malfoys are all sleep-deprived....) But the peacock, presumably because it is so gaudy, has many places in folklore. The bird was said to be sacred to Hera, wife of Zeus.[743] She was said to have placed the eyes of Argus in its tail after Hermes killed the hundred-eyed creature.[744] In Christian myth, the eyes in peacock's tail were sometimes said to be the all-seeing eyes of the Church.[745] Several Hindu goddesses, including Sarasvati goddess of poetry, are said to ride peacocks.[746] The bird, or its feathers, were regarded in several parts of Britain as an ill omen, perhaps forecasting rain or, more extremely, bankruptcy.[747] Islamic folklore claims that it once guarded the Gates of Paradise, but later lost the role.[748] Another Middle Eastern legend says that they stand on both sides of the Tree of Life, to represent humanity and nature.[749] In India, the peacock was said to eat snakes, making it an odd bird for a follower of Voldemort to own. The birds are said to be ashamed of their feet, and to hide them and shriek when they see them or they are seen (Thompson A2232.7, "Peacock given ugly feet to avoid arrogance").[750] Peacock feathers seem to have been considered particularly suitable for arrows in the Middle Ages, (when Sir Richard at the Lee wishes to give Robin Hood a gift, he offers arrows *fletched with peacock feathers;* "The Gest of Robyn Hode," stanza 132; Waltz-Gest, p. 42) but this is probably just because they are decorative, not because of any intrinsic qualities.

Peeves: see POLTERGEIST.

The PENSIEVE

Of the Pensieve, as described in Rowling, there is little trace in folklore. (The name itself is a neologism, reportedly from French *penser, to think,* and *sieve,* which strains, sorts, or separates.[751]) But consider giving it another name: the well of memory. This is certainly what a pensieve is: a well which summons memories. And *that* is an attested item. Norse myth tells of the well of Mimir, which held all knowledge; Odin gave up one of his eyes to drink from it.[752] And in Greek myth the spring Mnemosyne was supposed to restore memories.[753] (Contrast Lethe, which is a water of forgetting, but while that might be useful for rejected lovers, it's not going to be much help in catching Voldemort!) There are also prophetic wells known in England.[754]

PETER PETTIGREW'S FINGER

No, this is not a joke. It has folkloric significance. Peter Pettigrew was not the first to sacrifice a body part in order to excuse his behavior. "Thief cuts off own arm as an alibi" is Thompson K407.2.1; "cutting off part of own body," J213.3.2. Also somewhat similar is a tale-type with no proper title; Thompson numbers it 313 and calls it "The Girl as Helper in the Hero's Flight." A girl helps a man flee from something-or-other. He then (somehow) kills her, cuts off her finger, and (somehow) brings her back to life. When her father enchants a set of girls to look like her, he is able to identify her by the missing finger.

The British version of this is called "The Green Man of Knowledge,"[755] although in this version the girl never dies and her finger is merely broken, not cut off.

Another relevant Thompson motif is D702.1.1, "Cat's paw cut off; woman's hand missing," known from the Lohengrin legend.[756]

PETRIFICATION

There is no general Thompson motif for petrification, but "Petrification as curse" is M458, "Petrification by glance" is D581; "Petrification by magic" is D231; there are several other petrification motifs.

The word *petrify* means, literally, to make stone (Greek πετρος, *petros*=rock; hence Peter was the rock on which Jesus would build the church; Matthew 16:18). But why such a term? From the Greek Gorgons, whose gaze turned to stone.[757] There were three of them, two of them immortal; Perseus slew the third one, Medusa, and carried off her head. He did this by looking at her in a mirror.[758] (Shades, obviously, of how various people survived looking at the BASILISK in the *Chamber of Secrets*. There is also something quite similar in the German romance *Daniel von dem blühenden Tal,* or "Daniel of the Flowering Valley," by "Der Stricker," in which Daniel uses a mirror to acquire a Gorgon-like head and use it against his enemies.[759])

Petrification occurs in other myth systems as well. Lot's Wife is turned into a pillar of salt in Genesis 19:24. In Norse myth, when the dwarf Alvís answers all of Thor's questions, Thor turns him to stone rather than let him marry his daughter. Jackson, p. 157; Rose, p. 11, notes that Thor planned the whole thing so that the rising sun would fall on the dwarf and turn him to stone at the right time. A Peruvian legend has it that giants who had built the great buildings of Tiahuanaco (near Lake Titicaca) were turned to stone when the sun first came into existence.[760]

The theme of turning to stone was used by Tolkien in *The Hobbit*, where Gandalf tricked the three trolls to turn into stone at daybreak (which was also when Thor did his trick). However, this theme does not appear in *The Lord of the Rings;* one suspects Tolkien would have liked to have dropped the idea.

C. S. Lewis has the White Witch turn her enemies to stone in *The Lion, the Witch and the Wardrobe,* although Aslan is able to reverse this.

The Potterverse version of petrification is not like any of these, except maybe Lewis's. In the *Chamber of Secrets*, the victims aren't really made into stone; it's more like hard-rubber-ization — "rigorization," perhaps. And the process is reversible. It is noteworthy that the BASILISK can petrify victims; this is not inherent in the basilisk legend.

The PHILOSOPHER'S STONE

The "Philosopher's Stone" is the correct title for the magical item which Rowling's American publishers, for sales reasons (apparently thinking that insulting readers' intelligence will increase sales), incorrectly renamed "The Sorcerer's Stone," as in *Harry Potter and the Philosopher's/Sorcerer's Stone*. (To be fair, more than sixty different names were given for the Philosopher's Stone,[761] so what's one more among friends?) There are no historical references to the Sorcerer's Stone, but the Philosopher's Stone is well-known indeed to alchemists.

The earliest reference in alchemy texts to the Philosopher's Stone *(lapidens philosophorum)* is usually attributed to Zosimus around 300 C.E.[762] It is described simply as something that could turn other metals (especially lead) into gold.[763] (Apparently no one realized that, if they did enough of this, gold would become cheap.) In the mystic way that is typical of alchemy, it was called "a stone which is not a stone."[764]

The Philosopher's Stone was known in English by about the four-teenth century. The manuscript Boston, MA, Massachusetts Historical Society Winthrop 20 C contains a long poem about it (169 lines) which begins:

> Now every man In hys begynnyng
> Thynke hys god swete heven kyng
> If y wylt Rede here A none
> The workyng of þe phyloȝophers stone…[765]

> *Now every man in his beginning*
> *Thank his good sweet heaven[ly] king.*
> *If you will read here anon*
> *The working of the Philosopher's Stone.*

This is from about the same time as Chaucer. There is a good bit of alchemy in Chaucer's *Canon's Yeoman's Tale,* including one section where he gives instructions for turning quicksilver (mercury) into silver. There are references to philosophers and their work in this part of the tale (e.g. line 1122), although no direct reference to the Philosopher's Stone. The end of the tale also refers to some of the philosophical discussion that underlay alchemy.[766] A few scholars think Chaucer was in favor of alche-my,[767] but most apparently believe that he was making fun of a discipline where the instruction manuals always seemed to turn incomprehensible right around the stage where the real trick should have been revealed.[768]

Since the Stone didn't exist anyway, it was easy to pile extra prop-erties onto an object which originally had relatively limited use. This was especially so since alchemists used extremely figurative language in their texts, so metaphors for the stone's properties could be taken to be actual characteristics. So the Philosopher's Stone, in addition to having the property of transmutation (as we would now call it), was later said to cure diseases and grant immortality, or was used to produce the Elixir of Life which could accomplish the same end. Details are, of course, lacking.

Rowling took over the latter trait more or less intact — and never explained how Nicolas Flamel got away with hiding the Stone and not giving others access to it.

Flamel was a real alchemist, although his methods were pretty du-bious. He didn't start out in alchemy; his first work was as a scrivener (scribe, secretary, copyist). In his work, he came across an alchemical text. Like all alchemical texts, it was pretty vague, but he supposedly managed to figure out how to make the Philosopher's Stone. He went on to get rich, leave large charitable bequests — and leave behind an empty grave.[769] So it was assumed that his claims were true: he had managed to create a Philosopher's Stone, since he clearly became rich and conceivably became immortal.

One minor problem: We have *The Book of Abraham the Jew*, which supposedly was Flamel's source, and it has a recipe for the Philosopher's Stone[770] — and no one else can get it to work.

The idea of an item that somehow extended life was, of course, extremely common. "The Fountain of Youth" is proverbial. English folklore makes relatively little use of the motif — but there are interesting variations. For instance, in the ballad "Tam Lin"[771] a human sacrifice extends the life of the Queen of Fairy; for this, see also the entry on HORCRUXES.

In the *Philosopher's Stone* we learn that the Stone is red. This reflects the beliefs of alchemists. The ancient Greeks knew of seven metals — gold, silver, copper, tin, lead, iron, and mercury. (They also knew zinc, but they didn't *know* they knew it.) They viewed mercury as a sort of metallic principle.[772] They also were aware of the element sulfur, which was yellow and so was treated as a sort of a yellow principle.[773] Gold is a yellow metal, so naturally, if you combine a metallic principle with a yellow principle, you get gold, right?[774]

Well, no; what you get is mercury sulfate (HgS), or cinnabar — as the ancients should have known, because they extracted mercury by heating cinnabar![775]

See also AMULETS; IMMORTALITY.

The PHOENIX

Although the only phoenix we meet in the Harry Potter books is Fawkes, who lives in Dumbledore's office, *Fantastic Beasts* reports that the birds nest on mountain peaks and live in Egypt, China, and India. (Finding a habitable mountain peak in Egypt for it to live on is left as an exercise for the reader.) Classical legend says that there was only one phoenix, but obviously there are more in the Potterverse.

Even though they were not native to England, there are interesting tales about the Phoenix from an early date. The Old English *Exeter Book*

(Exeter Cathedral Library MS 3501, known to have been in existence by 1072), contains a long poem called "The Phoenix," which tells us that in its season "the bird burns along with his nest in the grip of the fire.… Yet after a space of time, life returns to him anew."[776] The bird seems to have been a symbol of resurrection in the late fourteenth century — because it is born from its grave, it made obvious sense to equate it with Jesus, since he too was born from his corpse.[777] So we find the Gawain-poet, in his memorial of the toddler Margaret (very possibly his own daughter), writing

> We calle hyr Fenyx of Arraby,
> Þat, freles, fleȝe of hyr Fasor.…[778]
> "We call her Phoenix of Arabia,
> That, faultless, flew away from her creator."

Much the same image occurs in Chaucer's *The Book of the Duchess,* memorializing Blanche, Duchess of Lancaster:

> Trewly she was, to my yë,
> The soleyn fenix of Arabye,
> For ther livyth never but oon,
> Ne swich as she ne knowe I noon.[779]
> "Truly she was, to my eye,
> The sole phoenix of Arabia,
> For there lives only one [at any time],
> Nor such as she have I ever known even one."

Tales of the phoenix also occur in tales from India, Egypt, Japan, Arabia,[780] and China (where they are male and female,[781] again meaning that there are more of them than one) — plus of course Greece and Rome. The Greek name φοινιξ, *phoinix,* derives from the word for purple-red (related to the word *Phoenician*[782]), which explains why the bird is often thought of as red. The idea of the Phoenix is thought to have originated in the east and migrated west (Shakespeare called it "The Arabian Bird," which title is also found in Herodotus and Pliny[783]) — indeed, the most famous early western reference locates it in Egypt but says it came from Arabia.[784] The story of the bird burning itself and being reborn from the ashes is classical, found as early as Herodotus.

The idea of a bird carrying a person to the upper world, as in the *Chamber of Secrets,* is Thompson Type F62.1. Resuscitation by burning is Thompson E15. A bird's tears restoring sight (similar to the healing power of Rowling's phoenix) is D1505.5.1.

There is a Jewish folktale regarding a Phoenix-like bird called a "Milcham." Supposedly, after Eve ate of the Tree of Knowledge, she induced all other creatures, except the Milcham, to eat the fruit as well. The Milcham, being sinless, retained its immortality — it was even given a special hiding place to guard it from evil — except that it melts or burns away every thousand years, re-hatching from its egg.[785] Some rabbis thought this bird was referred to in Job 29:18,[786] but the Hebrew text (which uses the word לוֹח, *khol)* is translated "sand" in most versions, and few even footnote the reading "phoenix" —although the *New Revised Standard Version,* perhaps the most authoritative available today, reads "the phoenix" in the text, "sand" in the margin; the *Revised English Bible* has "sand" in the text, "phoenix" in the margin. This interpretation is apparently ancient; the pre-Christian Greek Septuagint version rendered the passage in Job *phoinix,* which could mean *phoenix* but is usually thought to mean a *palm tree.* But did the Jewish legend inspire the translation or the translation inspire the legend?

The Phoenix is not as popular in modern fantasy as, say, dragons. Edith Nesbit used the creature with great success in her book *The Phoenix and the Carpet* — a book which Rowling knows and cites as an influence[787] (it has been suggested that the reason Fawkes is given that name is because the phoenix in Nesbitt's book came to life on Guy Fawkes day[788]) — but few others give it much attention. C. S. Lewis seems to allude to it briefly in *The Magician's Nephew,* where a large bird with a scarlet-crested head and purple tail is seen watching over the tree of healing, but he does not actually call it a phoenix, and its only role is to look at Digory Kirke to remind him of his task.

PIGWIDGEON

Not a folklore character but rather an elf in Michael Drayton (1563–1631)'s long poem "Nymphidia," where the name is given as "Pigwiggen":

> Pigwiggen was this Fairy Knight,
> One wondrous gracious in the sight
> Of fair Queen Mab, which day and night
>   He amorously observed ;

Which made King Oberon suspect
His service took too good effect,
His sauciness and often checkt,
    And could have wished him starved.

Although almost all mentions of Pigwidgeon derive from Drayton, the name is older: "The name is also given to a constable mentioned in *Selinus,* a tragedy, vaguely attributed to Robert Green, published in 1594."[789]

Since Drayton's elves were tiny (when Pigwiggan and Oberon go to battle over Queen Mab, they ride on earwigs), "Pigwidgeon" is a reasonable name for a small owl.

Pixies: see CORNISH PIXIES.

POGREBIN

Russian погребин. As told in *Famous Beasts,* it is a demon found in Russian folklore. It is also a Russian surname; perhaps one shouldn't get too close to someone with that name![790]

POLTERGEIST

The name is German, and means literally a "noisy spirit"[791] — a description that certainly fits Peeves. Poltergeists are not much known in genuine British folklore, presumably because they are so like the traditional Boggart.

Polyjuice Potion: see DOPPELGÄNGER.

PORLOCK

A creature mentioned several times in *Fantastic Beasts,* where it is described as a small hairy biped which watches over horses. It is said to live in the Dorset area of England and in southern Ireland. There is a *town* named Porlock in Somerset, just north of Dorset, and that Porlock famously home of the "Person from Porlock" who interrupted Samuel Taylor Coleridge in his writing of "Kubla Khan." Is Porlock, the town, named for the creature called a Porlock? The town's name is very old; when William the Conqueror had the Domesday Book compiled in 1086, Porlock was entered (under the name "Portlac"); it was held by one Drogo (presumably a Saxon), who held it from the sheriff Baldwin of Exeter; one Algar had held it before the Conquest, when it was worth £4.[792]

The Hopping Pot

In *Beedle's* story "The Wizard and the Hopping Pot," we see a wizard attribute many of his skills (at least as he reveals them to Muggles) as coming from his "lucky cooking pot." Legends about such a pot might be the source of tales of such Amulets as the Cauldron of Plenty (for which see the Deathly Hallows) and Froda's Magic Mill (for which see the chapter on Folklore).

The idea of an inanimate object which reveals someone's faults is perhaps most familiar now in the guise of Pinnochio's nose. There is also the reed that reveals a king's secrets whispered to the wall (Thompson motif D1316.5) and the harp or fiddle made of a dead woman's body which sings the tale of her murder in the ballad "The Twa Sisters";[793] as "The Singing Bone," this is Thompson tale-type 780 and motif E632.

The Price

There is a cost to saving the world.

Odin gave up his eye.[794]

Prometheus was bound.[795]

In Tolkien, Frodo loses a finger, and he cannot remain in Middle-Earth; "I tried to save the Shire, and it has been saved, but not for me. It must often be so, Sam, when things are in danger: some one must give them up, lose them, so that others may keep them."[796]

In LeGuin's Earthsea, Ged loses his powers.

In Alexander, Taran and Eilonwy give up immortality.

In Dickens's *A Tale of Two Cities,* which is said to have been a major influence on Rowling,[797] the hero Sydney Carton goes to the guillotine to save another man's life — ending with the famous words "It is a far, far better thing that I do, than I have ever done; it is a far, far better rest that I go to than I have ever known."

In the *Deathly Hallows*, Harry has to be prepared to die — although, ultimately, Rowling lets him off the hook completely. (Cheap, tawdry ending....) On the other hand, Lily Potter legitimately paid the price.[798]

The name "The Price" is not always used; sometimes it may be called "The Sacrifice"[799] or similar. Joseph Campbell made it part of his Great Classic Folk Theme, the "Monomyth." This is the primary topic of

Campbell's *The Hero with a Thousand Faces;* he sums up the story this way: "A hero ventures forth from the world of common day into a region of supernatural wonder: fabulous forces are there encountered and a fabulous victory is won; the hero comes back from this mysterious adventure with the power to bestow boons on his fellow men."[800]

Campbell himself compares this to a rite of passage, with stages "separation–initiation–return"; observe that Harry grows up during his adventures; also, he loses his parents, goes to Hogwarts, dies, and comes back from the dead.

Note how, when Harry returns to the "real" world near the end of the *Deathly Hallows,* he brings a boon of immunity to destructive magic. This is relatively unusual in fantasy; Tolkien and Alexander and LeGuin all show their heroes saving the world, but not bestowing direct gifts.

Of all the folklore themes mentioned in this work, the "monomyth," and its cost, may be the most controversial — or, at least, the one which has prompted the most speculations. Is it really a matter of folklore? Does it arise out of some deep human urge, or out of history, or something else? A strong case could be made that Campbell overstated his case — that the "monomyth" is not a universal *plot.* But it does seem to be a set of universal *motifs,* of which "The Price" is one of the most compelling. The best-known example of "the Price," and one of the earliest, is Jesus on the cross (1 Corinthians 6:20 actually says "you were bought with a price" — and at one point Lupin makes this very point to Harry regarding his parents' sacrifice: "Your parents gave their lives to keep you alive, Harry. A poor way to repay them…"[801]). Campbell tends to downplay the Christian example,[802] and the Norse and Greek analogies show that the idea predated the actual life of Jesus, but it seems clear Rowling had it in mind.

Campbell's view seems to have the emphasis a little wrong — he includes among his Thousand Heroes of whom the Monomyth was told both Jason and Aeneas,[803] who did not pay a price. Also, in Christianity, the gifts of the Questing Hero are not bestowed after the fact; it is the sacrifice itself that brings redemption. Similarly, Frodo saves the world by destroying the ring, not by returning to the Shire. And Harry destroys Voldemort, ultimately, by being willing to die. True, Odin dispenses his wisdom after giving up his eye, but on the whole successful epics concentrate on the cost, not the after-effects, of the heroic act. Hence the name "The Price."

The parallels between Harry and Jesus are significant, with the parallels between Harry's story and the account in the Gospel of Matthew being particularly close:

Potter Story	Matthew
In response to a prophecy, Voldemort seeks to destroy Harry, who might overthrow him.	In response to a forecast by the Magi, Herod the Great seeks to destroy Jesus, who is the foretold King of the Jews (Matthew 2:1–18).
The young Harry is forced to move to another home, the Dursleys'.	The young Jesus is forced to move to another home, Nazareth (Matthew 2:19–23).
Harry is tempted by Voldemort to change sides, but refuses.	Jesus is tempted by Satan to change sides, but refuses (Matthew 4:1–17).
Harry builds a circle of friends.	Jesus builds a circle of apostles (Matthew 4:18–22).
Harry as a teen comes into public view and begins to change the world, but is widely doubted and questioned.	Jesus as a young man comes into public view and begins to change the world, but is widely doubted and questioned.
Harry is sought by the authorities.	Jesus is sought by the authorities (Matthew 26:3–4, etc.).
Harry voluntarily is captured and is killed by his enemy.	Jesus voluntarily is captured and is killed by his enemies (Matthew 26:45–46, etc.).
Harry comes back to life and undoes much of the evil done by Voldemort.	Jesus comes back to life and undoes much evil (Matthew 28:1–10, etc.).

See also THINGS BOUGHT AT TOO HIGH A COST.

PROPHECIES FULFILLED ONLY BECAUSE SOMEONE TRIES TO PREVENT THEM

Thompson M370; Type M371.6.1 is "abandonment to avoid fulfillment of prophecy."

Voldemort tries to kill Harry because of the prophecy about him, and so sets up his downfall. Unlikely as it sounds, this is a widespread folklore type.

The classic example of this is the tale of Oedipus, who killed his father and married his mother. (Note that Rowling played with both Oedipal themes; see KILLED HIS FATHER AND MARRIED HIS MOTHER). Greek myth contains many other variants on prophecies coming true only because of attempts to avoid them coming true, very often involving infants who were cast away. In the tale of Troy, Paris was exposed because it was foretold that he would cause Troy's destruction[804] — and, being brought up in ignorance of his history, he ended up abducting Helen and causing the Trojan War. Acrisius cast his daughter Danae and her son Perseus adrift because of an oracle; Perseus later unknowingly slew Acrisius during an athletic competition at Larissa, where Acrisius had fled because of the prophecy.[805] Herodotus reported a tale that Cyrus the Great's grandfather Astyges, told that his daughter Mandane would bear a child who would supplant him, first gave Mandane a husband below her station, then had her child exposed;[806] Cyrus would later overthrow Astyges and found the Persian Empire.

The Irish tale of Deirdre of the Sorrows begins with a druid's prophecy that she would cause great slaughter. King Conchobhar therefore had her hidden away; she grew up to be a great beauty, over whom many battles were fought and many men, including her beloved Naoise, slain.[807]

Christian legends give us the tale of Barlaam and Josaphat, in which it is foretold to heathen King Abenner that his son Josaphat will become a Christian, causing Abenner to isolate his son and so set up the circumstances in which the philosophically-inclined Josaphat is converted by the hermit Barlaam.[808]

Perhaps more relevant is a story that Josephus told about Moses:[809] A diviner informed Pharaoh that a Hebrew child would humble Egypt. So Pharaoh ordered all Hebrew children killed — and set up the conditions which led to Moses humbling Egypt.

The tale of MacBeth as given by Shakespeare and his sources has certain similarities with this theme — and even more to Voldemort's misinterpretation of prophecy. Just as MacBeth misunderstands some of the prophecies he hears, such as that about no man of woman born being able to harm him, so Voldemort misunderstands the portion of the prophecy he hears. To be sure, very little of Shakespeare's retelling of the tale of the actual MacBethoc is regarded as actual history. But the motif of the act of prophesying causing the prophesy to come true is very widespread.

Tolkien several times examined the problem of a trying to avoid the working out of a prophecy. Galadriel warns against taking too much notice of the visions in her mirror, which are only possible and sometimes come true only when someone sets out to avoid them. In *The Silmarillion,* almost the last word on Túrin Turambar is "Master of Doom by Doom Mastered"[810] — his constant attempts to avoid his *wyrd* (doom, fate, destiny) serve to bring it about. Tolkien wrote that "a man that flies from his fear may find that he has only taken a short cut to meet it."[811] How true of Voldemort: devoting all his effort to avoiding death simply resulted in him dying young.

For prophecy to be possible, of course, the future must already be, in some sense, fixed and known. There are three general classes of insight into the future: prophecy, divination (which might include ARITHMANCY), and time travel. Prophecy is ancient, being found in the Bible (the first use of the noun "prophet" in the King James Bible is in Genesis 20:7; the first use of the verb "prophesy" is in Numbers 11:25). Divination, which differs from prophecy in that it is a human attempt to gather information as opposed to being a direct message from a god, is widely attested in the ancient world as well (and is condemned in the Bible). It is also the only form of forecasting in which it was common for the diviner to cast the oracle based on how much he or she was paid — "[C]omplete trust was placed by the ancients in the art of the seer whose interpretation of signs frequently influenced the pattern of events. Like today's professional footballers, good seers changed sides for high prices."[812] The idea of time travel is newer; although there were a few dream visions and peculiar instances such as Mark Twain's *A Connecticut Yankee in King Arthur's Court,* the first real time travel story was H. G. Wells's 1895 story *The Time Machine.*[813] That tale, however, was about time travel into the future and back, which meant that it did not involve the problem of the "time paradox" (i.e. doing something which changed the past and so destroyed the future). Robert A. Heinlein's *By His Bootstraps* was probably the first story to give us a time circularity, in which the future self deliberately arranges for the actions of his past self, which we see in the *Prisoner of Azkaban* when the older Harry releases the patronus that saves his younger self from the dementors.

Observe that Rowling — alone among authors I am aware of — has used time travel (in the *Prisoner of Azkaban*), prophecy, *and* divination (the last of which is said to work, at least sometimes, even if not when practiced by Professor Trelawney). Rowling also handles each part properly — Hermione works hard to hide her possession of her Time Turner, and clearly understands the idea of the past, present, and future selves (although Harry never gets it), plus Rowling carefully dovetails the events at the end of the *Prisoner of Azkaban* so that the past selves never realize that they are being influenced by their future selves.

The prophecies of Sybill Trelawny have one characteristic which is found in the classical Greek and Roman sibyls: the voice in which her true prophecies are uttered is not her own. When Æneas comes to consult the sybil of Cumae, he enters a cave with a hundred passages and a hundred gates, and speaks in a voice that is "more than mortal."[814]

PTOLEMY

One of the famous wizards whose chocolate frog card Harry collects on the Hogwarts Express in the *Philosopher's Stone*. Unlike most of those other wizards, Ptolemy was a real person. As with Agrippa, the real question is, *which* real person. Ptolemy was a very famous name in antiquity; one of Alexander the Great's top subordinates was Ptolemy son of Lagos, and after Alexander died, Ptolemy took over Egypt. All of the following kings of Egypt for more than two hundred years were named Ptolemy; the queen we call Cleopatra (properly Cleopatra VII, because the women of the Ptolemaic dynasty were all named Cleopatra or Berenice) was the daughter of Ptolemy XI (known as "Auletes" or "the Flute-Player") and the older sister of Ptolemy XII and Ptolemy XIII. The first half-dozen of these Ptolemies are referred to as the "King of the South" in chapter 11 of the Book of Daniel, with no attempt to distinguish when one king was succeeded by another.[815]

But the likeliest candidate for Ptolemy is surely the later Egyptian scientist Ptolemy, known in Latin as Claudius Ptolemaeus. Little is known of his life, but he lived in Alexandria, Egypt in the second century.[816] His chief importance is as a compiler: He took the results of Greek astronomy and put them together in one package.[817] He used primarily Hipparchus as a source.[818] This book came to be known as the *Almagest,* after its Arabic name, and was one of the great scientific books of the Middle Ages. Unfortunately, most of the information in it was wrong; Ptolemy believed (as did most people at the time) that the sun orbited around the earth, and worked out the motions of the planets on this basis (forcing him into a very complex system of "epicycles," or spheres within spheres[819]). Also, he accepted the estimate of the earth's size by Poseidonius, rather than the more accurate calculation by Eratosthenes. This blatant (and rather ridiculous) error, which could easily have been avoided, caused Christopher Columbus to insist that the earth was smaller than it was, and hence to insist that the American continent was part of Asia. Ptolemy also gave information about astrology, found in book called the *Tetrabiblios.*[820]

Thus Ptolemy was very famous, but very, very inaccurate. Astronomy was a Hogwarts subject (although nowhere are we shown anything about what is learned in astronomy class, or *why* Hogwarts students learned it), so perhaps Ptolemy was a resource they used. If so, their astronomy classes must have left a great deal to be desired. Maybe astronomy was taught by tradition, the way Divination was taught, not because it worked.

PUMPKINS

Harry Potter's world is full of uses of pumpkins, with pumpkin juice (as if there were such a thing) being the most common. This is somewhat surprising, since the association of the pumpkin with magic is more typical of America than Britain. On All Hallow's Eve (Halloween), a lighted pumpkin is supposed to protect against evil — especially if it had been planted on Good Friday.[821] The source of this legend is not clearly known.

Carving vegetables into head shapes at Hallowe'en is attested in Scotland, but there, the vegetable involved is a turnip (as large as possible). These were supposed to repel witches. After the holiday, the turnip was mashed together with potatoes to make "clapshot," which also contained money and other small prizes.[822]

The name "Jack-O'-Lantern" for a carved pumpkin may be a misnomer; a "Jack-O'-Lantern" is also a ghost. The American tale "How Jack Became a Jack-O'-Lantern" doesn't mention pumpkins — it sounds more like the explanation for the HINKEYPUNK, which lure travelers into swamps. Jack sells his soul to the Devil, but when the Devil comes after seven years to claim his soul, Jack nails the fiend's hand to the wall, and the Devil has to promise to let him live out his life. When Jack dies of old age, Heaven will not take him. Sent down to Hell, the Devil refuses to have him enter; he is too smart. Instead, he throws a ball of fire at Jack. Now Jack wanders around, carrying the fire, a Jack-O'-Lantern.[823]

In China, pumpkins were widely associated with fertility treatments, probably because they grew larger and faster than most other gourds,[824] but there is no sign of this in the Potterverse.

The Quest Hero: see **The UGLY DUCKLING.**

Quirrell, Quirinius: see **TWO-FACED FIGURES.**

Ramora

The Ramora is described as a fish living in the Indian Ocean which could anchor ships. This pretty well matches the Muggle description: "In Latin the Ramora was known as the *Delaya,* in Greek the *Echeneis* (the Ship Holder). It was a little Fish which could keep a ship anchored in the strongest wind or fiercest storm."[825] The Latin name is a joke, but the Greek one is real: εχενηις, "*a small sea-fish,* supposed to have the power of holding ships back, Lat[in] *echeneïs, remora,*"[826] a name used e.g. by Aristotle. The beneficial nature described in *Fantastic Beasts* is not so clear; supposedly the fish helped win the Battle of Actium for Octavian (the future Emperor Augustus) by holding back the ship of his enemy Mark Antony. It is sometimes linked with the sea urchin,[827] presumably because the sea urchin is known in Latin as *echinus.*

There is a non-magical fish, the remora (family name *Echeneidae*), which like the ramora will anchor itself to other fish or to boats — but at most it will slow them down a little.

The Entrance to Ravenclaw House

According to *The Deathly Hallows,* to gain admission to Ravenclaw house one must answer a question, with the question being (based on our limited samples) philosophical, complicated, often open to multiple responses, and presumably not soon repeated.

The obvious analogy to a doorward requiring an answer is to Thebes and the Sphinx, although the Theban Sphinx had only a few questions (perhaps only one), not a whole personality test of them.[828] It is interesting that the Sphinx Harry meets in the *Goblet of Fire* asks riddles and will not let Harry past unless he answers correctly, because that is also what the Theban Sphinx did. The SPHINX would not let anyone enter Thebes unless he could answer her riddle, and anyone who tried the riddle and got it wrong was devoured. (How the SPHINX kept up its strength in the case of such a presumably-limited diet is never explained.) Oedipus solved the riddle and saved the city — and hence became its king.[829]

There is a weaker, reverse, analogy to the quest of the Holy Grail, where knights coming to the Fisher King are expected to ask a question (but generally fail to ask it).[830]

"Guardians of the Threshold" are a common mythological theme (consider Cerberus, the archetype of FLUFFY), but having them ask riddles rather than just, say, attack, seems to be more popular in modern fiction than ancient.[831]

As for riddles themselves, they are found in many cultures. Aristotle himself discussed them more than two thousand years ago. The famous British manuscript *The Exeter Book* (Exeter Cathedral Library MS 3501, known to have been in existence by 1072) contains a large collection in Old English. Some of these, such as #25, can be, shall we say, spicy. The answer to this is "An onion:"[832]

> I am a wondrous thing: women expect me to bring joy, and I serve those who are close to me. I hurt no one except the person who kills me. My stem is tall and erect — I stand up in bed — and I have whiskers below that. Sometimes a pretty country girl — presumptuous lass! — wants to get a grip on me. She assaults my red self and grabs my head and holds me in a tight place. She will soon feel the effects, this curly-haired girl who has grabbed me; her eyes will be wet!

The Sloane Manuscript (British Library, Sloane MS. 2593, c. 1430) contains the "Riddle Song" which begins "I have a yong suster" ("I have a young sister"), with lines like "She sente me the chery Wythouten any ston" ("She sent me the cherry without any stone"; the response is that a cherry has no stone when it is in the blossom).

You've probably heard the riddle that begins "As I was going to St Ives, I met a man with seven wives." Riddles of the same type are known as far away as Russia: "Four cats are sitting, opposite each cat there are three cats. How many of them are there?"[833] In Norse myth, Odin and the giant Vafthrúdnir played a riddle game, which Odin won by asking an improper riddle.[834] Thus Ravenclaw is following a very ancient tradition in using riddles as an entry guard.

RED CAPS

Described in the *Prisoner of Azkaban* as small goblinoid creatures found where blood had been shed, the Redcap is traditionally a "malicious goblin found in the borders of Scotland. His name derives from his habit of dying his hat in human blood, and he inhabits ruined castles or any dreary place where atrocities have been committed. He can be overcome by a cross."[835] "Redcap lived in old ruined peel towers and castles where wicked deed had been done, and delighted to re-dye his red cap in human blood. William Henderson... described him as 'a short thickset old man, with long prominent teeth, skinny fingers armed with talons like eagles, large eyes of a fiery-red color, grisly hair streaming down his shoulders, iron boots, a pikestaff in his left hand, and a red cap on his head.'"[836] Some reports say that he committed his murders by dropping rocks on victims' heads, but that he could be driven off with a crucifix or reciting from the Bible.[837] Other names for these creatures, or something very like them, are Redcombs, Bloody Caps, Dunters, and Powries.[838] "Redcap (Redcomb) murders for blood" is Thompson F363.2. Other locales have other, less dangerous, creatures also called redcaps.

RE'EM

Described in *Fantastic Beasts* as giant oxen with golden hair, the re'em is curious because its two characteristics have come down to Muggles as *two different creatures,* one an animal with golden hair, the other a giant ox. The latter of these is is entirely real and even goes by the same name: ראם, *re'em,* occurs nine times in the Hebrew Bible (Numbers 23:22, 24:8, Deuteronomy 33:17, Job 39:9–10, Psalm 22:21, 39:6, 92:10, Isaiah 34:7). The King James Bible always translates it "unicorn" (see the entry on the UNICORN), based on a wild guess made by the Greek and Latin translators of the Hebrew, but the only reason for this ancient rendering is that most Biblical references to the *re'em* mention its horn(s). It was almost certainly the *bos primigenius,* the aurochs or wild ox, ancestor of the domestic ox,[839] the last of which is thought to have died in 1627.[840] This was an immensely strong creature, so the idea that drinking its blood would give strength, as described in *Fantastic Beasts,* is reasonable.

The hair of the aurochs of course was not golden — but Jason and the Argonauts are supposed to have sought the Golden Fleece of the Ram of Phrixus.[841] Jason did this partly to claim the throne of Iolcus, which was rightfully his, and partly to defend himself from Pelias, who held the throne.[842] The story of Jason, the *Argo,* the Golden Fleece, and Medea is too long to tell here — it is the subject of a whole book, Apollonius of Rhodes's *The Voyage of the Argo* — but it seems reasonable that the story of the Golden Fleece and of the golden-haired *re'em* are inter-related. ("Quest of golden fleece," Thompson H1332.1; "Ram with golden fleece," Thompson B101.3, R175.1).

Hebrew folklore eventually had more to say about the re'em, claiming that there were only two of them alive at any given time, living half a world apart, meeting only once every seventy years for purposes of mating, whereupon the parent animals died.[843] During Noah's flood, it was said to be too big to fit in the ark, so Noah towed it along behind.[844]

REMUS

In Roman mythology, Remus was the twin brother of Romulus.[845] Allegedly they came from the line of Aeneas,[846] the Trojan hero who had survived the city's sack, but this seems to be a case of two legends badly glued together. The two were children of a Vestal Virgin, Rhea Silvia,[847] who obviously had broken her vows of virginity. In at least one account, she didn't have much choice; Mars, the God of War, was the father.[848] Nor had she had much choice about becoming a Vestal; it was forced upon her by her uncle — who had usurped her father's throne and didn't want her raising children to overthrow him.[849] This King Amulius ordered her children to be exposed.[850] They were suckled by a wolf[851] before being rescued by a herdsman. (Note that a child raised by wolves was sometimes called a werewolf, as in the ROMANCE of William of Palerme; see under WEREWOLVES.) The boys grew up strong, and began to build a city, but eventually Remus teased Romulus, and Romulus killed him.[852]

Since Remus was suckled by wolves, it is an obvious name for a werewolf. So is "Lupin," since the Latin word for wolf is "lupus"; compare the English word "lupine."

See also HERMIONE.

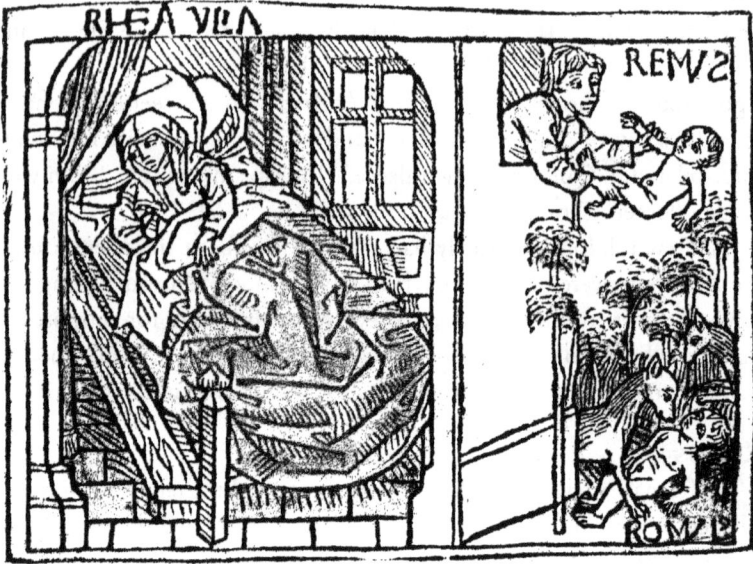

Woodcut of Rhea Silvia bearing the boys Romulus and Remus, who are throw out to the wolves. From an edition of Boccaccio's De Mulieribus Claris *printed by Johannes Zainer around 1474. Source: Wikimedia Commons.*

The Resurrected Hero

In the *Deathly Hallows*, Harry dies and comes back to life. Sound familiar? The reference is to Jesus. Duh. But compare Gandalf in Tolkien's *The Lord of the Rings*; also the tale of Persephone, who spent half of each year in Hades but then returned to the upper world.[853] In Sumerian and Babylonian legend, Ishtar/Inanna goes to the land of the dead and returns.[854] The Egyptian story of Isis tells of her reviving her son Horus and reassembling and reviving the body of Osiris.[855] British legend has John Barleycorn (or The Corn King), cut down, roasted, thrown away, then growing back every year.[856] The folktale "The Juniper Tree" also has a hint of this motif.[857] A related story is found in Scandinavian versions of the ballad known in English as "The Twa Sisters" (Child #10) or as the Grimm story of "The Singing Bone" (Thompson motif E632, tale 780): A woman is murdered, a musical instrument made from her corpse, and the instrument sings out the truth. In English, the story ends there, but in the Scandinavian versions, she comes back to life.[858]

On the other hand, the Norse tale of Balder has no happy ending; after the beloved god Balder is slain by the blind god Hod, abetted by the nasty god Loki, the gods beg Hel, Queen of the dead, to let him come back. She agrees — if every living thing weeps for him. All do except for a giantess, Thokk, and the whole thing fails.[859] This is in some ways reminiscent of the tale of Orpheus and Euridice, known from Ovid and Virgil: Euridice is slain by a snake, and Orpheus goes to Hades to try to bring her back. His music wins the right to take her back to life — if he never looks back on the return from Hades. But, at the last moment, he looks at her, and she is lost to him forever.[860]

Other famous gods and heroes who visit the Land of the Dead and come back (without bringing someone back to life) include, from classical legend, Hercules, Odysseus, Theseus, and Aeneas (who uses it for Necromancy; in the underworld, his dead father Anchises shows him the Rome of the future to tell Aeneas of his duty and destiny[861]); in the *Kalevala,* Vainamoinen; and in the Norse myths, Odin, who hangs himself for nine days (as a sacrifice to himself, according to some).[862] Also, once again looking at Tolkien, Aragorn goes to the Paths of the Dead and returns.

Rowling's version, since it involves Harry simply coming back, with no cost (see the Price) and no circle of life, falls closest to the Christian version.

The Resurrection Stone: see under The Deathly Hallows.

Riddles, Riddle of the Sphinx, Riddle Games: see under The Entrance to Ravenclaw House.

Ritual of Desecration

A ritual which puts a permanent blight on an area (sort of a magical sowing with salt) or of placing a curse on an object or person.[863] The creation of a Horcrux is an obvious ritual of desecration; the act itself is horrific, and the resulting object is dangerous to destroy (as Dumbledore learned in trying to deal with the Resurrection Stone) and dangerous to keep (as we learn both from the diary and the locket); note that, in this, a horcrux resembles Tolkien's One Ring. The idea of the ritual of desecration is found in many mythologies; in the west, the idea probably goes back at least to Thyestes raping his own daughter to gain revenge on his brother Atreus.[864] Christians who persecuted witches in the middle ages claimed that traditional witch initiations involved a ritual of desecration: stepping on a crucifix and declaring "I deny the Creator of heaven and earth. I deny my baptism. I deny the worship I formerly paid to God. I cleave to thee, Satan." The new witch would then perhaps be given a secret NAME, and might kiss a representation of Satan's rear end.[865]

C. S. Lewis used a Ritual of Desecration as a plot device in *That Hideous Strength;* the N.I.C.E. staff tried to get Mark Studdock to desecrate a crucifix — which caused him to wonder if there was actually some basis to Christianity.

Medieval ROMANCE

In the Introduction, I label the Harry Potter books a Romance. But what *is* a romance? It's *not* what we think of today as a romance novel, which is mostly about sexual love. Beyond that, finding a definition has been difficult:

"The exact definition of a romance is elusive. A few authors have insisted that it be 'romantic' — that is, that it be about love, perhaps specifically 'courtly love,' or the quest for the unattainable beloved. Another suggestion is 'a tale of knightly prowess, usually set in remote times or places and involving elements of the fantastic or supernatural.' 'Courtesy' is often a key element. Some claim that romances are 'inextricably linked with feudalism,' or that their roots are entirely in the Arthurian story."[866]

"Not only do they present wonders not found in the real world, but they also depict a world of superlatives: of the most beautiful ladies, the bravest knights, the fiercest opponents, the ugliest ogres, even, as in Chrétien de Troyes's *Lancelot,* 'the most beautiful tombs' and 'a sycamore tree of unequalled beauty....' Among the superlatives is often the truest love. The term 'romance' itself, from *roman,* originally referred to the French language, which was descended from Latin or the Roman language.... The term came to mean a story or a tale told in French, without the modern associations with love. Ultimately it was applied to the types of tales told by the French; and since many of the early French *romans* or romances told of knightly deeds and great loves, the word *roman* or 'romance' eventually came to be associated with such tales."[867]

"Finally, it is claimed that 'the romance moves largely amidst abstractions.... The problems of actual life are carefully avoided; the material treated consists, rather, of the fanciful problems of the courts of love and situations arising out of the new-born chivalry.'"[868]

"The sense of beautiful fragility, of something so precious and yet so precarious that it should outweigh our normal feelings of justice and propriety, is part of our response to many romances."[869]

"[P]erhaps we should say that a romance has only two requirements: it must feature a hero doing an extraordinary task, and it must be for a worthy cause. It may be Gawain marrying a hag to save Arthur, as in *Sir Gawain and Dame Ragnall*.... It may be Gawain (again) accepting with courage the danger of a fatal blow in *Sir Gawain and the Green Knight*. It may be a lover offering up his life for love (sort of the Official Worthy Cause of the Middle Ages) in *Floris and Blancheflour*. It may be Robin Hood rescuing a knight from poverty in *The Gest of Robyn Hode*. Or it may be Orfeo travelling to the underworld to bring back his beloved. In every instance, it is the story of a hero finding and maintaining what Chaucer calls his 'trouthe' — his troth, but far more than simply a vow. It is his pledged word, it is his integrity, it is his loyalty, it is his purpose, his place in the universe, his way of learning to be true to himself."[870] The best summary may be that it is a story of maintaining a high ideal in a hostile and wondrous world. This obviously is what Harry does. (Well, except for all those times he lies his head off.)

See also LOVE CONQUERS ALL.

The Room of Requirement: see under HOGWARTS: THE EDIFICE.

Ancient Runes: see under BEEDLE THE BARD.

Sacrifice: see **The Price**.

St. Mungo's

In all likelihood, the wizarding hospital is named "St. Mungo's" because it's such a silly-sounding name to English speakers. But "Mungo" is a genuine Scottish name — Mungo Park, for instance, did important scientific exploration of the East Indies and the Niger River of Africa; he was killed in 1805. But the most important Mungo was surely St. Kentigern, who in the sixth and early seventh centuries brought Christianity to the Strathclyde region of southwestern Scotland and the Cumbria area of northwestern England; he is especially associated with Glasgow. He was also known as "Mungo," or "Saint Mungo,"[871] and there were dedications to him under that name. (Although the two names seem very different, "Kentigern" means "hound-lord" and "Mungo" means "hound," so they are in fact related.) Because he lived so long ago, however, we have very little real knowledge of him life and work. Kentigern wasn't noted as a healer — his most noteworthy miracle was recovering a ring that had been thrown into a river — but almost every saint of that era has at least *some* healing miracles attributed to him, so it isn't really unreasonable to name a medical complex after him.

Salamanders

We see a salamander in the *Chamber of Secrets*, where the Weasley Twins catch one and try to get it to swallow fireworks. The book describes it as "smouldering." In the *Prisoner of Azkaban*, Hagrid puts them in a bonfire.

Most Muggles, if they know salamanders at all, think of them as a small, harmless amphibian. But there are hints of the wizarding salamanders in classical legend — they were spirits of fire (and strongly poisonous). "It was regarded as the elemental being of fire (as GNOMES were the elemental beings of earth; sylphs (air) and undines or nymphs (water)." Pliny said salamanders sought hot fires in order to breed,[872] although others claimed they was sexless and used them as a symbol for chastity; in heraldry, they were used to represent courage, since they could face the fires of affliction.[873] Salamanders were said to be very cold, and to have served as a fire-*quencher:* "A sort of lizard, fabled to live in fire, which, however, it quenches by the chill of its body."[874] Despite this report, other Muggle legends see it as a fire-starter.

The note in *Fantastic Beasts,* that they need a fire to live but can survive for some time outside of it if fed pepper, has no parallel in Muggle writings.

(Harry's) SCAR

"And so shall the rightful king be known." The words are J. R. R. Tolkien's, referring to Aragorn, but they are a common theme in folktale. Havelok the Dane, for instance, was recognized as king by a family birthmark ("recognition by birthmark" is Thompson H51.1; "recognition by scar" H51).[875] Nor was he the only hero who was were recognized by a lover or follower by birthmarks — indeed, the body of King Harold II was supposedly recognized by this means by his common-law wife Edith Swan-neck after the Battle of Hastings. And in the Arthurian tale of the *Vulgate Merlin,* the true and false Guineveres, who had the same father and were born on the same night, could be told apart only because the true Guinevere had a royal birthmark.[876] Heirlooms also serve this purpose (Thompson H96), and there are many instances of "hidden monarchs" being recognized based on a feat only they can perform — as Arthur supposedly pulled the sword from the stone[877] and Odysseus could bend his great bow that no one else could pull[878] (Thompson H331.4.2). Still, birthmarks are safer because they cannot be given away and are hard to fake. Terry Pratchett satirized this with his tales of the hidden King Carrot in the "Discworld" series. Birthmarks were often credited to a prenatal experience of some sort, such as a shock or evil act against the mother.[879] Harry Potter does not have such a birthmark, but his scar serves a similar function: A mark, which he has had from an early age, which makes him instantly recognizable. (Harry's uncontrollable hair is also unusual, but it doesn't seem to have any special function.)

A scar could also be an example of religious stigmata, although this seems unlikely since Harry bears his scar *before* he can take on the symbols of Jesus.

SEA SERPENT

Thompson B91.5, X1396.1. *Fantastic Beasts* accuses Muggles of "hysterical" accounts of the dangers of sea serpents. And certainly there are Muggle tales of battles with monsters of the deep, e.g., Beowulf fought the *mere-fixa* (sea-fishes; "creatures of the deep"; line 546) and the *feond-scaða* (*feond-scatha,* variously rendered, "multi-colored," "foul-enemy," "great sea-monster"; line 554);[880] to the latter name compare Tolkien's dragon "Scatha the Worm." And there is the classical story of the sea-creatures which appeared to be floating islands which would then dive and drown any humans who had landed on them; known in Latin as the *aspidochelone,* or *asp-turtle,* in Old English (and J. R. R. Tolkien) this became "Fastitocalon": "To him, floating creature of the mountainous oceans, the name Fastitocalon is given. His appearance is like shaly rock such as crumbles along the water's edge surrounded by sand-dunes… so that travellers on the ocean wave that they are looking with their eyes upon some island; and then they tie up the high-prowed ships to the false land…. When… he feels that the travellers are resting secure in him… then forthwith into the salt wave he goes with them… and makes for the bottom, and then in a cavern of death consigns them to drowning, the ships with the men."[881]

But the charge in *Fantastic Beasts* is still somewhat unfair — it appears that *sailors* have left few accounts of sea serpents. At least, it appears that there are no English-language sailor songs at all which mention sea serpents. It has been suggested that most of the alleged sightings are really of giant squid.[882] It has also been suggested that the idea goes back to the Babylonians, a people who did not even live by the sea, let alone sail on it! The Akkadian monster Tiamat "was a female dragon" and "goddess of the deep"[883] who was also the mother of the Babylonian gods. The god Marduk slew Tiamat in the Akkadian account of the *Enûma eliš*,[884] which is widely believed to be related to the account of the creation of the world in Genesis 1. After the battle, Marduk made seas, earth, and heavens from her corpse.[885] However, Tiamat seems to be mentioned only in the *Enûma eliš*,[886] not in any other ancient Mesopotamian literature, so we probably shouldn't consider her to be the archetype of much that follows.

The Bible refers on several occasions (Job 3:8, 41:1, Psalm 74:14, 104:26, 27:1) to Leviathan (לִוְיָתָן), which may be another name for this pre-creation serpent-being but may simply be another sea-monster.[887] It is thought to be the same creature as the "Lotan" of Ugaritic myth, but "Ugaritic texts give no detailed description of Leviathan" either, telling us primarily that the god Baal

> [S]mote Lotan the fleeting serpent,
> Annihilated the tortuous serpent
> The tyrant (?) with seven heads.[888]

But the Bible gives very little information about Leviathan. Only later did Jewish legend start to fill in details, and these non-scriptural stories might explain the fear of sea serpents: "Leviathan's monstrous tusks spread terror, from his mouth issued fire and flame, from his nostrils smoke, from his eyes a fierce beam of light; his heart was without pity. He roamed at will on the surface of the sea...."[889] One account claimed that it ate as a meal a creature more than five hundred miles long![890]

Perhaps the easiest explanation for the sea serpent is that it is an elaboration of a curious fact about dragons: they are "almost universally associated with water, especially deep pools and wells."[891] Put a water-loving dragon in the ocean and what do you get? A sea serpent....

Serpents: see under DRAGONS; NAGINI; PARSELMOUTHS; SEA SERPENT.

SEVEN

Why did Voldemort want seven horcruxes?

It is a powerful magic number. It also has deep religious significance — the Bible begins with the seven days of creation of Genesis (hence our seven days of the week), and the Apocalypse at the end is a tale of seven seals being unsealed. "The number seven was sacred among the various Semitic people, as well as among many other peoples.... Among the Egyptians, seven gradually succeeded four as the favorite holy number.… In Mesopotamia seven was holy from earliest times.… Seven plays such an important role in the O[ld] T[estament] that only the chief features of its use can be noted here.… It is hard to say what the numerous symbolic uses of seven in the Bible have in common. Perhaps the simplest and most comprehensive generalization that can be made is that seven denotes completeness, perfection, consummation."[892]

Also, there were seven classical planets (the Moon, the Sun, Mercury, Venus, Mars, Jupiter, Saturn).

But it is especially noteworthy that there are seven deadly sins (pride, lust, envy, anger, covetousness, gluttony, and sloth)[893] and seven Christian virtues (faith, hope, and love, plus the Cardinal Virtues prudence, justice, temperance, and fortitude).[894] Thus one might argue that with each Horcrux Voldemort made, he gave in to another deadly sin and lost another virtue. The greatest virtue, and the last, and the one that defeated him, was Love. (See Love Conquers All.)

"Seven as magic number" is Thompson D173.1.3.

The Shrieking Shack

The Shrieking Shack was said to be the most haunted place in Britain. Astounding, given that no ghosts ever came out of it! Someone managed an amazing advertising campaign. In any case, it has competition for the title: "'The most haunted house in England' was the epithet bestowed on Borley Rectory when public interest around the world made it one of the legends of the twentieth century. Its international fame began with a *Daily Mirror* article which began 'Ghostly figures of headless coachmen and a nun, an old-time coach… which appears and vanishes mysteriously, and dragging footsteps in empty rooms.'"[895] No doubt many other places have made similar claims.

Skrewts, Blast-Ended: see under Manticore.

Horace Slughorn

Odds are, if you've met the word "slughorn" anywhere other than in Rowling, it is in Robert Browning's poet "Childe Roland to the Dark Tower Came," which ends

> Dauntless the slug-horn to my lips I set,
> And blew "Childe Roland to the Dark Tower came."

It appears that Browning got the word from the eighteenth century poet Thomas Chatterton — and it appears that Chatterton for practical purposes invented the word, using it for an instrument used in battle, perhaps some form of trumpet.

But a "slug-horn" is, according to the dictionaries, a genuine English (or at least Scots) word, a somewhat worn down form of *slog(g) orne,* which when even further worn down became the word "slogan." (The original, according to several dictionaries, is the Scots Gaelic *sluagh-ghairm, company-shout, war-cry.*) But *slough/slog/sloʒ* has multiple meanings in Scots, including a valley or a petty person. So "Slughorn" *could* be a selfish person who blows his own horn. And *that* fits Horace Slughorn quite well.

On the other hand, a "slug" is an animal which moves slowly — and hence a person who didn't move quickly or expend much energy was also a slug, and Slughorn, although in fact a hard worker, certainly didn't go anywhere quickly!

Snakes: see under **Dragons; Nagini; Parselmouths; Stag.**

Snidget, Hunting the: see **Hunting the Snidget.**

Snitch, Golden: see under **Hunting the Snidget.**

The Sorcerer's Stone

There really isn't much to say about this. "The Sorcerer's Stone" is a fake title. It's the name Rowling's American publishers used for "The Philosopher's Stone" because they didn't think their readers would want to read about the real thing. For background about the actual item, see the Philosopher's Stone.

The Soul

This perhaps doesn't file under folktales, but the anthropology of life after death is interesting. Rowling obviously would have us believe in a single body and a single soul and no other part. This contrasts, e.g., with traditional Chinese belief in two souls, the *po* or animal soul (which gives life) and the *hun* or personality.[896] Some African and African-American beliefs also involve two souls, the bodily spirit and the true soul, or "dream soul."[897]

202 .*. The Soul

Early Greek belief, as found in the *Odyssey*, describes an afterlife of sorts, in Hades, where the dead exist but have no real personality or memory.[898] This is very similar to the earliest afterlife described in the Hebrew Bible, where all the dead go to Sheol (for more on this, see The Afterlife and Catching a Train); the modern Jewish tradition of an afterlife is derived mostly from the sect of the Pharisees, and arose quite late; even in the time of Jesus, the sect of the Sadduccees denied an afterlife or resurrection (Matthew 22:23, Mark 12:18, Luke 20:27, Acts 23:8).

Christian belief regarding souls and life after death is a good deal more complicated than the early Greek or Jewish view. There was a debate in late Greek circles over whether the person had two parts, body (σωμα, *soma*) and soul (ψυχη, *psyche*) or three; body, soul, and spirit. All three words are found in the New Testament, with some of the same degree of uncertainty as to meaning.[899]

Interestingly, the *psyche* as used by Homer is the animating spirit; it departs when the body dies, and the self is destroyed. It manifested itself as an ειδωλον, *eidolon*, an image, a seeming — in effect, a ghost. This perhaps explains, in part, the rather wistful words of Nearly Headless Nick about the afterlife in the *Order of the Phoenix*. He is merely an *eidolon*, and does not have the true knowledge of the *psyche*.

The New Testament version of the *psyche* is that which gives both life and personality, and which is not destroyed with the body. This view of the soul as a key to who a person is, it seems to me, fits well with Rowling's concept of Voldemort and the damage he was doing to his soul: by the time he has made multiple Horcruxes, his emotional life is very defective and his self has been devoted entirely to selfish ends — an ironic reversal, because what we call "selfish" behaviors are in fact the act of one who is self-less! It thus makes some sense that it requires murder to create a Horcrux — only the destruction of a *psyche* has enough power to damage a *psyche* (although the damage, if it occurs, is very bad). Voldemort, unlike Eutyches, no longer has an intact *psyche* in him.

There is one incidental question here: Do Muggles have souls? At the end of the *Goblet of Fire*, the Muggle Frank Bryce is one of those who appears during the duel between Harry and Voldemort, but at the end of the *Order of the Phoenix*, Nearly Headless Nick tells Harry that only wizards can become ghosts. This would seem to imply some sort of fundamental difference about the souls of wizards.

The Sphinx

Thompson B51. In the *Goblet of Fire,* a sphinx is one of the obstacles in the maze. This is a standard role for the creature; *Fantastic Beasts* says that sphinx have been used for centuries as guardians. This is a close match for Muggle legend, because the sphinx is a traditional "guardian of a threshold" — the classical legend of Oedipus and the Sphinx has the Sphinx ask a riddle of anyone who would enter Thebes (Thompson H541.1.1, "[Oedipus] solves the riddle of the Sphinx"; H761 is "the riddle of the Sphinx").

Image believed to be of Oedipus pondering the riddle of the Sphinx. From a vase in the Vatican, believed to date c. 475 B.C.E. Source: Wikimedia Commons.

The origin of the Sphinx legend is hard to trace. In Egypt, the great carving known as the Sphinx is thought to go back to the Old Kingdom, which makes it more than four thousand years old. This certainly makes it the oldest representation of the Sphinx, but little is known about what the contemporary Egyptians said about it; it may have represented the god Horus. The Egyptian version is a "figure with the body of a lion and the head of a man, woman, hawk, or ram. The sphinx was a symbol of the sun in ancient Egypt.... The Greek sphinx, in contrast to the Egyptian, has a body which is part dog, accompanied by the tail of a snake, the wings of a bird, the paws of a lion, and a female head and voice."[900] The Sphinx of the Potterverse resembles the Egyptian version; the creature in the *Goblet of Fire* is described as being a jumbo-sized lion with a woman's head.

The cherubim mentioned repeatedly (90 times) in the Hebrew Bible have been called "winged sphinx-like creatures common to the mythological art and iconography of the ancient Near East,"[901] but it is not clear if either creature inspired the other.

For more on the Sphinx's riddle, see The Entrance to RAVENCLAW HOUSE. Note that the Sphinx in the Hogwarts maze, like the Oedipus tale, asks a riddle — and declares it will attack any who get the answer wrong. But, unlike in the tale of Oedipus, the Hogwarts Sphinx steps aside happily when Harry correctly answers her riddle. Her riddle is also far less philosophical than the Theban sphinx.

Spiders: see ACROMANTULA.

STAG

In many cultures, human beings have an animal totem of some sort. For wizards, the totem arguably becomes real: their totem is the animal which forms their patronus. Who could doubt, e.g., that Voldemort's patronus is a snake?

Which makes it fascinating that Harry's patronus is a stag, because "The stag is pre-eminently a solar symbol, at war with the chthonic serpent. The stag trampling on the Serpent, like the eagle with the snake in its talons, depicts the conflicting opposites, positive and negative, the final triumph of good over evil, of light against darkness and the spirit over matter."[902] Thus the very fact that Harry's patronus is a stag is indicative of his future conflict with — and triumph over — Voldemort.

The Taboo Name: see The NAME.

Dudley Dursley's TAIL

In the *Philosopher's Stone,* Hagrid hexes Dudley Dursley so that the latter develops a tail. This is interesting because, during the medieval period, there was a legend that Englishmen had tails, an idea seemingly first mentioned (among surviving sources) in Walter Bower's *Scotichronicon.* A legend that the people of Kent had tails as a result of the murder of Thomas Becket was widespread.[903] As late as the nineteenth century, English children might be told that Cornishmen had tails.[904] Perhaps this legend suggested Dudley's tail, or tale, or whatever it was. To be sure, the legend of humans with tails usually seems to have envisioned someone with a tail like a monkey's, whereas Dudley has a pig's tail. But the logic of giving him a pig's tail is obvious....

It might be possible to give some people a tail using an engorgement charm. Humans in fact do have a vestigial tail, the coccyx. On a few people, this grows long enough to be visible at the base of the spine. This is a minor plot point in Crossley-Holland's *The Seeing Stone.* The human tail is never long enough to be visible at any distance or require special clothing to conceal — but maybe if you enlarged it just right....

The Tale of the Three Brothers: see Meeting DEATH ON THE ROAD.

Talismans: see AMULETS.

(Reading the) Tea Leaves

Although the expression "reading the tea leaves" is often used for fortune-telling, the actual *act* does not seem to be widely attested; the first mention of something like it is from June 1726, and is a case of one Mrs. Cherry, who practiced "that Occult Science of Tossing of Coffee Grounds," not reading tea leaves.[905] The first clear reference to reading tea leaves is perhaps in chapter 10 of Oliver Goldsmith's *The Vicar of Wakefield*.[906] Early forms of tea, however, were made into dried soups along with materials such as ginger, onions, salt, and animal Blood.[907] The latter two ingredients, in particular, have magical power; the mixture might be particularly suited to divination. Did Professor Trelawny use a special tea mix?

There was apparently a procedure used by the "spey-wives" of Scotland to read the leaves: "To prepare a cup for a reading, swirl the last of the tea around in a clockwise direction and wish or think about what you want to know before inverting the cup over the saucer. The tea leaves should be left sticking inside the cup. The fortune teller can then 'read' the tea leaves by interpreting the shapes that they have made. Tea leaves towards the top of the cup represent things that are going to happen soon, those towards the bottom may happen later."[908]

See also under Prophecies Fulfilled only because someone tries to prevent them.

Temptation: see And Lead Us Not Into Temptation.

Things Bought at Too High a Cost

The concept is simple: A good thing that must be purchased at the price of an evil.[909] Gordon Bok's retelling of *The Play of the Lady Odivere* is an example: Odivere, who is Christian, wins his wife by swearing the Odin's Oath — a bargain in which the swearer gets what he desires, but loses something in return. Odivere wins the woman, even though she was in love with the King of the Selkies; he pays the price when she turns unfaithful; condemned for adultery, she is saved from execution when she is rescued by the seal-king, leaving Odivere without any companion.

> And Odivere is a lonely man,
> Weary of fame and fortune both,
> And aye, and sore he rues the day
> He ever took the Odin's Oath.

The similarity to some versions of the Arthurian legend, in which Lancelot steals the love of Arthur's wife, is obvious — and some versions of the latter tale have Arthur marrying Gwenhwyvar out of lust or other bad reasons, although no oath is mentioned.

The idea lies at the very heart of *Sir Gawain and the Green Knight:* Just what punishment should Gawain bear for lying to the host about the belt that would allegedly preserve his life? There is a small price, which is why the Green Knight cuts him — but only a small one, which is why Gawain survives. (It seems likely that this is an inspiration for the climax of *The Lord of the Rings* as well. Tolkien — who not only knew but edited *Sir Gawain* — shows Frodo just falling short of destroying the One Ring, and as a result suffering the loss of a finger, just as Gawain fell just short of fulfilling his bargain and so had his neck cut.)

The price for a wrong choice can be far higher. The archetypal example is the eating of the tree of knowledge of good and evil. A good thing is gained: Knowledge. But the cost is expulsion from Eden and the loss of immortality (Genesis 3:1–24). The Faust legend is a variation on this. Many tales of wish-fulfillment follow the same form.

Most often, it seems to me, the thing bought for a price is either power or life. In Tolkien's universe, Morgoth acquires power and becomes accursed. In *The Lord of the Rings,* claiming the Ring would bring power but destruction of the self. When the Kings of Numenor cling to life, their rule becomes harsh and their lives unhappy.

Tolkien had an even more folkloric version of "things bought" of the tale in "Aotrou and Itroun," in which Aotrou makes an agreement with a fairy so that his barren wife may have children — but then refuses to honor his agreement to marry the fairy himself. This tale has obvious parallels with everything from "Rumplestiltzkin" (Thompson C432.1) to the Arthurian ROMANCE of "The Wedding of Sir Gawain and Dame Ragnall" (closely related to "The Wife of Bath's Tale").

Alexander plays even more with the idea; most of the books of his series have some example of something bought at too high a cost. The best example of all is Morda buying (he thinks) immortality but at the cost of his humanity. Ursula K. LeGuin's *The Farthest Shore* also has an example of a man trading a normal life for a poor form of immortality.

And that is the motivating theme of the Harry Potter books: Tom Riddle desires life, but at too high a cost. To preserve his own life, he takes the lives of seven others. In the end, it costs him his humanity. (It is interesting to note that there are mythologies, and apparently psychiatric complexes, involving snakes as some sort of agent of death, and "Most snakes representing death also represent the souls of the dead."[910]) Harry, confronted with much the same choice as Voldemort, is willing to give up his life — a motif straight out of the Gospels: "For those who want to save their own life will lose it, and those who lose their own life for my sake will find it" (Matt. 16:25; see also "And Give His Life as a Ransom for Many").

Anything I say after that must be something of an anticlimax, but this topic has been the subject of much twentieth century literature. Perhaps the most direct example is LeGuin's short story "The Ones Who Walk Away from Omelas." Omelas is a great and storied city, a wonderful home, a place of beauty and happiness and love for all. For all... save one. By a bargain with The Powers, Omelas is granted happiness — as long as one lost soul is left alone and neglected and suffering. Undoubtedly, the *total* happiness of the residents of Omelas is increased by the torture of this single sufferer. But is it worth it? Some would say not.

Chaucer played with this in several of his tales, notably "The Franklin's Tale" (arguably the best Romance among his writings) and "The Wife of Bath's Tale," although both these tales are more about *trouthe* and *gentilesse* — loyalty, truthfulness, honesty, and nobility. But "the Franklin's Tale" is also about a rash promise which threatens loyalty — it is something *given away* at too high a cost. Dorigen, the heroine, promises to be untrue to her husband if the man courting her, Aurelius, can do the impossible. Which he manages to do — and then what is Dorigen to do?

This, in a sense, brings us back to Voldemort and Harry. Voldemort sought life at any cost — and managed to maintain a sort of existence for sixty or seventy years. But his life was one of boredom and loneliness and abandonment, and the last fifteen years of that time brought him pain and weakness and complete helplessness. Consider what would have happened had Harry and Voldemort indeed died on the same day, at the end of the books. Harry would at least have died having known Ginny and Hermione and Ron, and having experienced love and friendship. Which was better? Sixty years of Voldemort's life, or eighteen of Harry's?

See also Achilles's Choice.

THREE

"By far the most widespread of the traditionally significant numbers."[911] A surprising number of things in the Potter series come in threes. Harry, Ron, and Hermione. The DEATHLY HALLOWS. The Triwizarding schools and the Triwizard Tasks. The Three Brothers in the tale of that name, for which see Meeting DEATH ON THE ROAD. This is interesting because three is a good folkloric and religious number — the number of the Trinity, as well as the Hindu pantheon of Brahma, Shiva, and Vishnu,[912] and the Irish fates Badb: Nemain, Macha, and Morrigu, and the classical trio of the brothers Zeus, Poseidon, and Hades. Even the personality is often said to have three parts, whether body, soul, and spirit (for which see the SOUL) or *id, ego,* and *supergo.*

"Three as magic number" is Thompson motif D1273.1.1. "Three Magic Objects" is Thompson tale 566.[913] Other stories of magic triplets include The Table, the Ass, and the Stick (563); The Knapsack, the Hat, and the Horn (569; Grimm #54), and The Three Snake Leaves (612).

Many folktales have three major characters, often three brothers (Thompson 654) or three sisters, who face similar tasks but respond to them differently. Often the youngest comes out on top; "Victorious Youngest Son" is Thompson L10; "Victorious Youngest Daughter" is L50. There are also the Three Little Pigs. Less desirable is the song of the Miller's Three Sons, in which the dying miller will give his mill to the son who will be most dishonest.[914]

The trio of Harry, Ron, and Hermione makes me think of various trios in Homer, such as Odysseus, Diomedes, and Athena; or Odysseus, Telemachus, and Penelope (or Athena); see the note under Folklore.

None of which, of course, proves that Rowling assigned any real significance to the number three. The biggest advantage of having a group of three may be that a committee of three will always have a majority....

The Tale of the Three Brothers: see Meeting DEATH ON THE ROAD.

Time Travel: see under PROPHECIES FULFILLED ONLY BECAUSE SOMEONE TRIES TO PREVENT THEM.

Toads: see under FAMILIAR.

TRANSFIGURATION

Transfiguration classes didn't originate with Rowling; "Domestic beast transformed into person" is a series of Thompson units starting with D330, and human beings are made into animals in D110, and one of LeGuin's Nine Masters of Roke is the Master Changer, responsible for teaching how to change humans (and other things) into other forms. Unlike Rowling's transfiguration, LeGuin's changes bring a danger: it is easy to become accustomed to the altered form and stay there. This idea goes back to the ancient tale of Acteon, who was transfigured into a deer and eaten by hounds; this is Thompson Q415.1.1. C. S. Lewis's *The Lion, the Witch, and the Wardrobe* also uses a sort of transfiguration, by the White Witch, although that seems more like a disguise than an actual change. In Alexander, Orddu, Orwen, and Orgoch threaten transfiguration but don't seem to do it; Morda, however, accomplishes the feat. The Thompson list includes a whole series of transfiguration motifs in addition to those listed above, such as D170, human to fish; D151.9, human to magpie; and, perhaps most significant in a Harry context, D191, human to snake.

The idea of transfiguration is the dominant subject of Ovid's *Metamorphoses*,[915] which is one of the more important collections of classical mythological tales. The story of Peleus and Thetis (the parents of Achilles) is particularly relevant. Another famous case of transfiguration, involving gender rather than species, is the transformation of the prophet Tiresias from man to woman and back.[916] (Observe that, in Rowling, we have no indication of whether transfiguration can involve a gender shift.) In one version of the story of Alexander the Great, Alexander was not the son of his official father Philip III but of an Egyptian magician Nectanebus, who transfigured himself into the shape of the god Ammon and impregnated Alexander's mother Olympias.[917]

In one of the versions of the tale of the Irish hero Oisín, the boy's mother is turned into a deer after he is conceived, and he is raised in the forest for several years before he is found by his father Fionn MacCumhaill.[918]

There are a number of English folk songs on the theme. "The Twa Magicians"[919] involves an attempted rape, with the woman transforming herself herself into various things and the man matching her spell for spell. This tale is very similar to the Welsh tale of Taliesin and Ceridwen,[920] for which see MERLIN. The folk ballad "Tam Lin"[921] also features many transformations, although in this case the Queen of Elfland is transforming Tam against his will.

The folk tale of "The Magician and His Pupil" (Thompson 325) is widespread, although not common in English guises. "A father sends his son to school to a magician. The father may have the son back if, at the end of one year, he can recognize the son in the animal form to which the magician will have transformed him. The boy learns magic secretly, and he escapes from the magician by means of a magic flight. He either transforms himself frequently, or else he casts behind him magic obstacles."[922]

The first published version of this tale may have been Straparola's 1553 version "Maestro Lattantio and His Apprentice Dionigi,"[923] although the tale of Taliesin is clearly an older version of the theme.

Shape-changing witches were part of British folklore for centuries. It was said that, if a witch took an injury while in animal shape, the wound would still exist when she re-assumed human shape. This was one means by which alleged witches were identified. See Thompson motif D702.1.1, "Cat's paw cut off; woman's hand missing," found in the Lohengrin legend.[924]

We see a different transfiguration in Geoffrey of Monmouth's version of the story of Arthur, in which MERLIN transfigures Uther into the shape of Gorlois to give him access to Ygraine.[925]

In the *Goblet of Fire,* we see the false Mad-Eye Moody punish Draco Malfoy by transfiguration (see under DRAGONS). This use of changing is attested in several of the ballads as a hellish punishment; in "The Cruel Mother" (Child #20), a mother who murders her child is sentenced to seven years as a bird, an eel, and such, ending with seven years in Hell; in "The Maid and the Palmer" (Child #21), a woman who has disposed of her children must spend years as a stepping-stone, bell-clapper, and so forth.[926]

Observe that, although there are many words for this sort of thing, Rowling chooses to use the one that is part of the Christian vocabulary — Jesus was "transfigured" on the mountaintop.

See also ANIMAGUS.

Triwizard Tasks: see LABYRINTH and The LAKE.

TROLLS

Thompson F455 and following. In the Muggle world, the troll seems to have originated in Scandinavian folklore. It is well known for hiding under bridges and attacking those who cross; their "characteristic weakness" is that they cannot face direct sunlight[927] (note how Tolkien's trolls in *The Hobbit* are turned to stone, although the trolls in *The Lord of the Rings* have been bred to overcome this). Descriptions of trolls in folklore seem to be rather vague — which makes sense for creatures who come out only in darkness! Of course, it may be due to the fact that, according to *Fantastic Beasts,* there are three types. It is not agreed whether trolls are giant humanoids or dwarf-like; it has been suggested that they were originally giants but that later folklore "shrank" them.[928] Our leading sources are Norwegian folktales, but they aren't entirely consistent. Early in "The Golden Castle That Hung in the Air,"[929] a troll-child gets lost and seems willing to be friendly with a boy. The boy brings the troll-child home, and the parent is almost pathetically grateful. These trolls seem friendly. Yet, later in the story, we find three trolls, one with three heads, one with six, one with nine, each holding a human girl prisoner and all willing to eat humans; the hero needs to drink a strength potion to lift their weapons. All three sound a similar refrain, much like our "Fee, Fie, Foe, Fum, I smell the blood of a Christian man" (Thompson G84). It seems likely that this motif originated somewhere else — because the same girls, multi-headed trolls, and swords appear in "The Three Princesses in the Mountain-in-the-Blue"[930] and "Soria Moria Castle,"[931] although the framing stories are different.

In "The Companion,"[932] there are three "troll-hags" and a male troll, but they are singularly ineffective and the male troll is beloved of a princess; they seem unpleasant but not too inhuman. The famous tale of the "Three Billy Goats Gruff" says that the troll had eyes big as saucers and a nose as long as a poker, and calls it "big," but gives no other description.[933] In the story of "The Ash Lad Who Had an Eating Match with the Troll,"[934] the troll is very strong but very stupid, and we aren't told much else. "Taper-Tom Who Made the Princess Laugh" speaks of a man with legs of different lengths who was short as a boy when he stood on the short leg, tall as a troll when he stood on the longer.[935] In "Butterball," a "big, tall troll-hag" walks around with her head under her arm and is easily tricked by a fat little boy.[936]

Some troll stories were based on classical legends, with trolls replacing other monsters. In "The Boys Who Met the Trolls in the Hedal Woods," there are three trolls who "were so big and tall that their heads were level with the tops of the fir trees"[937] — but the heart of the tale is that they have only one eye among the three of them, and the boys survive by snatching it. This is surely derived from the tale of Perseus and the Graeae (Thompson H1332.3, Perseus seeks Gorgon's head), so these may not be "native" trolls. Similarly, a troll owns a castle in the Norwegian tale of "Squire Per" — and, like one of Tolkien's trolls, dies upon seeing the sun.[938] But "Squire Per" is a Norwegian take on "Puss in Boots," and in the Charles Perrault version of that tale, the horrid creature is an Ogre who is eaten by the cat.[939] A third instance of a classic story showing up Norwegian folklore with a troll added is "White-Bear-King-Valemon,"[940] which is a Cupid-and-Psyche variant in which the hero is turned into a white bear by a "troll-hag," and has to be rescued by the loyalty of a girl.

Trolls are sometimes equated with the "Trows" in the northern isles off Scotland (the words are certainly of the same origin), although the latter are less hostile to humans;[941] trows are often listed as fairies, not monsters.[942] Although sometimes skilled at certain sorts of mechanical tasks, trolls are generally not regarded as being very bright — note how the troll is outsmarted in the tale of the Billy Goats Gruff. Thus Rowling's trolls seem pretty typical: Big, dumb, and seemingly not fond of the outdoors.

An enchanted mist is sometimes called a "troll mist,"[943] but there seems to be no explanation for this usage.

Two-Faced Figures

In the *Philospher's Stone*, we see a two-faced person, Quirrell/Voldemort — one head facing forward, another back. Quirrell/Voldemort hides this peculiarity. Usually, in myth, it is not hidden. In classical legend, Janus was a two-faced god who looked forward and back.[944] Even more like Voldemort is the Hindu god Ganesha, since (in a few accounts) he has two faces, one face being an elephant head, the other a face of S(h)iva the destroyer. To be sure, the usual description makes him simply a human with an elephant's head.[945]

Other than the simple fact of two-facedness, there seems to be no connection between Quirrell/Voldemort and either Janus or Ganesha. But the image is pretty memorable all by itself.

The Ugly Duckling

Thompson L140 and following. Hans Christian Anderson wrote the story which gave this tale-type its name in 1845, but the concept is older — in a way, it goes back to the tale of Joseph in the book of Genesis. The idea is of someone who is rejected as a youth but grows up to be beautiful and desirable in some way or other. Folk tales of Ugly Ducklings are very common, often happening to youngest sons (who are often the third or seventh child). Even Cinderella is sometimes an Ugly Duckling.[946]

J. R. R. Tolkien once admitted that "nothing moves my heart (beyond all the passions and heartbreaks of the world) so much as 'ennoblement' (from the Ugly Duckling to Frodo)."[947]

Both Harry and Hermione are ugly ducklings — Hermione twice over, because we learn in the *Goblet of Fire* that she is quite pretty when she makes the effort (making her literally an ugly duckling), plus she is a muggle-born who nonetheless proves to be one of the greatest of magicians. Harry is one in the sense that the Dursleys reject him but he goes on to great things.

W. H. Auden had a fascinating comment about Ugly Ducklings: "[T]here are two types of Quest Hero. One resembled the hero of Epic; his superior *arete* [excellence, manliness, heroism; Greek ἀρετή] is manifest to all. Jason, for example, is instantly recognizable as the kind of man who can win the Golden Fleece if anybody can. The other type, so common in fairy tales, is the hero whose *arete* is concealed. The youngest son, the weakest, the least clever, the one whom everybody would judge as least likely to succeed, turns out to be the hero when his manifest betters have failed. He owes his success, not to his own powers, but to the fairies, magicians, and animals who help him, and he is able to enlist their help because, unlike his betters, he is humble enough to take advice, and kind enough to give assistance to strangers who, like himself, appear to be nobody in particular."[948]

Harry is victorious because he has Hermione, and Ron, and Ginny, and at the end he can call upon the spirits of his parents and others. Had Voldemort realized he had the Resurrection Stone, would he have had anyone to call with it?

See also The UNWANTED CHILD.

The UNBREAKABLE VOW

The oath that must be fulfilled is in many ways similar to an unbreakable curse. The main difference is that the curse is imposed by another, whereas the vow is voluntary (although it is presumably possible to imperius a person into an unbreakable vow. Is such a vow binding? That is, does the power of the vow depend on the act of making the vow or upon the will of the person taking it? We have no data; it's an interesting theological question). Rowling's unbreakable vow bears some faint similarity to the *geas* or *geis* of Irish myth,[949] which could be very costly — e.g. Cuchulain's doom was sealed as a result of a condition he had to fulfill.[950] Curses are too common in folklore for us even to take up, and Rash Promises are almost as frequent (in the article on Medieval ROMANCE, for instance, both "The Franklin's Tale" and *Sir Orfeo* are plotted around Rash Promises). The list below includes only a handful of examples.

There is a story in English folklore of a woman named Joan Flower, accused of witchcraft. When on trial in Lincoln in 1618, she apparently took an oath that she was no witch, and asked that God choke her on the piece of bread she was about to eat if she were. She ate the bread, choked, and died. Which still might be better than being burned or pressed to death....[951]

In the Bible, we see Saul suffer for a rash vow; in 1 Samuel 14, a great victory for Israel is largely negated because Saul forced the Israelites to vow to fast before the battle. There are also some rather nasty Biblical oaths involving a woman being tested to see if she is faithful to her husband (no tests for the husband, though, no, siree...). The church later suppressed the Biblical ritual (the "water of purification," in which the woman drank probably-polluted water to see if it made her sick), but the Carolingians came up with another version.

We see a clever manipulation of the oath in the story of Tristan and Isuelt, in which Isuelt declares under oath that no one has been between her legs except King Mark and the beggar who carried her across a stream — who happens to have been Tristan. Thus Isuelt feels the need to keep her oath while causing others to interpret it in a different way.

There is a parallel in Tolkien to the Unbreakable Vow: the Oath of Fëanor in *The Silmarillion*. This is not a vow which kills the one who fails to keep it; rather, it is vow of destruction of the soul. In Tolkien, the taking of such an oath is tremendously destructive.

Compare also the Blood Oath, mentioned in the entry on Blood.

UNDERGROUND ADVENTURES

It is interesting to observe how many of Harry's battles take place underground. Those in the *Philosopher's Stone,* the *Chamber of Secrets,* and the *Order of the Phoenix* are explicitly underground. And the key event in the *Half Blood Prince* is arguably in Voldemort's cave, not at Hogwarts. The *Goblet of Fire* has its climax above ground but in the dark; so too the *Prisoner of Azkaban,* plus the Shrieking Shack is entered by an underground tunnel. Even in the *Deathly Hallows,* the key scene takes place in the dark forest, and when Voldemort curses Harry, Harry ends up in something that resembles King's Cross Station — an "Underground" station! (And one, we might add, with a very Christian name.) This theme of fighting in the dark is common in fantasy: The climax of Tolkien's *Lord of the Rings* takes place in Mount Doom, in a dark so vast that not even the Phial of Galadriel can light it; in *The Hobbit,* the event that makes all the rest possible is Bilbo's finding of The Ring in a blind cavern. LeGuin's Earthsea sees Ged meet Tenar in the underground labyrinth, and Ged and Arren making their last effort in the ever-dark realm of the dead. MacDonald's *The Princess and the Goblin* is set mostly underground. Odysseus goes into darkness in Hades in the *Odyssey.* Beowulf's fight with Grendel's mother also takes place underground (and under water).[952] The ballad "Thomas Rymer" shows Thomas visiting Faërie, where

> For forty days and forty nights
>   He wade thro red blude to the knee,
> And he saw neither sun nor moon,
>   But heard the roaring of the sea.[953]

In other words, the ballad takes him to an other-worldly realm that seems to be underground. "Tam Lin" also hints at an underground location,[954] and the entrance to Faërie is underground in *Sir Orfeo*.[955]

The dark is a metaphor for evil in the Bible; indeed, "God is light and in him there is no darkness" (1 John 1:5). A Christian tradition, with no Biblical backing, says that Jesus descended into Hell — into the dark regions below the earth.

Even *Alice's Adventures in Wonderland* takes place "down the rabbit hole," although the place Alice lands seems to be above-ground and is well-lit.

It is not self-evident that the location of the adventures makes any real difference, but still, Harry usually fights the Dark Lord in the dark. By implication, Harry is usually fighting on Voldemort's territory. Which, like so many things in the Potter books, has some Christian parallels: when Jesus is about to be arrested, he declares that "the ruler of this world is coming" (John 14:30; compare John 16:11) — in other words, he is (as C. S. Lewis once put it) invading "enemy" territory.

UNICORN

Thompson B13. Unicorns are an old Muggle tradition. The Greek word is μονοκερατος/μονοκερως, *monokeratos/monokeros,* one-horn. The first certain reference seems to be in Aristotle,[956] although Ctesias apparently had heard Persians talk of them (he said the horn was white at is base, black in the middle, red at the tip).[957] This *one-horn* word shows up seven times in the LXX Greek translation of the Hebrew Bible (Numbers 23:22, Deuteronomy 33:17, Job 39:9, Psalms 21/22:21, 28/29:6, 77/78:69, 91/92:10), and *unicornis* is used in the Latin Vulgate, the official Bible of the medieval Catholic Church, in Psalms (although *rhinoceris* is its more usual translation elsewhere). Both Greek and Latin were incorrect renderings; the Hebrew word (ראם, *re'em*) does not refer to a unicorn but rather to a wild ox or aurochs — and is also the name of the similar magical beast, the RE'EM. But the Vulgate reading was used as justification for belief in unicorns in the Middle Ages.

The result was a tremendous amount of bogus lore. Most of it is European — there is a Chinese "unicorn," but it has the body of a deer, not a horse, and may have scales; it may not even be a mammal.[958]

European bestiaries said that the unicorn was attracted to virgin girls but repelled by all other humans.[959] The horn of the unicorn had great restorative powers, equal almost to the PHILOSOPHER'S STONE.[960] A poisoned drink served in a unicorn horn, e.g., would lose its poisonous power,[961] and a ground-up horn could cure leprosy and plague. It was also considered to be an aphrodisiac.[962] Unfortunately, unicorns were too fast to catch; they had to be lured by a virgin (or else induced to ram their horns into a tree, where it could be sawed off or the beast killed[963]). (In one Norwegian tale, "The Golden Castle that Hung in the Air,"[964] it is induced to cooperate by being fed a large supply of beef and pork.)

The unicorn was sometimes identified with Jesus, although there isn't the slightest Biblical basis for this and the Catholic church eventually banned this sort of symbolism. A legend has it that the Unicorn went extinct in Noah's Flood because it could not or would not enter the Ark,[965] or because it was thrown from the Ark and drowned (Thompson A2214.3).

In the Potterverse we find that this lore is only partially correct. Unicorn blood, rather than horn, is the life-giving substance, although unicorn horn and hair also have their uses in magic. (The bit about drinking the blood to give life is very likely a riff on the Christian eucharist, which is considered to involve drinking the blood of Christ, at least symbolically.[966]) The bit about virgins seems to be an exaggeration of the fact, reported in *Fantastic Beasts,* that the unicorn is shy and is more willing to approach women than men.

The unicorn was a popular heraldic beast, and was used in the royal shield of Scotland; apparently it was James I who adopted it.[967] Hence Lewis Carroll's use of the characters of "The Lion and the Unicorn."

Most objects described as unicorn "horns" in our world seem to have been narwhal tusks,[968] which are not horns but teeth. The horn of the rhinoceros, also so used, is hair.

In some legend systems there is only one unicorn, just as there is only one phoenix. Obviously this is not the case in the Potterverse.

The UNWANTED CHILD

Harry is not welcome at the Dursleys's. This is an extraordinarily common motif; Rowling has said that one of her favorite books as a child was *The Little White Horse,* which is the tale of an orphan, Maria

Merryweather.[969] Charles Dickens, another author Rowling read, populated most of his novels with characters who not only aren't wanted but who are orphans.[970] He didn't invent the idea, though; it's widespread in folktales, with "Cinderella" being the most famous example. In that case, it is a stepmother who does not welcome a stepchild, and that is the most usual form of the tale (this is basic biology — a stepparent has no reason to invest resources in children not his or her own. It is interesting to observe that Vernon Dursley, who is not related to Harry at all, is even more cruel than Petunia Dursley, who is Harry's aunt). But the motif of an unwanted child has many variants in the Thompson list:

A511.2.1 — Abandonment of Hero at Birth

L10 — Victorious Youngest Son

L100 — Unpromising Hero

S31 — Cruel Stepmother

We might even add L111.2.1 — Future hero found in a basket. Examples of this are Moses in the bullrushes (Exodus 2:3–5), Amadis of Gaul,[971] and Scyld Scefing at the beginning of *Beowulf*. Sargon of Akkad, one of the earliest of the great kings of Mesopotamia, claimed to have been set adrift in a basket by his mother;[972] similarly the Hindu hero Karna.[973] The baby Siegfried is said to have floated out to sea when his basket fell into a river.[974] The great (and mostly legendary) bard Taliesin was placed in a bag and tossed into the sea by his mother.[975] Although most stories of King Arthur's birth make him the son of Uther and Ygraine, there is a story in which he is found in a basket at sea.[976] One version of the tale of Romulus and Remus, the founders of Rome, has them set adrift in a river.[977] Some would compare this with Jesus being found in a manger by the shepherds. (Of course, there is also a legend that Judas Iscariot was cast away in a boat in a basket — see KILLED HIS FATHER AND MARRIED HIS MOTHER![978]) As is often the case, Rowling picked the most Biblical alternative: Dumbledore set up Harry's adoption, as Miriam set up Moses's.

The Orphan Hero is everywhere — I believe it was Orson Scott Card who once argued that all romance/fantasy heroes are adolescents, but what he really meant is that they have no family to nail them down. As early as 1871, "the English anthropologist Edward Tylor argued that many… [hero tales] follow a uniform plot, or pattern: the hero is exposed at birth, is saved by other humans or animals, and grows up to become a national hero."[979] Otto Rank claimed that the Standard Hero Tale tends to begin as follows: "The hero is the child of most distinguished parents, usually the son of a king. His origin is preceded by difficulties, such as continence, or prolonged barrenness, or secret intercourse of the parents due to external prohibition or obstacles. During or before the pregnancy, there is a prophecy, in the form of a dream or oracle, cautioning against his birth, and usually threatening danger to the father (or his representative). As a rule, he is surrendered to the water, in a box."[980]

Not every tale follows this exact script (e.g. there aren't many king's sons in most of the tales we read today, although the English made a hero, undeservedly, of Richard I son of Henry II), but we see something similar in many modern fantasies. Examples:

Harry Potter has no parents.

Alexander's Taran has no parents.

Crossley-Holland's Arthur is separated from his parents. So was Malory's King Arthur (although not the Welsh Arthur, really).

LeGuin's Ged's mother is dead and his father is distant; Tenar is separated from her parents and cannot hope to find them.

In Tolkien, Frodo's parents are dead. Aragorn's father died when he was an infant, and his mother also died young (an analogy, interestingly, to Tolkien himself; his father died when he was four and his mother when he was twelve[981]).

Even Jesus was brought up by his stepfather — and the stepfather resented it. (See not only the Gospel of Matthew but also "The Cherry Tree Carol,"[982] in which the pregnant Mary asks Joseph for cherries and is told "let the father of the baby gather cherries for thee" until God intervenes.)

See also The UGLY DUCKLING.

Vampire

A very popular motif today, but not one with much of a folklore pedigree (to be sure, it doesn't have much place in the Harry Potter books, either; they are mentioned on occasion, but we don't really meet any except Sanguini, who appears briefly at Slughorn's party in the *Half-Blood Prince*). Supposedly only one author, William of Newburgh, mentioned vampires in Britain prior to 1875 — and even these don't sound much like our modern idea of vampires; the word "leech" has been suggested.[983] The popularity of vampires today, and many of their characteristics, seems to go back mostly to Bram Stoker's *Dracula* (1897), which of course has its roots in tales from Transylvania (in Romania) and Hungary. Pickering, p. 307, says that the name "Dracula" is thought to go back to the Wallachian ruler Vlad IV Tepes (reigned 1456–1462), known as "Dracula" — truly a fascinating name, because "drăculeț" in my Romanian dictionary as meaning "devilkin," i.e. "little devil" or "child of the devil" (the Romanian word for "devil" is "drac") and Romanian is derived from Latin, in which "draco" meant "dragon." Thus Vlad Dracula, Vlad the Impaler (so-called for his tendency to penetrate his victims with a sharpened stake); Schevill, pp. 205–206), was Vlad the Little Devil and Vlad the Dragon. But classical legend had the *mormos,* which also came out to bite children although seemingly not to drink their blood.[984] It has been suggested that the idea of vampires drinking blood is a perversion of the Catholic doctrine of transubstantiation,[985] but this is only speculation.

Some support for vampire legends comes from cases where corpses were exhumed and found to have blood on their lips or in their mouths. But this turns out not to be evidence; when a body decomposes and bloats, blood can be forced out of the blood vessels and into the mouth region.[986]

Some accounts claim that vampires are the reawakened souls of heretics, criminals, or suicides,[987] but this idea seems to have been largely dropped in modern folklore.

Veela

Veela are a race of South Slavic fairies; in the *Goblet of Fire,* Fleur Delacour comes from France, but their association with the Bulgarian Quidditch team is more natural; there are several stories of them in Serbian folklore.[988] It is possible that the Veela have secrets not known to English experts, because very little proper study has been made of Slavic folklore.[989] Still, the *idea* of a magically, overwhelmingly seductive creature is common. The Sirens in the *Odyssey* are a partial analogy (although they were not human in appearance). So are the succubi.[990] Magic to enhance desirability is known as *glamour,* and is well-known in Scottish folklore.[991]

The veela itself is more often known as the vila, or sometimes the willi or vala or völva — and they were more than mere seductresses: "a variety of spirit feared for its malevolence toward the living. They were usually identified as the ghosts of unbaptized children or of virgins, fated to roam the earth forever, and were rumoured to force mortals they came across to dance to death."[992] "The Vile (singular *Vila)* of the Serbs were shape-shifters and could transform themselves into serpents or swans."[993] In particular, they are said to have danced in circles, and those breaking the circle were forced to dance until they died.[994] (This rather resembles tales of the Nereids as found in modern Greek folklore,[995] although the Nereids of classical folklore were different; they were associated with the sea and sailors.)

Although usually known for bringing trouble to mortals, there are occasional reports of veela coming to the aid of individual humans. They were said to have great knowledge of the properties, including healing properties, of flowers and herbs. The most famous veela was probably Raviyoyla/Ravioyla, who played a large part in rescuing Prince Marko in the Serbian epic of the same name.[996] Indeed, Marco's mother is said to have been a veela,[997] so there is precedent for human/veela marriages.

The plural of "vila" is "vile." Puccini's first opera, *Le Villi,* is about veela.

Veil (of Death), Beyond the Veil of Death: see The DOOR OF
  DEATH.

Vila: see VEELA.

The VOICE THAT ONLY ONE CAN HEAR

In the *Chamber of Secrets,* only Harry can hear the voice of the BAS-
ILISK. This has real world parallels in the victims of schizophrenia, who
may hear voices. Or think of Jeanne d'Arc/Joan of Ark (who, to be sure,
also showed most of the signs of schizophrenia. At least, she does if you
aren't Catholic…). But the idea is very old. Thomas the Rhymer (Thomas of Ercildoune), for instance, is sometimes said to have been called
by such a voice. So were the Old Testament prophets — Elijah heard
a "still, small voice" or a "voice of sheer silence" at Mount Horeb in 1
Kings 19:12. And, even more importantly, Saul of Tarsus either heard
voices, or saw a vision, or something, in his conversion in the Book of
Acts: "Those who were with me saw the light but did not hear the voice
of the one who was speaking to me" (Acts 22:9; to be sure, in Acts 9:7,
they hear the voice but fail to see a light that Saul/Paul sees).

These are mostly voices with positive messages. But what did, say,
Jack the Ripper hear?

Wands, Magic Wands

Although the White Witch uses a wand in C. S. Lewis's *The Lion, the Witch, and the Wardrobe,* the wand is not the typical tool of the traditional magic-worker. Insofar as there is one, it is probably the staff — carried both by Gandalf in Tolkien's *The Lord of the Rings* and by Ged and the other graduates of Roke in LeGuin's Earthsea books. "Even now the 'magic wand' is the common property of the stage-magician, while in all popular and learned literary tradition, from Shakespeare's Prospero to Milton's Comus or Terry Pratchett's Diskworld, the staff is the distinguishing mark of the wizard."[998]

Or perhaps the wand is for *evil* magic and the staff for good? Looking again to Lewis, the magician/star Coriakin carries a staff, rather than a wand, in *The Voyage of the Dawn Treader.*

One might speculate that the association between the wizard and the staff came about because it takes wizards a very long time to learn their craft, so that they might need a stick to lean on by the time they learned it.

The idea of the wizard's tool is ancient; while there is no artifact particularly associated with magic in the Bible (e.g. the Witch of Endor, in 1 Samuel 27, seems to operate by sheer spiritual power, as does Simon Magus in Acts 8:9–24), both Aaron and the Egyptian magicians use a staff or a rod (Exodus 7:8–12, where both Aaron and the magicians turn their utensils into snakes). Later in the Exodus story, "The rod of Aaron acted an oracular part in the contest with the princes; laid before the ark [of the covenant], it budded and brought forth almonds.... [This divinatory role] became liable to abuse; thus Hosea rebukes the chosen people.... 'My people ask counsel at their stocks [rods], and their staff declareth unto them'"⁹⁹⁹ [Hosea 4:12]. The word "wand," in fact, does not appear in the Bible in any form (at least not in the King James Bible, the Revised Standard Version, or the New Revised Standard New Testament).

Dagda, in Irish myth, had a staff which could both kill and bring back to life.¹⁰⁰⁰

In Greek myth, the minor goddess CIRCE used a wand to transform Odysseus's men into pigs.¹⁰⁰¹ Otherwise, the closest thing to a magical implement is probably the caduceus of Hermes, which is a modified staff or wand; it's hard to say which. But the Greeks and Romans, like the Jews, were occasionally guilty of rabdomancy, or divining by means of a rod.¹⁰⁰² Even today, we still are familiar with the phrase "divining rod."

In Norse myth, All-Father Odin usually carries a staff.¹⁰⁰³ We do find a few instances of magic wands in the Norse myths, however. In the For Scírnis, or "Skirnir's Journey," the god Freyr falls in love with Gerd (Gerth), and sends his servant Skirnir to woo her. He offers gifts such as golden apples, and threatens her with a sword. When those don't work, he declares, "One touch of my magic wand will make you mind";¹⁰⁰⁴ the wand (called a "taming wand" in one translation)¹⁰⁰⁵ can exile the victim to a place of torture. Eventually Gerd agrees to meet Freyr, although not for that reason.

Even more interesting, "Gandalf" is J. R. R. Tolkien's simplified form of the name "Gandálfr" in the Dvergatal, and Tolkien seems to have concluded that the name means "staff-elf" or "wand-elf," and to have created Gandalf and his wizardry on that basis!¹⁰⁰⁶

There are a few wands in English folklore. In folk song, Allison Gross used a wand to convert the balladeer into a snake,¹⁰⁰⁷ and there is mention of a golden wand in the ballad/ROMANCE "King Arthur and King Cornwall."¹⁰⁰⁸ That seems to be about it.

Welsh lore perhaps has them — the tale of Math son of Mathonwy, in the Mabinogion, sees the magician Math using his wand to change the forms of various people and to determine if his niece is a virgin. (The side effect of that is the birth of Dylan the sea-child.) But this wouldn't have been known to English audiences until Lady Charlotte Guest published her translation of the Mabinogion in the nineteenth century. And, even there, it is not clear whether the Welsh word should be translated as "wand" or "rod" — Guest,[1009] Gantz,[1010] and Jones[1011] all translate it as "wand,"but Patrick R. Ford prefers "rod."[1012]

The flexibility of a willow wand has a place in folklore, although not because it is magical. The folk song "The Bitter Withy" describes the young Jesus being lashed with willow twigs/wands for misbehaving (see the entry on the Whomping WILLOW). The twigs involved would probably have been considered to have magical powers afterward — but there is no reason to think all willow wands would be so endowed.

It appears that the magic wand entered English consciousness through the French fairy tales of Charles Perrault. The Fairy Godmother in Perrault's "Cinderella" uses a wand — a motif which does not occur in the Grimms' German version of Cinderella; that version has magic, but the magic comes from her dead mother's grave.[1013] The widespread popularity of the magic wand shows the influence of Perrault's tale.

The magic wand is Thompson D1254.1; there are only six other listed wand motifs: "Wand transformed to other object," D451.6.1; "wand transforms," D572.4; "King's wand," P19.4.0.1; "Wand locates hidden treasure," D1314.2; "Quest for magic wand," H1342.0.1; "Wands of life and death," D1663.1.

Weasley, Ginny: see GINEVRA.

The WEIRD SISTERS

The Weird Sisters are a musical group that appears notably at the Yule Ball in the *Goblet of Fire*. And it seems a perfectly reasonable name for a pop band. But it is also the name applied to the three witches in Shakespeare's play *Macbeth:*

> The weïrd sisters, hand in hand,
> Posters of the sea and land...[1014] [posters=those who travel post-haste]

Thus "weird sisters" was a name for a band of witches, so it is a particularly suitable name for a witch band.

But there is more to the name "Weird sisters" than we might think. Holinshed, Shakespeare's source for the action in *Macbeth*, describes them as "three women in strange and wild apparel, resembling creatures of elder world."[1015] The earliest printed text of Shakespeare in fact spells that line "The weyward Sisters, hand in hand."[1016] The spelling "weyard" is also used, and it is suspected that "weyard" is how the word was pronounced by Shakespeare's company.

This is important, because, to Shakespeare, "weird" did *not* mean "strange" or "odd." The weird sisters are the sisters of *wyrd* — the Old English word for "fate." Or "doom." Or "destiny." It is a word of very broad meaning. And it doesn't mean that the victim of *wyrd* is stuck with it, as if it were simply destiny — *wyrd* can be overcome.[1017] *Beowulf* says explicitly that *wyrd* often favors the man it has not doomed. This in fact is a very good description of the situation facing Harry and Voldemort: The prophecy says that "Neither Can Live While the Other Survives," but it does not specify who will survive. It was Harry's resolute determination to do what was good and right that caused *wyrd* to favor him and help him defeat Voldemort.

Thus it was a fateful decision to have the Weird Sisters play Hogwarts in the year Voldemort returned.

Werewolves

Thompson D113.1.1. The origin of werewolf legends is not known; although one version of the classical legend of Lycaon tells of him being turned to a wolf by Zeus as punishment for trying to trick the god into cannibalism,[1018] this is not true lycanthropy (depending on the version of the tale, either the victim was made a wolf forever, or had to spend eight years as a wolf and then permanently reverted to humanity); in any case, Zeus then destroyed most humans, so the lycanthropes would have been killed.[1019]

Plato has a legend of a people in Arcadia who turned into wolves, but in their case, it came about as a result of eating human flesh in a sacrifice to Zeus Lykaios;[1020] this again is unlike the standard werewolf legend and may have been a story out of Plato's head.

The earliest recorded versions of a person who went back and forth into wolf form seem to date from about the eleventh century. It has been suggested that the idea arose because of warriors who wore wolfskins or carried other wolf totems into battle.[1021]

It has been further suggested that "Little Red Riding Hood" is the remains of a werewolf fable. Note its similarity to Rowling's theme of Fenrir Greyback (Fenris Ulf?) waiting to catch unsuspecting victims. Another interesting parallel is the story of "The Griesly Bride." The female werewolf is courted by a man. On their wedding night, she sneaks out into the snow. He follows — and she turns, and pursues, and kills him.

In classical legend, Autolycus the maternal grandfather of Odysseus was said to be an un-catchable thief, and some versions say that he could transform himself[1022] — presumably to a wolf, given his name (*auto-ly-cus=self-lyc[anthrope]*).

It is not certain whether the compound "were-wolf" is significant. "Were-" sometimes means "man-," as in "weregild," "man-gold," the price a murderer had to pay to the relatives of the murdered man. But there is evidence that the word *werewolf* does not derive from the word Old English root *were-*.[1023]

Werewolf legends are unusual in England but common in Germany. Although Gervase of Tilbury claimed in 1211 to have tales of English werewolves, his examples were in fact all French.[1024] Simpson and Roud suggest that werewolf legends are rare in England because wolves are extinct in Britain. There was a Middle English alliterative ROMANCE ti-tled "William of Palerne," sometimes called "William the Were-wolf," but it is obscure. It is, in any case, a rather literal translation (into al-literative verse) of the French "Guillame de Palerme"; it is another tale based not on English legend but on French. Besides, William is not actually a werewolf but a human child briefly fostered by wolves after being exposed by his parents — a tale reminiscent in its beginning of the story of Romulus and REMUS. It also contains a couple of men who end up disguised as bears, being fed by another "werewolf." It's all very confusing....

Although the lower classes in England would have known little about werewolves, the upper classes might have known them from one of the Breton *lais* of Marie de France: "In *Bisclavret,* Marie turns to the folk-lore of lycanthropy.... Antecedents of Marie's story include versions in Pliny's *Historia naturalis* and Petronius's *Satyricon;* her version in turn seems to have influenced episodes in the later medieval *Lai de Melion* and *Roman de Renert le Contrefait.* In Marie's hands, the story of the man compelled by fortune *(aventure)* to spend part of his existence as a beast of prey in the forest becomes a parable about the force of bestiality that exist within human nature and how they should (and should not) be confronted, used, or transcended."[1025] The *lai* itself tells us

In Breton, the *lai's* name is *Bisclavret* —
the Normans call it *Garwaf [The Werewolf]*.
In the old days, people used to say —
and it often actually happened —
that some men turned into werewolves
and lived in the woods.
A werewolf is a savage beast;
while his fury is on him
he eats men, does much harm,
goes deep in the forest to live.[1026]

In this account, the werewolf suffers for much more than one day a month; "during the week he would be missing for three whole days."[1027]

A Danish ballad, "The Nightingale," also known as "The Feathered Maiden" or "Nilaus Erlandsen," has a blood-chilling story of a woman turned into a nightingale and her brother turned into a wolf, with him being told he would remain a wolf until he could destroy his avian sister. (Wimberly, p. 60. Lisa Null set an English translation of this to music and recorded it on her album "The Feathered Maiden and Other Ballads." The original is thought to date from around 1580.) One suspects that many werewolf tales began this way: with a one-time enforced Transfiguration — permanent if the story had a tragic ending, temporary if the conclusion was happy.

The association of werewolves with the full moon seems to be newer; it was not part of traditional werewolf tales.[1028] But there is perhaps a vague sort of logic to it, if we treat lycanthropy as a disease. There were diseases with periodic recurrence — malaria is one, that comes in waves as new parasites break out. The Romans even called it "quartan fever" because they thought the worst symptoms occurred every four days.

The association with the moon is harder to explain, but most early civilizations used lunar rather than solar calendars. Many cultures made the Moon a god; in Babylonian myth, e.g., she was Sin and a major part of the pantheon.[1029] The Jewish calendar is still lunar; the new moon was a festival in early Israel, and the name for the new moon (שדח) means "renewal."[1030] This makes it logical, in a way, that the full moon would bring out werewolves; if the new moon is a holy day, then its inverse, the full moon, ought to be unusually unholy. In the Middle Ages, the full moon was widely thought to worsen the symptoms of insanity,[1031] so that is additional reason to expect it to worsen the conditions of werewolves.

The likeliest conclusion is that the werewolves of the Potterverse are a motif Rowling assembled from very disparate materials.

It has been suggested that the modern popularity of werewolf tales and Gothic fiction (and, more recently, of the walking dead and ZOM-BIES and such) can be traced back to the works of Thomas Gray, who is best remembered for "Elegy Written in a Country Churchyard" but who in 1761 published poems imitating Icelandic sagas that started a sort of horror movement.[1032]

See also REMUS.

WHICH SIDE ARE YOU ON?

In *The Lord of the Rings*, J. R. R. Tolkien gives us a world in which all Elves are good (although this gets a little more complicated in *The Silmarillion*). All orcs and trolls are evil. Similarly, in the Narnia books, C. S. Lewis presents creatures such as hags and werewolves as irreconcilably evil.

Both Tolkien and Lewis show humans and dwarves as having choices. So, to Tolkien, do hobbits, and probably ents as well. We know that the Valar (angels) can go bad, since Melkor and Sauron are of that kindred; this is explicit in the schools of Christian thought that make Satan a rebellious angel. What is the difference between creatures with a choice to do good or evil and creatures without it?

One thought is that creatures created by God are free — this obviously covers humans, and it covers dwarves as well, to Lewis. But to Tolkien, dwarves were created by Aulë; how do they differ from orcs, created by Morgoth? Is it that God accepted the dwarves? But could not God accept a repentant orc?

And what about a dementor? Does *it* have a choice? The dementors are described as *needing* human emotions as their equivalent of food. Are they actually more evil for feeding on their sort of diet than we are for feeding on beef — or even wheat?

This is not an entirely modern question. One version of the birth of MERLIN makes him the child of a virtuous woman who was forcibly impregnated by a demon. The forces of evil hoped he would be on their side — but, being half-human, he had a choice, and he chose good.[1033]

The Bible has an even more curious twist on this. Although Jesus is without question on God's side, we still see the Devil try to tempt him in Matthew 4:1–11/Luke 4:1–13; there is also a brief summary in Mark 1:12–13. Jesus has been fasting for weeks, and the Devil urges him to turn stones to bread, then to throw himself from the top of the Temple, then offers him all the kingdoms of the world if Jesus will only be his servant. Jesus turns aside each request with an Old Testament quotation. It is a curious situation — it is clear that the Devil would profit if Jesus would serve him, but nowhere does the Bible explain why Jesus would even consider doing such a thing when it violates his entire mission. It is much easier to understand why a human would go for something less than the most moral outcome.

Rowling casts several interesting twists on this. Humans, of course, have free will. Dragons, treated by Tolkien as irredeemably evil, she reduces to non-sentience, so they are not really at issue. She eliminates the inherent evil of werewolves — Lupin is a werewolf, but he still supports the "good guys" and presumably can still enter Rowling's version of heaven. But what can we say of house elves? They may desire to do what is good, but are forced by their slavery to do ill (as Dobby was); or they may desire to do harm, but also are bound to obey orders to do good (as Kreacher was). This is perhaps reminiscent of one of Paul's comments: "For I do not do what I want, but I do the very thing I hate.... I can will what is right, but I cannot do it. For I do not do the good I want, but the evil I do is not what I want to do" (Romans 7:15, 18–19). Paul attributes this to sin.

The issue of freedom of the will to avoid sin is a crucial one in Christian theology. The idea that one can, by individual will, make one's self sinless lies at the heart of the Pelagian doctrine (for which see the introduction); the extreme form of the other position, which goes back to Augustine of Hippo, is known as "total depravity," and is characteristic of the Presbyterian/Reformed faith. The typical Christian answer to the question is again expressed by Paul: "Work out your own salvation with fear and trembling, for it is God who is at work in you" (Philippians 2:12–13) — i.e. the Christians choose the good (or don't), but it is God who enables them to do it, thus preserving both free will and a measure of predestination. "Any alternative view, it is said, makes man a decisive contributor to his own salvation, and so in effect his own Savior."[1034] On this point I do not think Rowling would agree. Her attitude, if it can be guessed, is that it is the intent, not the deed, that counts toward salvation, and so Voldemort is doomed (as Dumbledore told Harry, "You cannot help"), but Dobby and Kreacher, despite years of service to the Malfoy and Black families, seem likely to be saved.

See also GOOD AND EVIL.

The Whomping WILLOW

I know of no other tale of trees actively attacking in the way the Whomping Willow does — but the Albanian Aërico was a spirit that lived in trees (especially the cherry) and attacked those who came too close[1035] — a creature that sounds like a sort of a cross between the Whomping Willow and a bowtruckle. Note also Tolkien's "Old Forest," where the trees move and Old Man Willow traps travelers. And Old Man Willow is down by the Withywindle — the winding willow river ("Withy"=willow).

So why the willow?

Willow legends are many. The ballad of "The Bitter Withy" tells an apocryphal tale of the young Jesus luring a group of cruel boys to their death. Mary then lashes him with willow twigs, leading the young Jesus to declare, "O the withy! O the withy! The bitter withy that causes me to smart, to smart, Oh! the withy it shall be the very first tree That perishes at the heart."[1036] (And, indeed, willows do often rot.) A child switched with a willow supposedly would cease to grow thereafter.

Tradition says that willow, the grieving tree, should not be brought into the house except on May Day.[1037] The association with grief supposedly went back to Psalm 137 — although this is probably a modern invention; it is not certain whether the Hebrew word in that poem means "willow" or "poplar" (the New Revised Standard version gives the first two verses of the psalm as "By the rivers of Babylon — there we sat down and there we wept when we remembered Zion. On the willows there we hung up our harps." But for "willows," in the text, they put "poplars" in the margin.

The Greeks had a number of legends about willow, associating it especially with goddesses.[1038] In Chinese legend, the willow was associated with love, and the wood repelled demons.[1039]

Willow was a good wood, supposedly, for magic Wands.[1040] It was considered magically powerful. So, perhaps, it makes sense to have a magical tree be a willow.

Or maybe the phrase just sounded good.

WINGED HORSE

According to *Fantastic Beasts,* there are many sorts of winged horses, although the only one we experience in the Potter books is the Thestral. And the Thestral isn't just a horse with some bird parts glued on its shoulders (which wouldn't make a flying horse anyway; bird-type wings don't have the *lift);* thestrals are also invisible in certain instances and have other magic properties. It seems likely that some creatures labelled "winged horses" arose by ordinary biological means, but that others were conjured up by wizards.

Muggles have some experience with winged horses, which are Thompson B41.1, but few if any cultures know of more than one kind. The archetypal winged horse is Pegasus, which was said to have arisen from the blood which fell from Medusa's neck when she was slain. Pegasus was tamed by Bellerophon, who with help from Athena and Poseidon managed to put a bridle on the animal. Bellerophon was able to kill the Chimaera by flying above it on Pegasus and dropping arrows on it.[1041]

Pegasus also carried thunderbolts for Zeus, and returned to divine service after the death of Bellerophon. It eventually became one of the constellations.[1042]

In Islamic tradition, a white horse, Al Borak/Buraq, was said to have carried the prophet Mohammed into the heavens. It was sometimes said to have wings.[1043]

Witch, Witches, Witchcraft, Witch Hunts: see Wizards.

WIZARDS AND WIZARDRY

Here is an interesting question: Why are the incantations in the Harry Potter series in Latin?

It's not an idle question. Although tales of magic-workers are found in most cultures around the world, there is no concept of wizardry in classical (Greek and Latin) mythology. "Classical MYTHOLOGY lacks such a basic item in the [fantasy] genre's repertoire as the WIZARD."[1044] There are gods and demigods, but there are no humans who, by means of learning, have gained a control of "magic." (Maybe this is *because* there were so many gods and demigods; there were enough of them to do all the tricks anyone needed....) So the real reason the magic words are as they are, presumably, is that Rowling knew Latin...

Still, where did "Wizards" come from? The word is found 11 times in the King James Bible, all in the Old Testament (Leviticus 19:31, 20:6, 27; Deuteronomy 18:11, 1 Samuel 28:3, 9; 2 Kings 21:6, 23:24; 2 Chronicles 33:6, Isaiah 8:19, 19:3; *witch* and related terms occur nine times). But these are not what we would call magic-users; the New Revised Standard Version usually translates the word as "medium," and the Revised English Bible paraphrases Leviticus 19:31, 20:6, 27 to command against involvement with ghosts and spirits. In Deuteronomy, the Revised English Bible offers "necromancer," which has been suggested as a better translation by many scholars; the rendering "pythoness" has also been proposed.[1045] These "witches" and "wizards" were specifically those who used magic to converse with, or held power over, the dead.

The word "wizard," or "wysard," is Middle English, a *wyse* (wise) person. MERLIN is the presumed prototype. There are hints that wizards began as alchemists — Michael Scot, the "Wizard of Balwearie" (born *c.* 1175, died *c.* 1230), is described as a "physician, philosopher, and astrologer" who learned from Arabic scientific texts; some of the legends about him resemble those around Faust.[1046] In general these wizards seem to be innocent of "witchcraft" in the Church (i.e. evil) sense. It strikes me that our old-man-with-a-beard-and-staff image is a combination of people like Scot with the Norse image of Odin. Dumbledore, by this definition of wizardry, is a wizard, and Hermione a sort of a female version. Voldemort is something else; he is a wizard in the Biblical sense. Harry, frankly, is neither sort.

"The Old English word 'witch' meant 'one who casts a spell,'"[1047] so it could be used for "good" or "bad" MAGIC — but tended to refer to the latter.

There is a current debate over whether the medieval notion of "witchcraft" existed. This is not to deny the existence of the modern "Wiccan" movement, which certainly exists, although its antiquity is debatable ("Wicca. This Old English masculine noun meaning 'male witch, wizard' was curiously misinterpreted by Gerald Gardner's followers as an abstract noun meaning 'witchcraft....'"[1048] Many think the movement arose out of the teachings of people such as Margaret Murray rather than out of an actual tradition[1049]). The question is whether the "witches" who suffered in medieval witch hunts were in fact anything other than unfortunates with nasty neighbors. Were there actually people who rode with the Devil (or tried to), held sabbats, and were otherwise rebels against Christianity? Russell Hope Robbins "saw the entire persecution as a make-work project for otherwise under-employed inquisitors who were running short of *Waldensians* and *Albigensians* to burn."[1050] But, of course, many people *believed* that there were witches — a belief which predated Christianity[1051] — and so the folklore of witches evolved.

Although there are witches in balladry, they do not seem to have been part of any professional movement or religious sect: "the ballad witch, or, better, simply the worker in magic, may be regarded as a 'lay' magician — one who is acquainted with magical procedure but who, so far as the ballad story goes, has recourse to the black art merely as a means of gaining her own private ends. There is, to be sure, an occasional example of an old crone or 'witch-wife' who… imparts her supernatural knowledge to another, but this need not imply witch cults or organizations."[1052] In ballads as in fairy tales, wicked stepmothers were very commonly the source of black magic.[1053]

Historically, it was Pope Gregory IX (1227–1241) who first declared that witches be treated as heretics.[1054] It was not until 1484 — after the invention of printing! — that Pope Innocent IV put beliefs about witches on a formal church footing. The *Malleus Malefacarum,* which described how to deal with them, came five years later, written by a pair of clerical authors whose financial dealings, at least, were anything but honest.[1055] It claimed that, although witchcraft could be done by either sex, women were more likely to fall into it[1056] — no big surprise given that the authors of the *Malleus* were supremely bigoted men in a church that *still* doesn't ordain women.

David Buchan claimed that all the witches encountered in balladry were female,[1057] and although this is exaggerated, it is clearly true that the majority of ballad magic-workers were female. "The Twa Magicians," Child #44, volume I, pp. 399–403, features a male rapist who is a magician and a female victim who is also a magician. Some versions of "Lady Isabel and the Elf-Knight," Child #4, volume I, pp. 22–62, feature an "outlandish knight" who may also be a magician.

And, of course, there was that sentence in the Torah: "you shall not suffer a witch to live" (Exodus 22:18). Hence witches, as heretics, were condemned to be burned, even if the only evidence against them was a confession obtained under torture. Or even the lack of the same. But it

took centuries for civilization to overcome its prejudice; the last reported witch-burning was in Poland in 1793.[1058]

There were cases of witch trials in the medieval period — the trial of
Jeanne d'Arc being a famous example — but supposedly the law was not
finally codified until 1542,[1059] then repealed in 1736.[1060] The law seems
to have resulted in an upsurge of cases against old women; many of the
cases prior to that (including d'Arc's) were largely political.[1061]

Rowling admits the existence of witches, obviously, and mentions the
witch persecutions, obviously, but her witches and wizards are certainly not the devil-worshipping, promiscuous, disfigured creatures of the
Malleus Malefacarum.

Indeed, it is noteworthy that the witches in our folktales do not resemble the church's definition. *The Wizard of Oz* is largely motivated
by witches, but there is no sign of the Devil. The wicked character in
"Hansel and Gretl" is usually described in English as a "witch," but the
actual text of the Grimm version simply calls her a "woman as old as the
hills" or a "very old woman;"[1062] Thompson labels the tale-type 327 as
"The Children and the Ogre," not mentioning witches. Ballad character
Allison Gross is "the ugliest witch i' the north country," but she is not
involved with the devil; she wants the singer to love her — and although
she can successfully turn him to a serpent, she cannot make him bend to
her will![1063] "The Broomfield Hill" features a witch-woman, but she helps
the heroine avoid unchastity.[1064]

For discussion of how many wizards there are in most folktales, and
in the Potterverse, see under MAGIC.

WIZENGAMOT

Dumbledore, in the years before he split with the Ministry of Magic,
was the Chief Warlock of the Wizengamot. As seen in the *Order of the
Phoenix,* it appears to be the British Wizarding world's court. Did it
always fill that role?

The title "Wizengamot" appears to be a variant on the ancient
"Witenagemot," which was the royal council of the pre-Saxon Kings of
England, often known by the short title the "Witan." This name is easily
explained: *Witan* is Old English for "wise," and *Gemot* is a "meeting" or
"gathering" — a root which still survives, in a small way, in the word
"moot." The "shire-moot," for instance, was the meeting of the residents

of a shire in England (over which a *scirgerefa,* a shire-reeve or sheriff, presided[1065]). J. R. R. Tolkien briefly mentioned the *Shire-moot* in the *Lord of the Rings* (although it is the Thane, not the Sheriff, who presided over the Shire-moot), and the *Entmoot* was an important event.

But the Shire-moot and Entmoot were relatively democratic — every hobbit or ent seems to have been eligible to attend. The Witenagemot was anything but democratic. The original idea seems to have been that the King gathered his high officials, partly to consult them but mostly to make sure they knew what he wanted. "The witan was regarded as vaguely representing the national will. This fact must not tempt today's reader to look upon the witan as a representative body in anything like the modern sense. The witan was always composed of men of wealth, wisdom, and prestige. It was indeed an aristocratic assembly and it looked after its own aristocratic interests and privileges. Rumbles of scholarly controversy are still heard about the extent to which the witan can be called a formal council. It certainly had no sense of unity, no fixed membership, no determinable composition. Although nobody possessed any official right to attend the witan there were several essential members such as the royal family, the archbishops, bishops, abbots, royal chaplains, the ealdormen and earls so powerful in the local shires, and several officials of the royal household. Apparently the king also summoned any eorls, gesiths [types of military leaders], or king's thegns [local rulers; lords of the manor] he wished to attend."[1066]

"The witan also acted as a high court, not of appeals but of first instance. It tried the cases of great men and causes important to the kingdom. In doing to, the witan of course interpreted and added to the body of customary law."[1067]

Thus the Wizengamot resembles the Witenagemot in that it consists of the most distinguished folk of the government, and that it held a judicial function, but differs in many important ways: it has a fixed composition, it has an official and defined function, and it does not answer to and is not summoned by a monarch (note that the Minister of Magic is *part of* the Wizengamot; he does not dictate to it).

These differences are substantial enough to make it seem unlikely that the Wizengamot was actually inspired by the Muggle institution. On the other hand, it seems just barely possible that the Wizengamot might have influenced Muggle folklore. The idea of the magical gathering together at a regular time for some important purpose is common — even in *Macbeth,* Shakespeare's three witches set up meetings. But the Wizengamot is more reminiscent of the "Fairy Rade," which often took place at Hallowe'en. Admittedly this sounds little like the solemn, stuffy meetings of the Wizengamot. But it is a time when the fairies gather to conduct their business.

Yeti

The Yeti is a curious member of the family of magical animals. For the most part, Muggles used to tell tales about magical beasts, but ceased to believe in them as the wizarding world has done a better job of concealing them. The Yeti is the reverse — hardly known at all until the Muggles invented mass communications, folklore about it exploded in the late twentieth century. Most Muggle folklorists regard it as primarily "fakelore."

Muggles correctly identify it as a creature of the Himalayas; although similar snow creatures may have been noticed as early as the time of Alexander the Great,[1068] the Yeti itself seems to have been first reported to the outside world in the 1950s. "The tradition itself appears to have had its origins in the Sherpa legend of a monkey king who converted to Buddhism and decided to live as a hermit in the mountains. It was his union with a female monster that resulted in the birth of the first yeti."[1069]

The females are sometimes referred to as "Ladni,"[1070] although this name is rarely heard in the popular reports.

ZOMBIE

Do zombies truly exist in the Potterverse? In chapter eight of the *Philosopher's Stone,* Professor Quirrell claimed that he had "gotten rid of" one, but there are several problems with this story. The notable one is that Quirrell claimed that this was where he had gotten his turban — it was a thank-you gift. But, of course, the real reason Quirrell wore the turban was to hide the fact that Lord Voldemort was living in his head. Even the students didn't believe this story, since Quirrell refused to give any other details. So we have no verified evidence of the existence of zombies.

One possibility is that people casually use the term "zombie," which is absurdly common in popular culture, to refer to INFERI, which are also reanimated dead. To be sure, Inferi are generally under a wizard's direct control, whereas the zombies of pop culture have some degree of autonomy, but that is a pop culture error. If zombies are real, their origin is genuinely similar to that of INFERI. They are said to have originated in Haitian voodoo (where the name is sometimes spelled "zombi" instead of "zombie"). If a dead body was robbed of its soul via dark arts, it could be reanimated, with the resulting creature walking with a stumbling gait, eyes cast down, mumbling or speaking in an unknown language. Zombies could be "cured" with salt, which would either cause them to vanish or to try to return to their graves.[1071]

One theory is that zombies are actual live people who were poisoned, so that they *thought* they had died, and were then drugged and enslaved to the *bocor,* or voodoo priest, who revived them. Haitian law recognized this concept to the extent that it forbids it,[1072] and it is claimed that the poison involved is the pufferfish venom tetrodotoxin,[1073] or TTX, but that isn't evidence that it actually happened. It is hard to believe that this process was actually worth the effort, because the venom of the pufferfish (also known as the fugu) is very toxic; coma follows ingestion by minutes or hours, and the death rate is fifty percent or higher.[1074] Plus it's a neurotoxin,[1075] so even the victims who survive may not be good for much afterward. The justification for slavery was mostly economic, and this isn't economic. There was a man, Clairvius Narcisse, who allegedly was subjected to this procedure in 1962,[1076] but it was very hard to find corroborating evidence. "In the cold light of scientific scrutiny, the evidence supporting the zombie powder theory is pretty weak."[1077]

Although Zombies are classically Haitian, they did come to be known outside that country, often with the name spelled "Zombi" rather than "Zombie." From Louisiana come tales of "The Zombi of Bayou Teche"[1078] and "The Zombi of Batture du Diable," among others. In the latter tale, the Zombi is indeed a walking dead person — he carries his head under his arm[1079] — but he is not harmful. In the former, the Zombi is a magic-worker.

BIBLIOGRAPHY

Fantasy Works

Note: Most of these works have gone through many editions; I have not tried to supply complete bibliographic information.

Alexander: Lloyd Alexander, *The Chronicles of Prydain* (*The Book of Three, The Black Cauldron, The Castle of Llyr, Taran Wanderer, The High King*).

Card: Orson Scott Card, the "Ender" series (*Ender's Game, Speaker for the Dead, Xenocide, Children of the Mind,* and later sequels).

Crossley-Holland: Kevin Crossley-Holland, The "Arthur" series, *The Seeing Stone, At the Crossing-Places, The King of the Middle March, Gatty's Tale/Crossing to Paradise.*

Dickson: Gordon Dickson, *The Dragon and the George* and its sequels, *The Dragon Knight,* etc.

Herbert: Frank Herbert, *Dune* and its several sequels, e.g. *Dune Messiah, Children of Dune.*

LeGuin: Ursula K. LeGuin, *The Earthsea Trilogy* (now many more than three books, but the main ones are *A Wizard of Earthsea, The Tombs of Atuan, The Farthest Shore*). LeGuin's "Hainish" cycle of science fiction works also contains stories of genuine fantasy interest, such as *Rocannon's World* and *The Word for World Is Forest;* her essay collection *The Language of the Night* has much insight into the genre.

Lewis: C. S. Lewis, *The Chronicles of Narnia* (*The Lion, the Witch, and the Wardrobe, Prince Caspian, The Voyage of the Dawn Treader, The Silver Chair, The Horse and His Boy, The Magician's Nephew, The Last Battle*). The "Space Trilogy" (*Out of the Silent Planet, Perelandra, That Hideous Strength*) is also fantasy (in fact, arguably occult fantasy); although some claim these books as science fiction, and the first book does have some science fiction trappings, the third doesn't even make a pretense.

Niven: Larry Niven, the "Warlock" series, various short stories including *Not Long Before the End, What Good is a Glass Dagger,* and *The Magic Goes Away;* this has also become "shared universe" used by many other authors; there is no single collection.

MacDonald: George MacDonald, The "Curdie" Books, *The Princess and the Goblin* and *The Princess and Curdie;* also many other books of fantasy interest, such as *Phantastes* and *At the Back of the North Wind.* His short story *The Golden Key* is cited as influential by many Christian Fantasy authors.

Nesbit: E(dith) Nesbit, *The Psammead Series* (*Five Children and It, The Phoenix and the Carpet, The Story of the Amulet),* plus many other stories; also the short story collection *The Book of Dragons* (1900).

Pratchett: Terry Pratchett, the "Discworld" series of some thirty volumes; the most relevant to our purposes is *Guards! Guards!* (1989), which introduces us to then-Constable Carrot.

Tolkien: J. R. R. Tolkien, *The Hobbit* and *The Lord of the Rings* (also the posthumous *The Silmarillion* and such, but these are mentioned only rarely).

Zelazny: Roger Zelazny, *The Chronicles of Amber (Nine Princes in Amber, The Guns of Avalon, Sign of the Unicorn, The Hand of Oberon, The Courts of Chaos,* plus sequels and sidelights).

FOLKLORE, HISTORY, LITERATURE, AND MYTHOLOGY REFERENCE WORKS

Æschylus/Vellacott: Æschylus, *The Oresteian Trilogy* (i.e. *Agamemnon, The Choephori, The Eumenides),* translated by Philip Vellacott, 1956, slightly revised edition, Penguin, 1959.

Alcock: Leslie Alcock, *Arthur's Britain,* 1971 (I use the 1993 Penguin edition with a few minor changes).

Alexander, Marc: Marc Alexander, *A Companion to the Folklore, Myths & Customs of Britain,* Sutton Publishing, 2002.

Anderson: George K. Anderson, *Old and Middle English Literature from the Beginnings to 1485,* being Volume I of *A History of English Literature* edited by Hardin Craig, 1950, 1962; references are to the 1962 Collier paperback

Anelli: Melissa Anelli, *Harry, a History: The True Story of a Boy Wizard, His Fans, and Life Inside the Harry Potter Phenomenon,* Pocket Books, 2008.

ANET: James B. Pritchard, *The Ancient Near East, Volume I: An Anthology of Texts and Pictures,* 1958, being selections from *Ancient Near Eastern Texts Pertaining to the Old Testament,* 1950, 1955; references are to the Princeton paperback edition.

ApostolicFathers: *Early Christian Writings: The Apostolic Fathers,* translated by Maxwell Staniforth, 1976; references are to the 1986 Dorset Press hardcover

Aristophanes & Menander: *Aristophanes and Menander: New Comedy,* translated by Kenneth McLeish (Aristophanes's *Women in Power* and *Wealth)* and J. Michael Walton (Menander's *The Malcontent* and *The Woman from Samos),* Methuen Drama, 1994.

Arrowsmith: Nancy Arrowsmith with George Moorse, *A Field Guide to the Little People,* with illustrations bubyeinz Edelmann, 1977; references are to the Quality Paperback Book Club Edition. Note: This book appears to actually believe in its subject matter, but hey, modern hallucinations can be part of folklore too....

Asimov: Isaac Asimov, *Isaac Asimov's Biographical Encyclopedia of Science & Technology,* 1964, 1972; references are to the 1976 Equinox paperback.

Ault: Norman Ault, *Elizabethan Lyrics,* 1949; references are to the 1960 Capricorn Books edition.

Axelrod & Oster: Alan Axelrod & Harry Oster, *The Penguin Dictionary of American Folklore,* Penguin Reference, 2000.

Baggett & Klein: David Baggett and Shawn E. Klein, editors, *Harry Potter and Philosophy: If Aristotle Ran Hogwarts,* Popular Culture and Philosophy Series, Open Court Books, 2004.

BakerDictionary: Everett F. Harrison, Editor-in-chief; Geoffrey W. Bromiley, Associate Editor; Carl F. H. Henry, Consulting Editor, *Baker's Dictionary of Theology,* Baker Book House, 1960.

Baring-Gould-Mother: William S. Baring-Gould and Ceil Baring-Gould, *The Annotated Mother Goose: Nursery Rhymes Old and New, Arranged and Explained,* 1962, 1967; references are to the 1972 Meridian paperback.

Baring-Gould-Myths: Sabine Baring-Gould, *Curious Myths of the Middle Ages,* "new edition," 1894; references are to the 2005 Dover paperback reprint

Beahm: George Beahm, *Muggles and Magic: J. K. Rowling and the Harry Potter Phenomenon,* Hampton Roads, 2004.

Benet: William Rose Benet, editor, *The Reader's Encyclopdedia,* 1948 (this is the first edition, published in four volumes by Crowell with continuous pagination; there have been at least four editions since, but as all of them reduce the amount of folklore and replace it with modern kinky stuff, I have continued to refer to Benet's own edition).

Bennett & Gray: J. A. W. Bennett, *Middle English Literature,* edited and completed by Douglas Gray and being a volume of the Oxford History of English Literature, 1986; references are to the 1990 Clarendon paperback.

Benson & Foster: Larry D. Benson, Editor, revised by Edward S. Foster, *King Arthur's Death: The Middle English* Stanzaic Morte Arthur *and* Alliterative Morte Arthur, TEAMS Middle English Texts Series, Western Michigan University, 1994.

Beowulf/Chickering: Howell D. Chickering, translator and editor, *Beowulf,* a dual-language edition (with Old English text and close Modern English parallel plus introduction and notes), Anchor, 1977.

Beowulf/Heaney: Seamus Heaney, *Beowulf: A New Translation,* 2002; reference here is to the copy in *Beowulf, A Verse Translation,* a Norton Critical Edition, translated by Seamus Heaney and edited by Daniel Donoghue, Norton, 2002. (The same volume also contains Tolkien-Beowulf).

Bethard: Wayne Bethard, *Lotions, Potions, and Deadly Elixirs: Frontier Medicine in the American West,* 2004; references are to the 2013 Roberts Rinehart paperback.

Bettelheim: Bruno Bettelheim, *The Uses of Enchantment: The Meaning and Importance of Fairy Tales,* 1975; references are to the 1989 Vintage Books paperback edition.

Botkin: B. A. Botkin, editor, *A Treasury of Mississippi River Folklore,* with a foreword by Carl Carmer, Crown, 1955; references are to the undated American Legacy Press reprint.

Bowers: John M. Bowers, *The Canterbury Tales: Fifteenth-Century Continuations and Additions,* TEAMS Middle English Texts Series, Western Michigan University, 1992.

Bradley: S. A. J. Bradley, translator and editor, *Anglo-Saxon Poetry,* Everyman, 1982.

Brengle: Richard L. Brengle, *Arthur King of Britain: History, Chronicle, Romance & Criticism,* Prentice-Hall, 1964.

BriggsFairies: Katharine Briggs, *An Encyclopedia of Fairies: Hobgoblins, Brownies, Bogies, and Other Supernatural Creatures,* 1976; references are to the 1977 Pantheon paperback.

BriggsFolk-Tales: Katharine Briggs, *A Dictionary of British Folk-Tales in the English Language,* Part A: Folk Narratives, 1970; references are to the 1971 Routledge paperback that combines volumes A.1 and A.2.

Brøndstedt: Johannes Brøndsted, *The Vikings,* 1960; translated by Kalle Skov, Penguin Books, 1965.

BrownM: Mary Ellen Brown, *Child's Unfinished Masterpiece: The English and Scottish Popular Ballads,* University of Illinois Press, 2011.

BrownN: Nancy Marie Brown, *Song of the Vikings: Snorri and the Making of Norse Myths,* Palgrave MacMillan, 2012.

Burne: Charlotte Sophia Burne, *The Handbook of Folklore: Traditional Beliefs, Practices, Customs, Stories and Sayings,* 1914; references are to the 1995 Senate paperback.

Campbell: Joseph Campbell, *The Hero with a Thousand Faces,* 1949; references are to the Princeton/Bollingen paperback edition of the slightly revised 1968 second edition.

Card-Miracles: Orson Scott Card, *Cruel Miracles,* TOR Books, 1990. References are to Card's introduction to the short story collection.

Carpenter: Humphrey Tolpenter, *J. R. R. Tolkien: A Biography,* 1977; references are to the 2000 Houghton Mifflin paperback.

Chaucer/Benson: Larry D. Benson, general editor, *The Riverside Chaucer,* third edition, Houghton Mifflin, 1987 (based on F. N. Robinson, *The Works of Geoffrey Chaucer,* which is considered to be the first and second editions of this work).

Cheetham: Anthony Cheetham, *The Life and Times of Richard III,* with an introduction by Antonia Fraser, 1972; references are to the 1992 Shooting Star edition.

Child: Francis James Child, *The English and Scottish Popular Ballads,* ten volumes (now usually published as five); references are to the five volume Dover set.

Christie-Murray: David Christie-Murray, *A History of Heresy,* Oxford, 1976

Clifton: Chas S. Clifton, *Encyclopedia of Heresies and Heretics,* 1992; references are to the 1998 Barnes & Noble edition.

Clute/Grant: John Clute and John Grant, editors, *The Encyclopedia of Fantasy,* 1997; new addition with addenda, Orbit, 1999.

Clute/Nicholls: John Clute and Peter Nicholls, editors, *The Encyclopedia of Science Fiction,* Orbit, 1993, 1999.

Cohen-Carroll: Morton N. Cohen, *Lewis Carroll: A Biography,* 1995; references are to the 1996 Vintage Books paperback.

Cohen-LSRail: Norm Cohen, *Long Steel Rail: The Railroad in American Folksong,* University of Illinois Press, 1981.

Colbert: David Colbert, *The Magical Worlds of Harry Potter: A Treasury of Myths, Legends, and Fascinating Facts,* Lumina Press, 2001.

Cooper: J. C. Cooper, *Dictionary of Symbolic & Mythological Animals,* originally published 1992 as *Symbolic & Mythological Animals*; references are to the 1995 Thorsons paperback edition.

Cornfeld: Gaalyah Cornfeld (David Noel Freeman, Consulting Editor), *Archaeology of the Bible: Book by Book,* Harper & Row, 1976.

Cotterell: Arthur Cotterell, *A Dictionary of World Mythology,* 1979; references are to the 1997 Oxford Paperback Reference edition.

Crosland: M. P. Crosland, *Historical Studies in the Language of Chemistry,* 1962, 1978; references are to the 2004 Dover reprint.

Crump: Thomas Crump, *A Brief History of Science,* 2001; references are to the 2001 Carroll & Graff paperback edition.

Dante/Ciardi: Dante Alighieri, *The Inferno,* translated by John Ciardi, Mentor, 1954.

Darrow: Floyd L. Darrow, *The Story of Chemistry,* Chautauqua Press, 1928.

Dickens & Ross: Bruce Dickens and Alan S. C. Ross, editors, *The Dream of the Rood,* Methuen's Old English Library, 1934; references are to the corrected ninth (?) printing of 1965.

Dickerson & O'Hara: Matthew Dickerson & David O'Hara, *From Homer to Harry Potter: A Handbook on Myth and Fantasy,* Brazos Press, 2006 (references are to the 2007 third printing).

Domesday: *Domesday Book: A Complete Translation,* edited by Dr. Ann Williams and Professor G. H. Martin, Alecto Historical Editions, 1992; references are to the Penguin Classics 2003 paperback edition.

Douglas: Ronald MacDonald Douglas, *Scottish Lore and Folklore,* Beekman House, 1982.

Driver: *The Book of Exodus [In the Revised Version],* with Introduction and Notes by The Rev. S. R. Driver, D.D., 1911; references are to the 1929 Cambridge University Press edition.

Duriez: Colin Duriez, *The C. S. Lewis Handbook,* Baker, 1990.

Eberhard: Wolfram Eberhard, *A Dictionary of Chinese Symbols: Hidden Symbols in Chinese Life and Thought* (originally published in 1983 as *Lexicon chinesischer Symbole*), translated from the German by G. L. Campbell, 1986; references are to the 2003 Routledge paperback edition.

EddaLarrington: *The Poetic Edda,* translated and with an introduction and notes by Caroline Larrington, Oxford, 1996; references are to the 1996 World's Classic paperback.

EddaTerry: *Poems of the Elder Edda,* translated by Patricia Terry with an Introduction by Charles W. Dunn, University of Pennsylviania Press, 1990.

Ellis: Peter Berresford Ellis, *Dictionary of Celtic Mythology,* Oxford, 1992; references are to the 2004 Oxford University Press paperback.

Emsley: John Emsley, *Nature's Building Blocks: An A-Z Guide to the Elements,* Corrected edition, Oxford, 2003.

Finlay: Victoria Finlay, *Color: A Natural History of the Palette,* 2002 (I use the 2004 Random House paperback).

Flanders & Olney: Helen Hartness Flanders and Marguerite Olney, *Ballads Migrant in New England,* 1953; references are to the 1968 Books for Library reprint.

Ford: Paul F. Ford, *Companion to Narnia,* with a Foreword by Madelein L'Engle, Harper & Row, 1983.

Frankel: Ellen Frankel, *The Classic Tales: 4,000 Years of Jewish Folklore,* 1989; references are to the 1993 Jason Aronson Inc. edition.

Frazer: Sir James George Frazer, *The Golden Bough: A Study in Magic and Religion,* 1922; 1 volume abridged edition with index, 1963; references are to the 1978 Macmillan paperback.

Frith: Uta Frith, *Autism: A Very Short Introduction,* Oxford University Press, 2008.

Frye: Northrup Frye, *Anatomy of Criticism,* 1957; references are to the 2000 Princeton edition with a new foreword by Harold Bloom.

Gardiner & Wenborn: Juliet Gardiner & Neil Wenborn, editors, *The History Today Companion to British History,* Collins & Brown, 1995.

Gardner: Martin Gardner, *The Annotated Alice: The Definitive Edition,* being Charles Dodgson's (Lewis Carroll's) *Alice's Adventures in Wonderland* and *Through the Looking Glass* with annotations and notes by Gardner; 1960 *(The Annotated Alice),* 1990 *(More Annotated Alice);* 2000 *(The Definitive Edition,* published by Norton).

Gardner/Chickering: Emelyn Elizabeth Gardner and Geraldine Jencks Chickering, *Ballads and Songs of Southern Michigan,* University of Michigan Press 1939.

Gawain/Tolkien & Gordon: J. R. R. Tolkien and E. V. Gordon, *Sir Gawain and the Green Knight,* second edition revised and edited by Norman Davis, Oxford, 1967.

Gawain/Tolkien: J. R. R. Tolkien, translator, *Sir Gawain and the Green Knight * Pearl * Sir Orfeo,* with an introduction (and perhaps some light editing) by Christopher Tolkien, 1975; references are to the 1988 Ballantine paperback edition.

Geoffrey/Evans & Dunn: Geoffrey of Monmouth, *History of the Kings of Britain,* translated (from Latin) by Sebastian Evans and revised by Charles W. Dunn, with an introduction (1911) by Lucy Allen Paton, Dutton, 1958.

Gerritsen & van Melle: Willem P. Gerritsen and Anthony G. van Melle, editors, *A Dictionary of Medieval Heroes,* originally published as *Van Aiol tot de Zwaanridder: Personages uit de middeleeuwse verhaalkunst en hun voortleven in literatuur, theater en beeldende kunst,* 1993, translated from the Dutch by Tanis Guest, 1998; references are to the 2000 Boydell Press paperback.

Gilliver, Marshall, & Weiner: Peter Gilliver, Jeremy Marshall, and Edmund Weiner, *The Ring of Words: Tolkien and the Oxford English Dictionary,* Oxford University Press, 2006; references are to the 2009 paperback edition.

Goldstein: David Goldstein, *Jewish Folklore and Legend,* Hamlyn, 1980.

Granger: John Granger, *Harry Potter's Bookshelf: The Great Books Behind the Hogwarts Adventures,* Berkley, 2009.

Grant & Hazel: Michael Grant and John Hazel, *Gods and Mortals in Classical Mythology: A Dictionary,* 1973; reference are to the 1985 Dorset Press edition.

Graves & Patai: Robert Graves & Raphael Patai, *Hebrew Myths: The Book of Genesis,* 1963, 1964; references are to the 1983 Greenwich House edition.

Greene: Richard Greene, Editor, *A Selection of English Carols,* Oxford University Press, 1962.

Grimal: Pierre Grimal, *The Penguin Dictionary of Classical Mythology,* 1951, translated by A. R. Maxwell-Hyslop and edited by Stephen Kershaw, Penguin, 1986.

Haddawy: *The Arabian Nights,* translated by Husain Haddawy, based on the text edited by Muhsin Mahdi, Norton, 1990.

Hardwick: Charles Hardwick, *Traditions, Superstitions, and Folk-Lore (Chiefly Lancashire and the North of England),* 1872 (available on Google Books).

Harland & Wilkinson: John Harland, F. S. A, and T. T. Wilkinson, F. R. A. S., *Lancashire Folk-Lore: Illustrative of the Superstitious beliefs and practices, local customs adanusages of the people of the County Palatine,* Frederick Warne and Co., 1867 (available on Project Gutenberg).

Harmin: Karen Leigh Harmin, *J. K. Rowling: Author of Harry Potter,* Enslow, 2006.

Harris: Joseph Harris, editor, *The Ballad and Oral Literature,* Harvard University Press, 1991.

Hartman & Di Lella: Lois F. Hartman and Alexander A. Di Lella, *The Book of Daniel: A New Translation with Introduction and Commentary,* being volume 23 of *The Anchor Bible,* Doubleday, 1978.

Haskins: *The Headless Haunt and Other African-American Ghost Stories,* collected and retold by James Haskins, illustrated by Ben Otero, Harper Collins, 1994.

HastingsDictionary: *Dictionary of the Bible,* edited by James Hastings with John A. Selbie, John C. Lambert, Shailer Mathews. Charles Scribner's Sons, 1947. Frequently cited as *Hastings's Dictionary of the Bible.*

Hazlitt: W. C. Hazlitt, *Dictionary of Faiths & Folklore: Beliefs, Superstitions and Popular Customs,* 1905; references are to the 1995 Bracken Books paperback reprint.

Head: Victor Head, *Hereward,* Alan Sutton Publishing Ltd., 1995.

Henderson & Oakes: Joseph L. Henderson and Maud Oakes, *The Wisdom of the Serpent: The Myths of Death, Rebirth, and Resurrection,* 1963; references are to the 1990 Princeton paperback.

Herodotus: Herodotus, *The Histories,* translated by Aubrey de Sélincourt, revised and with an introduction by A. R. Burn, Penguin, 1954; revised edition 1972.

Hertzberg: Hans Wilhelm Hertzberg, *I & II Samuel,* translated by J. S. Bowden, Westminster Press, 1964 (translated from the second edition of the German *Die Samuelbücher,* 1960).

HesiodLoeb: *Hesiod [and] The Homeric Hymns and Homerica,* with an English Translation by Hugh G. Evelyn-White, Loeb Classical Library, 1914 (#57 in the Loeb Classical Library).

Hesiod & Theognis: *Hesiod and Theognis (Theogony • Works and Days • Elegies),* translated and with an introduction by Dorothea Wender, Penguin, 1973.

HolinshedHosley: *Shakespeare's Holinshed: An Edition of* Holinshed's Chronicles *(1587),* selected, edited, and annotated by Richard Hosley, G. P. Putnam's Sons, 1968.

Holt: J. C. Holt, *Robin Hood,* second edition, revised and enlarged, Thames & Hudson, 1989.

Holzer: Harold Holzer, *Lincoln: President-Elect,* 2008; references are to the 2009 Simon & Schuster paperback.

HomerIliad/Fagles: Homer, *The Iliad,* translated by Robert Fagles, with an introduction by Bernard Knox, Penguin, 1990. *Note: This book uses its own line numbering scheme for Homer; line numbers have been checked against the Richard Lattimore translation.*

HomerOdyssey/Fagles: Homer, *The Odyssey,* translated by Robert Fagles, with an introduction by Bernard Knox, Penguin, 1996. *Note: This book uses its own line numbering scheme for Homer; line numbers have been checked against the Richard Lattimore translation.*

Hooke: S. H. Hooke, *Middle Eastern Mythology,* Pelican/Penguin, 1963 (references are to the 1981 paperback edition).

HouseholdTreasury: [no author listed], *The Household Treasury of English Song,* T. Nelson and Sons, 1872.

Huttar: Charles A. Huttar, "Hell and The City: Tolkien and the Traditions of Western Literature," reprinted in Jared Lobdell, editor, *A Tolkien Compass,* Open Court Books, 1975.

Ifrah: Georges Ifrah, *Histoire universelle des chiffres,* 1981, 1994; English translation *The Universal History of Numbers: From Prehistory to the Invention of the Computer,* translated by David Bellos, E. F. Harding, Sophie Wood, and Ian Monk, John Wiley & Sons, 1998.

InterpretersDict: George A. Buttrick, Editor, *The Interpreter's Dictionary of the Bible: An Illustrated Encylcopedia,* in four volumes, Abingdon Press, 1962 (a fifth supplementary volume was added later).

Isaacs & Zimbardo: Neil D. Isaacs and Rose A. Zimbardo, editors, *Tolkien and the Critic: Essays on J. R. R. Tolkien's* The Lord of the Rings, University of Notre Dame, 1968.

Jackson: Guida M. Jackson, *Traditional Epics: A Literary Companion,* 1994; references are to the 1995 Oxford paperback.

Jaffe: Bernard Jaffe, *Crucibles: The Story of Chemistry: From Ancient Alchemy to Nuclear Fission,* 1930, 1942, 1948; fourth revised edition, Diver, 1976.

Jekyll: Walter Jekyll, *Jamaican Song and Story: Annancy Stories, Digging Songs, Ring Tunes, and Dancing Tunes,* 1907; references are to the 2005 reprinting of the 1966 Dover edition with essays by Philip Sherlock, Louise Bennett, and Rex Nettleford.

Jones: David E. Jones, *An Instinct for Dragons,* Routledge, 2000.

Josephus/Thackeray: H. St. John Thackeray, translator, *Josephus: Jewish Antiquities: Books I–IV,* the fourth volume in the 10 volume Loeb translation of Josephus (and #242 in the Loeb Classical Library), Harvard University Press, 1930.

Kennedy: Peter Kennedy, editor, *Folksongs of Britain and Ireland,* 1975; references are to the 1984 Oak paperback edition.

Kenyon: Sir Frederic Kenyon, *Our Bible and the Ancient Manuscripts,* revised by A. W. Adams and with an introduction by G. R. Driver, Harper & Brothers, 1958.

Kirk: Connie Anne Kirk, *J. K. Rowling: A Biography,* Greenwood Biographies, Greenwood Press, 2003.

Kittel: Gerhard Kittel, *The Theological Dictionary of the New Testament,* ten volumes, translated and edited (from the German) by Geoffrey W. Bromiley, with index volume by Ronald Pitkin, Eerdmans, 1976.

Knappert: Jan Knappert, *Indian Mythology: An Encyclopedia of Myth and Legend,* Diamond Books, 1991; references are to the 1995 Diamond Books edition.

Knight & Ohlgren: Stephen Knight and Thomas Ohlgren, editors, *Robin Hood and Other Outlaw Tales,* TEAMS (Consortium for the Teaching of the Middle Ages), Medieval Institute Publications, Western Michigan University, 2000.

Knight: Gareth Knight, *The Magical World of the Inklings: J. R. R. Tolkien, C. S. Lewis, Charles Williams, Owen Barfield,* Element Books, 1990.

Kronzek: Allan Zola Kronzek and Elizabeth Kronzek, *The Sorcerer's Companion,* Broadway Books, 2001; second edition, Broadway Books, 2004.

Lackey: Mercedes Lackey, editor, with Leah Wilson, *Mapping the World of the Sorcerer's Apprentice: An Unauthorized Exploration of the Harry Potter Series Complete Through Book Six* (originally titled *Mapping the World of Harry Potter),* Benbella Books, 2005.

Lacy: Norris J. Lacy, Editor, *The Arthurian Encyclopedia*, 1986; references are to the 1987 Peter Bedrick paperback edition.

Lang: Andrew Lang, editor, *The Blue Fairy Book,* 1889; references are to the 1965 Dover paperback.

Larousse: Alison Jones, *Larousse Dictionary of World Folklore Larousse*, 1995; references are to the 1996 paperback edition.

LarousseBiog: Magnus Magnusson, editor, *Larousse Biographical Dictionary,* fifth edition, 1990; originally published as the *Cambridge Biographical Dictionary;* references are to the 1994 paperback edition.

Laws: Malcolm Laws, *American Balladry from British Broadsides,* Publications of the American Folklore Society, Volume VIII, 1957.

Leach: MacEdward Leach, *The Ballad Book,* Harper and Brothers, 1955.

Leather, Ella Marie Leather, *The Folk-lore of Herefordshire,* 1912; references are to the 1992 Lapridge paperback.

Ledgard: *The Snake Prince and Other Stories: Burmese Folk Tales* collected and retold by Edna Ledgard, Interlink Books, 2000.

LeGuinNight: Ursula K. LeGuin, *The Language of the Night: Essays on Fantasy and Science Fiction,* edited and with introductions by Susan Wood, 1979; references are to the 1985 Berkeley paperback.

LewisMere: C. S. Lewis, *Mere Christianity,* a compilation of *The Case for Christianity, Christian Behavior,* and *Beyond Personality,* 1943, 1945, 1952. References are to the 1956 eighth printing of the Macmillan edition.

Liddell & Scott: Henry George Liddell, D.D., and Robert Scott, D.D., *A Greek-English Lexicon,* Fifth Edition, Oxford/Clarendon Press, 1864.

Lindahl Et Al: Carl Lindahl, John McNamara, and John Lindow, editors, *Medieval Folklore: A Guide to Myths, Legends, Tales, Beliefs, and Customs,* 2000; references are to the Oxford 2002 one-volume paperback edition.

Livo & Cha: Norma J. Livo and Dia Cha, *Folk Stories of the Hmong,* Libraries Unlimited, 1991.

Lobdell: Jared Lobdell, editor, *A Tolkien Compass,* Open Court Books, 1975.

Loomis: Roger Sherman Loomis, *The Grail: From Celtic Myth to Christian Symbol,* 1963; references are to the 1992 Constable edition.

Lupack: Alan Lupack, *The Oxford Guide to Arthurian Literature and Legend,* Oxford University Press, 2005, 2007.

Lüthi: Max Lüthi, *Once upon a time: On the Nature of Fairy Tales,* translated by Lee Chadeayne and Paul Gottwald with additions by the author and introduction and reference notes by Francis Lee Utley, 1970; references are to the 1976 Indiana University Press paperback.

Lyle: Emily Lyle, editor, *Ballad Studies,* D. S. Brewer/Folklore Society, 1976

Mabinogi/Ford: *The Mabinogi and other Medieval Welsh Tales,* Translated and Edited, with an Introduction, by Patrick K. Ford, University of California Press, 1977.

Mabinogion/Gantz: Jeffrey Gantz, translator, *The Mabinogion,* Penguin Books, 1976.

Mabinogion/Guest: Lady Charlotte Guest, translator, *The Mabinogion,* Dover, 1997, based on the 1906 edition of Guest's earlier translation.

Mabinogion/Jones: Gwyn Jones and Thomas Jones, translators, *The Mabinogion,* 1949, 1974, 1989, 1993; references are to the Everyman paperback edition.

Magnusson: Magnus Magnusson, *Scotland, The Story of a Nation,* Harper Collins/Atlantic Monthly, 2000.

MacInnis: Peter MacInnis, *Poisons* (originally published as *The Killer Bean of Calabar and Other Stories*), 2004; references are to the 2005 Arcade paperback.

Marie/Hanning/Ferrante: Marie de France, *The Lais of Marie de France,* translated and introduced by Robert Hanning and Joan Ferrante, Foreword by John Fowles, Dutton, 1978.

McCarter: P. Kyle McCarter, Jr., *I Samuel,* being volume 8 of *The Anchor Bible,* Doubleday, 1980.

Mercantante & Dow: Anthony S. Mercantante & James R. Dow, T*he Facts on File Encyclopedia of World Mythology and Legend* (in two volumes), second edition, Facts on File, 2004.

Mercantante: Anthony S. Mercantante, *Who's Who in Egyptian Mythology,* with a foreword by Dr. Robert S. Bianchi, Clarkson N. Potter, 1978.

Metzger: Bruce M. Metzger, *A Textual Commentary on the Greek New Testament,* third edition, United Bible Societies, 1971.

Miller: Robert P. Miller, editor, *Chaucer: Sources and Backgrounds,* Oxford University Press, 1977.

Mills: Maldwyn Mills, *Ywain and Gawain, Sir Peryvell of Gales, The Anturs of Arther,* J. M. Dent/Everyman, 1992.

Moorman: Charles and Ruth Moorman, *An Arthurian Dictionary,* University Press of Mississippi, 1978.

Moscati: Sabatino Moscati, *Ancient Semitic Civilizations,* being an English edition of *Storia e Civilta dei Semiti,* 1957; references are to the 1960 Capricorn Books paperback.

NewCentury: *The New Century Handbook of English Literature,* edited by Clarence L. Barnhart with the assistance of William D. Halsey, 1956; revised edition, Appleton/Century/Crofts, 1967.

Newman: *Folk Tales of Japan,* adapted by Shirlee P. Newman, Bobbs-Merrill, 1963.

Nicoll: W. Robertson Nicoll, general editor, *The Expositor's Greek Testament,* in five volumes; many editions; reference is to the 1951 Eerdmans edition.

Nigg: Walter Nigg, *The Heretics,* edited and translated (from German) by Richard and Clara Winston, 1962; references are to the 1990 Dorset edition. Based on Nigg's *Das Buch der Ketzer,* 1949.

Noel: Ruth S. Noel, *The Mythology of Middle-Earth,* Houghton Mifflin, 1977.

Norwegian: *Norwegian Folk Tales from the collection of Peter Christen Asbjørnsen and Jørgen Moe,* illustrated by Erik Werenskiold and Theodor Kittelsen, translated by Pat Shaw Iversen and Carl Norman, The Viking Press, 1960; paperback edition with same pagination by Pantheon, 1987?

Noth: Martin Noth, *Exodus,* translated by J. S. Bowden, Westminster Press, 1962 (translated from the German *Das zweite Buch Mose, Exodus,* 1959).

O hOgain: Dáithí Ó hÓgáin, *The Lore of Ireland,* Boydell Press, 2006.

Opie & Tatem: Iona Opie and Moira Tatem, editors, *A Dictionary of Superstitions,* 1989; references are to the 1999 Barnes & Noble edition.

Opie: Iona and Peter Opie, editors, *The Oxford Dictionary of Nursery Rhymes,* second edition, Oxford, 1951, 1973.

OvidMetamorphoses/Innes: Ovid, *The Metamorphoses,* translated and with an introduction by Mary M. Innes., Penguin, 1955.

OxfordCompanion: John Cannon, editor, *The Oxford Companion to British History,* 1997; second edition, Oxford, 2002.

OxfordFairyTales: Jack Zipes, Editor, *The Oxford Companion to Fairy Tales: The Western fairy tale tradition from medieval to modern,* Oxford, 2000.

OxfordMind: Richard L. Gregory, editor, *The Oxford Companion to the Mind,* Oxford, 1987. This is, of course, a very old volume by science standards, but I have tried to verify the statements online.

OxfordSaints: David Farmer, *The Oxford Dictionary of Saints,* fifth edition, 2003; references are to the 2004 paperback edition.

Parmelee: Alice Parmelee, *All the Birds of the Bible: Their Stories, Identification, and Meaning,* Harper & Brothers, 1959.

Partridge: Eric Partridge, *A Dictionary of Slang and Unconventional English* (combined fifth edition with dictionary and supplement), Macmillan, 1961.

PearlVantuano: William Vantuono, [editor and] translator, *Pearl: An Edition with Verse Translation,* University of Notre Dame Press, 1995.

Percy/Wheatley: Thomas Percy, D.D., *Reliques of Ancient English Poetry, Consisting of Old Heroic Ballads, Songs and Other Pieces of our Earlier Poets, together with some few of Later Date* (fourth edition, 1794), edited, with a general introduction, additional prefaces, notes, glossary, etc., by Henry B. Wheatley, F.S.A., three volumes, 1886; references are to the 1966 Dover paperback reproduction.

Pickering: David Pickering, *The Cassell Dictionary of Folklore,* Cassell, 1999

Pope: Marvin H. Pope, *Job,* being volume 15 of *The Anchor Bible,* Doubleday, 1965.

Porter: Roy Porter, consultant editor, *The Biographical Dictionary of Scientists,* second edition, Oxford University Press, 1994.

PlutarchAthens: Plutarch, *The Rise and Fall of Athens: Nine Greek Lives,* translated with an introduction by Ian Scott-Kilvert, Penguin, 1960.

RankEtAl: *In Quest of the Hero,* consisting of "The Myth of the Birth of the Hero," by Otto Rank; "The Hero: A Study in Tradition, Myth, and Drama, Part II," by Lord Raglan; "The Hero Pattern and the Life of Jesus," by Alan Dundes, with an introduction by Robert A. Segal, Princeton, 1990.

Ranke: Kurt Ranke, editor, *Folktales of Germany,* translated by Lotte Baumann and with a Foreword by Richard M. Dorson, University of Chicago Press, 1966; references are to the third impression of 1974.

Reagin: Nancy R. Reagin, editor, *Harry Potter and History* (Wiley Pop Culture and History Series), John Wiley & Sons, 2011.

Rees: Alwyn Rees and Brinley Rees, *Celtic Heritage: Ancient Tradition in Ireland and Wales,* Thames and Hudson, 1961; references are to the 1991 paperback reprint.

Ridpath: Ian Ridpath, editor, *A Dictionary of Astronomy,* second edition, Oxford University Press, 1997; second edition, Oxford University Press, 2007.

Roberts: Jane Roberts, *Guide to Scripts used in English Writings up to 1500,* 2005; references are to the 2008 British Library edition.

Rogers: Deborah Rogers, "Everyclod and Everyhero: The Image of Man in Tolkien," reprinted in Jared Lobdell, editor, *A Tolkien Compass,* Open Court Books, 1975.

Rose: Carol Rose, *Spirits, Fairies, Leprechauns, and Goblins: An Encyclopedia,* originally published as *Spirits, Fairies, Gnomes and Goblins: An Encyclopedia of Little People,* 1996; references are to the 1998 W. W. Norton paperback edition.

Rowling & Fraser: *Conversations with J. K. Rowling* by Lindsey Fraser, Scholastic Books, 2000–2001.

Saggs: H. W. F. Saggs, *The Greatness That Was Babylon,* Mentor Books, 1962

Sands: Donald B. Sands, editor, *Middle English Verse Romances,* Holt, Reinhart, and Winston, 1966.

Satin: Morton Satin: *Death in the Pot: The Impact of Food Poisoning on History,* Prometheus, 2007.

Schevill: Ferdinand Schevill, *A History of the Balkans: From the Earliest Times to the Present Day,* originally *History of the Balkan Peninsula,* no date but published *c.* 1920; references are to the 1991 Dorset Press hardcover reprint.

Scott: R. B. Y. Scott, *Proverbs • Ecclesiastes*, being volume 18 of The Anchor Bible, Doubleday, 1965.

Scrivener/Miller: Frederick Henry Ambrose Scrivener, *A Plain Introduction to the Criticism of the New Testament,* fourth edition revised by Edward Miller, George Bell & Sons, 1894.

Seyffert: Oskar Seyffert, *The Dictionary of Classical Mythology, Religion, Literature, and Art,* 1882; translated, revised and edited by Henry Nettleship and J. E. Sandys under the title *The Dictionary of Classical Antiquities,* 1891; references are to the 1995 Grammercy Books edition.

Shippey-Author: Tom Shippey, *J. R. R. Tolkien: Author of the Century,* 2002; references are to the 2002 Houghton-Mifflin paperback edition.

Shippey-Road: Tom Shippey, *The Road to Middle-Earth,* revised edition, Houghton-Mifflin, 2003.

Simpson & Roud: Jacqueline Simpson and Steve Roud, *A Dictionary of English Folklore,* Oxford, 2000.

Sisam & Tolkien: Kenneth Sisam, editor, *Fourteenth Century Verse and Prose,* combined with J. R. R. Tolkien, *A Middle English Vocabulary Designed for use with SISAM'S* Fourteenth Century Verse & Prose, Oxford, 1921, 1922, 1925.

Skene: W. F. Skene, *The Four Ancient Books of Wales,* Edmonston and Douglas, 1868; references are to the Kessinger print-on-demand reprint, *c.* 2010.

Smith: Goldwin Smith, *A Constitutional and Legal History of England,* n.d. but after 1979.

Snorri/Young: Snorri Sturluson, *The Prose Edda: Tales from Norse Mythology,* translated from Icelandic by Jean I. Young, University of California Press, 1954–1973.

Sokolov: Academician Y. M. Sokolov, *Russian Folklore,* translated by Catherine Ruth Smith, MacMillan, 1950.

Spartz & Schoen: Emerson Spartz and Ben Schoen with Jeanne Kimsey, *Mugglenet.com's Harry Potter Should Have Died: Controversial Views from the #1 Fan Site,* Ulysses Press, 2009.

Speake: Graham Speake, editor, *The Penguin Dictionary of Ancient History,* Penguin, 1994.

Steindorff & Seele: George Steindorff and Keith C. Seele, *When Egypt Ruled the East,* 1942; second edition (revised by Seele), 1957; reference is to the (paperback) sixth impression of 1968.

Stevens: John Stevens, *Medieval Romance: Themes and Approaches,* 1973; references are to the 1974 Norton paperback edition.

Stevens & Klarner: Serita Deborah Stevens with Anne Klarner, *Deadly Doses: A Writer's Guide to Poisons,* Writer's Digest Books, 1990.

Stone: Merlin Stone, *Ancient Mirrors of Womanhood: A Treasury of Goddess and Heroine Lore from Around the World,* 1979; references are to the 1984 Beacon Press paperback.

Storey: R. L. Storey, *The End of the House of Lancaster,* 1966, second edition 1986; references are to the 1999 Sutton revised second edition.

SuetoniusGraves: C. Suetonius Tranquillus, *Lives of the Twelve Caesars,* translated by Robert Graves as *The Twelve Caesars,* 1957; revised edition, Penguin, 1979.

SuetoniusLoeb: C. Suetonius Tranquillus, *Lives of the Twelve Caesars,* volume I [Julius Cæsar-Gaius] with a translation by J. C. Rolfe, Loeb Classical Library, 1913; revised edition with a new introduction by K. R. Bradley, Loeb Classical Library, 1998 (#31 in the Loeb Classical Library).

Swanton: Michael Swanton, translator and editor, *The Anglo-Saxon Chronicle,* 1996; references are to the 1998 Routledge edition.

SykesKendall: Egerton Sykes, *Who's Who in Non-Classical Mythology,* 1952; revised edition with new material by Alan Kendall, Oxford University Press, 1993.

TacitusAnnals: Tacitus, *The Annals of Imperial Rome,* translated by Michael Grant, 1956, 1959, 1971; references are to the 1982 Penguin paperback edition.

Tatar-Annotated: *The Annotated Classic Fairy Tales,* edited and with an Introduction by Maria Tatar, Norton, 2002.

Tatar-Classic: Maria Tatar, editor, *The Classic Fairy Tales,* A Norton Critical Edition, Norton, 1999.

Thompson-Folktale: Stith Thompson, *The Folktale,* University of California Press, 1946, 1977.

Thompson-Hundred: Stith Thompson, *One Hundred Favorite Folktales,* 1968; references are to the 1974 Midland Book edition.

Timbrell: John Timbrell, *The Poison Paradox: Chemicals as Friends and Foes,* Oxford, 2005.

Tolkien-Beowulf: J. R. R. Tolkien, "Beowulf: The Monsters and the Critics," being the Sir Israel Gollancz Memorial Lecture for 1936; this essay is probably the most-reprinted piece of Beowulf criticism ever, and is included in many volumes; reference here is to the copy in *Beowulf, A Verse Translation,* a Norton Critical Edition, translated by Seamus Heaney and edited by Daniel Donoghue, Norton, 2002. (The same volume also contains Beowulf/Heaney).

Tolkien-Fairy: J. R. R. Tolkien, "On Fairy Stories" (presented as a lecture in 1938, then in 1947 in *Essays Presented to Charles Williams,* then combined with "Leaf by Niggle" in the 1964 volume *Tree and Leaf*); I use the version published in *The Tolkien Reader*, Ballantine, 1966.

TolkienLetters: *The Letters of J. R. R. Tolkien,* selected and edited by Humphrey Carpenter with the assistance of Christopher Tolkien, Houghton Mifflin, 1981.

Tolkien-Sigurd: J. R. R. Tolkien, *The Legend of Sigurd & Gudrún,* edited by Christopher Tolkien, Houghton Mifflin, 2009.

Tolkien & Tolkien: John & Priscilla Tolkien, *The Tolkien Family Album,* Houghton Mifflin, 1992.

Tong: Diane Tong, *Gypsy Folktales,* MJF Books, 1989.

Turville-Petre: Thorlac Turville-Petre, *Alliterative Poetry of the Later Middle Ages: An Anthology,* Routledge, 1989.

VirgilLoeb: Virgil [Publius Vergilius Maro], *Virgil I: Eclogues, Georgics, Aeneid I–VI* (Loeb edition, Latin and English), translated by H. Rushton Fairclough, revised edition, Loeb Classical Library, Harvard University Press, 1916, 1935.

VirgilMcKail: Virgil [Publius Vergilius Maro], *Virgil's Works: The* Aeneid, Eclogues, *and* Georgics, translated by J. W. MacKail with an introduction by William C. McDermott, Modern Library, 1950.

Wagner: John A. Wagner, Editor, *Encyclopedia of the Wars of the Roses,* ABC*Clio, 2001.

Warner: Anne Warner, *Traditional American Folk Songs from the Anne & Frank Warner Collection,* Syracuse University Press, 1984.

Waltz-Gest: Robert B. Waltz, *The Gest of Robyn Hode,* Loomis House, 2012.

Waltz-Orfeo: Robert B. Waltz, *Romancing the Ballad: How Orpheus the Minstrel became King Orfeo,* Loomis House, 2013.

Watkins-Saints: Revd. Philip D. Noble, editor, *The Watkins Dictionary of Saints,* Watkins Publishing, 2007.

Wedeck & Schweitzer: Frederick M. Schweitzer and Harry E. Wedeck, *Dictionary of the Renaissance,* Philosophical Library, 1967.

Wells: Evelyn Kendrick Wells, *The Ballad Tree,* Ronald Press Co., 1950.

Westwood & Simpson: Jennifer Westwood and Jacqueline Simpson, *The Lore of the Land: A Guide to England's Legends, from Spring-Heeled Jack to the Witches of Warboys,* 2005 (I use the 2006 Penguin paperback edition).

Williams: Isobel E. Williams, *Scottish Folklore,* W. & R. Chambers, 1991.

Williamson: *The Wise & Foolish Tongue: Celtic Stories and Poems* Collected and Told by Robin Williamson, 1989; references are to the 1991 Chronicle Books edition.

Wimberly: Lowry Charles Wimberly, *Folklore in the English and Scottish Ballads: Ghosts, Magic, Witches, Fairies, the Otherworld,* 1928; references are to the 1965 Dover paperback edition.

Wise Et Al: Michael Wise, Martin Abegg, Jr., Edward Cook, *The Dead Sea Scrolls: A New Translation,* Harper Collins, 1996.

Wolffe: Bertram Wolffe, *Henry VI,* 1981; references are to the the 2001 paperback edition in the Yale English Monarch series with a new introduction by John L. Watts.

Zipes: Jack Zipes, *The Great Fairy Tale Tradition,* a Norton Critical Edition, Norton, 2001.

INDEX OF THOMPSON MOTIFS AND TALE-TYPES

Based on the list in Stith Thompson, *Motif-Index of Folk Literature,* revised and enlarged edition, volume 6.1 (A-K) and 6.2 (L-Z), Indiana University Press, N.D.

Unit	Name	See the entries on:
A486	Eumenides	(The true/taboo) Name
A511.2.1	Abandonment of Hero at Birth	Cruel Parents and Unwanted Marriages
A522.7	Spider as culture hero	Acromantula
A831.9	Earth created from Adam's body	The Afterlife and Catching a Train
A1958.0.1	Owl is baker's daughter punished…	Owls
A2214.3	Unicorn thrown from Ark and drowned	Unicorn
A2232.4	Griffin disdains to go on ark; extinct	Griffin
A2232.7	Peacock given ugly feet to avoid arrogance	Peacocks
A2301.2	Spider's body made larger	Acromantula
A2611.5	Mandrake from blood of person hanged	Mandrakes
A2721.2.1.4	Elder tree cursed for serving as cross	The Deathly Hallows
B11	Dragons	Dragons
B11.3.4	Dragons live beneath castle	The Chamber of Secrets; Merlin
B11.6.2	Dragons Guarding Treasure	Dragons
B13	Unicorns	Unicorn
B21	Centaurs	Centaurs
B41.1	Winged horse	Winged Horse
B42	Griffin	Griffin
B42.1	Hippogriff	Hippogriff
B51	Sphinx	Sphinx
B81	Mermaids	Mermaids/Men
B81.13.11	Mermaid captured	Mermaids/Men
B81.13.12	Mermaid lives under lake	Mermaids/Men
B91.5	Seaserpent	Sea Serpent
B101.3	Ram with golden fleece	Re'em
B102	Silver animals	Occamy
B121.3	Supernatural qualities/magic of cats	Cats
B147.2.2.4	Owl as bird of ill-omen	Owls
B165.1.1	Learning language when licked by a snake	Parselmouths
B215.5	Serpent language	Parselmouths
B217.5	Animal languages learned from dragon	Parselmouths

B272.7.1	Beam across door protects from witch	Broomsticks
B291.1	Bird as messenger	Owls
B292.8	Dog as guardian of treasure	Fluffy
B314	The Animal Brothers-in-law	Animagus
B542.2	Escape on flying horse	Hippogriff
B542.21	Transportation to fairyland on back of griffin	Griffin
B582	Mermen	Mermaids/Men
B646.1	Marriage to person in snake form	Animagus; Nagini
B1114	Hybrid Animals	Hybrids, Hybrid Animals
C432.1	Guessing name gives power over a creature/ Rumplestiltzkin/Tom-Tit-Tot	(The true/taboo) Name; Things Bought at Too High A Cost
C433	Eumenides	(The true/taboo) Name
D6	Enchanted Building	Hogwarts: The Edifice
D45.3	Two friends exchange forms	Doppelgänger
D56	Magic change in age	Old Age
D110	Human transformed into wild animal	Transfiguration
D113.1.1	Werewolves	Werewolves
D151.9	Transfiguration, Human to Magpie	Transfiguration
D170	Transfiguration, Human to Fish	Gillyweed, Transfiguration
D191	Transfiguration, Human to Snake	Transfiguration
D231	Petrification by magic	Petrification
D330	Domestic beast transformed into human	Transfiguration
D581	Petrification by glance	Petrification
D702.1.1	Cat's paw cut off; woman's hand missing	Peter Pettigrew's Finger; Transfiguration
D876	The Goose that Laid the Golden Eggs	(Golden) Egg, Occamy
D925	Magic Fountain	(The) Fountain of Fair Fortune
D1025.9	Magic seal skin	Animagus
D1041	Blood as magic drink	Blood
D1155	Magic Carpet	Flying Carpets
D1162.2.1	Hand of Glory	Hand Of Glory
D1254.1	Magic wands	Wands
D1273.0.1	Charm written in blood has magic power	Blood
D1273.1.1	Three as magic number	Three
D1273.1.3	Seven as magic number	Seven
D1316.5	Reed reveals King's secrets whispered to wall	(The Hopping) Pot
D1355	Love-producing magical objects	Love Potions
D1355.3.8	Dragonsblood as love charm	Dragon's Blood
D1472.1.7	Magic table supplies food and drink	The Deathly Hallows
D1505.5.1	Bird's tears restore sight	Phoenix
D1651.1	Bending bow as test	Folklore
D1651.10	Container for soul can only be split by man's own sword	Horcruxes
D1652.1	Inexhaustible Food	The Deathly Hallows
D1812.3.3.7	Cain drinks Abel's blood	Blood
D1812.5.0.5	Divination by condition of animal's liver	Necromancy
D1855	Postponing Death	Immortality
D1960.1	Seven Sleepers of Ephesus	The Chamber of Secrets
D1961	Argus has eyes all over body.	Hermione
D2061.2.3	Death by Pointing	Avada Kedavra

H1332.3	Perseus seeks Gorgon's head	Trolls
H1376.2	Youth Who Set Out to Learn What Fear Was	(The) Headless Hunt
H1381.3.5	Identical persons	Doppelgänger
J24.1	Do Not Marry a Girl From Abroad	Ethnic Purity
J213.3.2	Cutting off part of own body	Peter Pettigrew's Finger
J1730.1	Hero learns name only at first adventure	(The true/taboo) Name
K81.3	Inexhaustible Food	(The) Deathly Hallows
K305.1	Stealing Eggs from a Bird	(Golden) Egg
K407.2.1	Thief cuts off own arm as an alibi	Peter Pettigrew's Finger
K437	Hand of Glory	Hand Of Glory
K445	The Emperor's New Clothes	Babbitty Rabbitty
K544	Escape by alleged possession of external soul	Horcruxes
K606.1.1	Escape by playing magic music	Fluffy
K1349.10	Cap of Invisibility	(The) Deathly Hallows
L10	Victorious Youngest Son	(Meeting) Death on the Road; Three; Unwanted Child
L50	Victorious Youngest Daughter	Three
L100	Unpromising Hero	Unwanted Child
L111.2.1	Future Hero Found in a Basket	Unwanted Child
L140	Ugly Ducklings	(The) Ugly Duckling
M201.1.3	Pact with Devil signed in blood	Blood
M343	(Oedipus) killed his father	Killed His Father and Married His Mother
M344	(Oedipus) married his mother	Killed His Father and Married His Mother
M370	Prophecies Fulfilled only because someone tries to prevent them	
M371.0.1	Abandonment to avoid fulfillment of prophecy	Killed His Father and Married His Mother; Prophecies Fulfilled only because someone tries to prevent them
M416.2	Eternal life without eternal youth as curse	Immortality, Old Age
M458	Petrification as curse	Petrification
N271	Murder will out	Hand Of Glory; Horcruxes
N575	Griffin as guardian of treasure	Griffin
P203	Game with bones of ancestor	Blood
Q415.1.1	Acteon transformed to a deer, eaten by hounds	Transfiguration
Q556.2	The Mark of Cain	Mark of Cain
R121.5	Thread of Ariadne [leads] out of Labyrinth	Labyrinth
R175.1	Ram with golden fleece	Re'em
S31	Cruel Stepmother	Unwanted Child
S333	Ankles of exposed child pierced	Killed His Father and Married His Mother
T35.1	Fountain as Lovers' Rendezvous	(The) Fountain of Fair Fortune
T617.2	Hero learns name only at first adventure	(the true/taboo) Name
V311.3	Choice between life or heaven	The Afterlife and Catching a Train
X1396.1	Seaserpent	Sea Serpent
Z111	Death personified	(Meeting) Death on the Road
302	The Monster with His Heart in the Egg	Horcruxes
313	The Girl As Helper in the Hero's Flight	Peter Pettigrew's Finger

325	The Magician and his Pupil	Babbitty Rabbitty, Transfiguration
326	Youth Who Set Out to Learn What Fear Was	(The) Headless Hunt
327	The Children and the Ogre	Wizards
328	"The Boy Steals the Giant's Treasure" = "Jack and the Beanstalk"	(Golden) Egg
330	The Smith Outwits the Devil	(Meeting) Death on the Road
332	Godfather Death	(Meeting) Death on the Road
552	The Animal Brothers-in-law	Animagus
566	The Three Magic Objects	The Deathly Hallows, Three
591	The Thieving Pot	(The Hopping) Pot
654	Three Brothers	Three
763	Meeting Death on the Road	(Meeting) Death on the Road
780	The Singing Bone	Hand Of Glory; (The Hopping) Pot
850	Birthmarks of the Princess	(Harry's) Scar
882	Wager on Wife's Chastity	The Mirror of Erised
931	Oedipus	Killed His Father and Married His Mother
1640	The Brave Little Tailor	Folklore chapter

Index of Folklore and Early Literary Sources Cited

The Smith Outwits the Devil	(Meeting) Death on the Road
The Snake Prince	Animagus; Nagini
Snow White	Mirror of Erised
Soria Moria Castle (Norwegian)	Trolls
Squire Per (Norwegian)	Ogre, Trolls
Tale of Taliesin	Transfiguration
Taper-Tom Who Made the Princess Laugh (Norwegian)	Trolls
The Three Billy Goats Gruff (Norwegian)	Trolls
Three Princesses in the Mountain-in-the-Blue (Norwegian)	Trolls
Tiresias legend	Transfiguration
Tom-Tit-Tot	(The Taboo) Name
Tristan legend	Folklore; Love Potions; Unbreakable Vow
Urashima, the Fisherman (Japanese)	Old Age
Vasilisa the Fair (Slavic, especially Russian)	Broomsticks
Vortigern's Tower	Chamber of Secrets
White-Bear-King-Valemon (Norwegian)	Trolls
Why the Sea is Salt	Folklore
The Widow's Son and an Old Man	Horcruxes
The... Youth Who Set Out to Learn What Fear Was	The Headless Hunt
Ludovico Ariosto	
Orlando Furioso	Ginevra; Hippogriff
[Ballads/Songs]	
"Allison Gross"	Animagus; Wands; Wizengamot
"Babbity Bowster"	Babbitty Rabbitty
"Babylon"	Gillyweed
"The Bitter Withy"	Wands; (The Whomping) Willow
"Boar's Head Carol"	Hog's Head
"The Boy and the Mantle"	Mirror of Erised
"The Cherry Tree Carol"	(The) Unwanted Child
"The Cruel Mother"	Transfiguration
"The Death of Queen Jane"	Neither Can Live While the Other Survives
"The Gardner"	Gillyweed
"The Great Silkie of Sule Skerry"	Animagus
"King Arthur and King Cornwall"	Wands
"Kemp Owyne"	Animagus
"The Laily Worm and the Machrel of the Sea"	Animagus
"Lamkin"	Blood; Hand Of Glory
"The Maid and the Palmer"	Transfiguration
"A Maid in Bedlam"	Cruel Parents and Unwanted Marriages
"The Mermaid"	Mermaids/Men
"The Millers Three Sons"	Three
"Nilaus Erlandsen"	Werewolves
"The Queen of Elfan's Nourice"	(The Enchanted) Lake
"Sir Hugh, or The Jew's Daughter"	Blood
"Tam Lin"	Animagus; Horcruxes; Philosopher's Stone; Transfiguration; Underground Adventures; Wizengamot
"Thomas Rymer"	Underground Adventures
"The Twa Magicians"	Transfiguration

2 Kings 21:6	Wizards
2 Kings 23:24	Wizards
2 Chronicles 23:6	Wizards
Ezra 10:9–17	Ethnic Purity
Nehemiah 9:2	Ethnic Purity
Job 3:17	The Afterlife and Catching a Train
Job 29:18	(The) Phoenix
Job 39:9 LXX	Unicorn
Psalm 21:21 LXX (22:21 Hebrew/English)	Unicorn
Psalm 28:6 LXX (29:6 Hebrew/English)	Unicorn
Psalm 77:69 LXX (78:69 Hebrew/English)	Unicorn
Psalm 90:13 LXX (91:13 Hebrew/English)	Basilisk
Psalm 91:10 LXX (92:10 Hebrew/English)	Unicorn
Ecclesiastes 10:20	Owls
Psalm 137	(The Whomping) Willow
Isaiah 8:19	Wizards
Isaiah 19:3	Wizards
Isaiah 51:9	Sea Serpent
Isaiah 53:7–8	"And Give His Life as a Ransom for Many"
Isaiah 59:5 LXX	Basilisk
Ezekiel 38–39	Giants
Daniel 11	Ptolemy
2 Maccabees 12:26	Mermaids/Men
Matthew 2:1–18	(The) Price
Matthew 2:19–23	(The) Price
Matthew 4:1–11(+16–17)	And Lead Us Not Into Temptation; (The) Price; Which Side Are You On?
Matthew 4:18–22	(The) Price
Matthew 6:13	And Lead Us Not Into Temptation
Matthew 7:13	Door of Death
Matthew 16:18	Petrification
Matthew 16:25	Things Bought at Too High A Cost
Matthew 20:28	"And Give His Life as a Ransom for Many"
Matthew 26:3–4	(The) Price
Matthew 26:28	Blood
Matthew 27:51	(The) Door of Death
Matthew 28:1–10	(The) Price
Mark 1:12–13	Which Side Are You On?
Mark 1:16	Ethnic Purity
Mark 9:39	(The Taboo) Name
Mark 12:42–44	Fountain of Fair Fortune
Mark 14:36	"And Give His Life as a Ransom for Many"
Mark 14:50	"And Give His Life as a Ransom for Many"
Mark 15:4–5	"And Give His Life as a Ransom for Many"
Luke 4:1–13	Which Side Are You On?
Luke 11:4 KJV	And Lead Us Not Into Temptation
Luke 18:2–5	(The Hopping) Pot
Luke 22:43–44	"And Give His Life as a Ransom for Many"
John 5:2–5	Fountain of Fair Fortune
John 11	Healer-King
John 14:13–14	(The Taboo) Name

Geoffrey of Monmouth
History of the Kings of Britain (The) Chamber of Secrets;
(The) Deathly Hallows; Giants; Merlin;
Morgana; Transfiguration

Grimm Brothers
#15: Hansel and Gretl Beedle the Bard; Forbidden Forest;
Wizards
#17, The White Snake/Serpent Parselmouths
#20, The Valiant Little Tailor Folklore
#28, The Singing Bone Hand Of Glory; (The Hopping) Pot;
(The) Resurrected Hero
#47, The Juniper Tree (The) Resurrected Hero
#53, Snow White Beedle the Bard
#97, The Water of Life Deathly Hallows
#114, The Clever Little Tailor Folklore
#197, The Crystal Ball Crystal Ball
Homer
Iliad X.240–243 Folklore
Iliad X.277–278 Folklore
Iliad XX.73–74 (The Taboo) Name
Odyssey I.1 Folklore
Odyssey I.87 Folklore
Odyssey I.96–212 Folklore
Odyssey IV.12–14 Hermione
Odyssey V.182 Folklore
Odyssey V.382 Folklore
Odyssey X.237–243 Circe
Odyssey XI.29–30 The Afterlife and Catching a Train
Odyssey XI.36–37 Door of Death
Odyssey XXI.1–3 Folklore
Hesiod
Theogony 326 the Sphinx
Flavius Josephus
The Jewish War II.ix.2 (II.250) Prophecies Fulfilled only because
someone tries to prevent them

[Mabinogion]
Branwen Daughter of Llŷr Deathly Hallows
How Culhwych Won Olwen Giants; Hagrid and the Half-Giants
Math son of Mathonwy Wands
Owein, or The Countess of the Fountain Fountain of Fair Fortune
Peredur Chess
Pwyll Lord of Dyved Doppelgänger
Mother Goose's Melody Beedle the Bard
Ovid
Metamorphoses Transfiguration
Pelagius
"freedom to choose" Folklore
Plutarch
Life of Themistocles 12.1 Owls
Samuel Rogers
"Italy"/"Ginevra" Ginevra
[Romances]

Index of People, Places, and Items

Characters in the Potter universe shown in **bold**, e.g. **Potter, Harry; Longbottom, Neville.** Modern authors shown in *italics*, e.g. *Tolkien, J. R. R.* Characters not from Rowling have their source shown in parentheses, e.g. Baggins, Frodo *(Tolkien).* The key word in the name of the entry is capitalized, the rest in lowercase, e.g. "the taboo/true Name" should be sought under "Name," not "taboo" or "true." Kings are assumed to be English unless otherwise specified. No attempt has been made to include all mentions of "the trio" of Harry, Hermione, and Ron.

Orestes son of Agamemnon — Hermione; Killed His Father and Married His Mother; (the true/taboo) Name

Orpheus/Orfeo — the Door of Death; Fairy, Fairies; Fluffy; the (Enchanted, Merpeople's) Lake; Love Conquers All; Necromancy; the Resurrected Hero; (Medieval) Romance; Underground Adventures

Osiris (Egyptian god) — Necromancy

Othello *(Shakespeare)* — Folklore, Literature...

Ouranos — Killed His Father and Married His Mother

Owyne, Kemp — Animagus

Padfoot: see Sirius Black

Palantíri *(Tolkien)* — Crystal Ball

Palladium — Folklore, Literature...; Amulets

Pandora — And Lead Us Not Into Temptation

Papagena *(The Magic Flute)* — Folklore, Literature...

Papageno *(The Magic Flute)* — Folklore, Literature...

Paracelsus (Philippus Aurelius Theophrastus von Hohenheim) — Gnomes, Paracelsus

Paris, Prince of Troy — Hermione; Prophecies fulfilled only because someone tries to prevent them

Parvati, Hindu goddess — Padma and Parvati Patil

Patil, Padma — Padma and Parvati Patil

Patil, Parvati — Mummy, Padma and Parvati Patil

Patronus — Familiar, Stag

Paul, Apostle — Love Conquers All; the Voice that Only One Can Hear

Pegasus (flying horse) — Chimaera, Winged horse

Pelagius, Pelagian Heresy — Folklore, Literature...

Peleus, father of Achilles — Transfiguration

Penelope *(Homer)* — Folklore, Literature...; Three

Persephone, Greek goddess — the Resurrected Hero

Perseus — the Deathly Hallows; Petrification; Prophecies fulfilled only because someone tries to prevent them

Perseval, grail knight — Dumbledore

Peter, Simon, disciple of Jesus — Petrification

Petitcreiu (dog in the Tristan legend) — (The Taboo) Name

Pettigrew, Peter — Blood; the Healer-King; (The Taboo) Name; Peter Pettigrew's Finger

Peverell, Antioch, Cadmus, and Ignotus — (Meeting) Death on the Road

Philosopher's Stone — Amulets; The Philosopher's Stone

Pigwiggan (Drayton) — Fairy, Fairies; Pigwidgeon

Pigwidgeon (owl) — Pigwidgeon

Pinnochio — the hopping Pot

Plato — the Soul, Werewolves

Pluto (Latin god and place of the Afterlife) — see Hades

Polo, Marco — Boggart

Polyjuice Potion — Doppelgänger

Ponce de León, Juan — Immortality

Potter, Lily Evans — Deep Magic and Deeper Magic; Green/Green Eyes; Love Conquers All; Magic; the Price

Potter, Harry — Introduction; Folklore, Literature…; Achilles's Choice; The Afterlife and Catching a Train; "And Give His Life as a Ransom for Many"; And Lead Us Not Into Temptation; Blood; Doppelgänger; the Mark of Cain; the taboo/true Name; Neither Can Live While the Other Survives; the Price; Prophecies fulfilled only because someone tries to prevent them; Things Bought at Too High a Cost; Three; the Ugly Duckling; Underground Adventures; the Unwanted Child; the Voice that Only One Can Hear

    as Brave Little Tailor — Folklore, Literature…; the Resurrected Hero; Wizards and Wizardry

    as type of Jesus — "And Give His Life as a Ransom for Many"; the Price; the Resurrected Hero; (Harry's) Scar; Things Bought at Too High a Cost

    as Ugly Duckling — Folklore, Literature…; the Ugly Duckling

    patronus of — stag

Pridwen, Arthur's shield — the Deathly Hallows

Pratchett, Terry — (Harry's) Scar; Wands

Prometheus — the Price

Psyche *(Story of Cupid and Psyche)* — And Lead Us Not Into Temptation; Animagus; Nagini; Trolls

Ptolemy, Claudius — Ptolemy

Ptolemy I son of Lagos, king of Egypt — Ptolemy

Ptolemaic dynasty of Egypt — Ptolemy

Puck (Robin Goodfellow) *(Shakespeare)* — Boggart; Cornish Pixies; Dobby; Fairy, Fairies

Punchkin — Horcruxes

Puss in Boots — Cats

Pwyll Lord of Dyved *(Mabinogion)* — Doppelgänger

Quidditch — Introduction

Quirrell, Professor — Two-Faced Figures, Zombie

Rachel wife of Jacob — Mandrakes

Ragnall, Dame — And They All Lived Happily Ever After; (Medieval) Romance

Ragnarok — the Last Battle

Rapunzel — Love Conquers All

Ravenclaw, Rowena — Hengist of Woodcroft

    Diadem of — Amulets

Remus, brother of Romulus — Remus; the Unwanted Child

Renwein, daughter of Hengist — Hengist of Woodcroft

Resurrection Stone — the Deathly Hallows

Reuben son of Jacob — Mandrakes

Rhea Silvia — Remus

Richard I — the Healer-King

Riddle, Tom Marvolo: see **Voldemort**

Riddle, Tom Sr. — Blood, Love Potions

Robbins, Russell Hope — Wizards and Wizardry

Rocannon *(LeGuin)* — Horcruxes

Rogerio *(Ariosto)* — Hippogriff

Roland *(Chanson de Roland)* — Folklore, Literature…

Romulus, founder of Rome, and Remus — Remus; the Unwanted Child

Ron, Arthur's lance — the Deathly Hallows

Rowena, daughter of Hengist — Hengist of Woodcroft

Rumplestiltzkin — the taboo/true Name; Things Bought at Too High a Cost

Sammath Naur *(Tolkien)* — Folklore, Literature…

Samson — Horcruxes

Samuel (Biblical prophet) — Necromancy

Thor, Norse god — Hagrid and the Half-Giants; Petrification

Thrym, Frost Giant — Hagrid and the Half-Giants

Thyestes, killer of Agamemnon — Ritual of Desecration

Tiamat — The Afterlife and Catching a Train; Sea Serpent

Tibert the Cat — Cats

Tiresias — Transfiguration

Titania *(Shakespeare)* — Fairy, Fairies

Tithonus — Immortality

Titus, Roman Emperor — the Door of Death

Tolkien, J(ohn) R(onald) R(euel) — Introduction; Modern Fantasies and Citations; Folklore, Literature…; The Afterlife and Catching a Train; And Lead Us Not Into Temptation; And They All Lived Happily Ever After; Animagus; Crystal Ball; the Dark Lord; the Deathly Hallows; Deep Magic and Deeper Magic; Dragons; Fairy, Fairies; the Forbidden Forest; Giants; Goblins; Hagrid and the Half-Giants; the Healer-King; Hogwarts: the Edifice; Horcruxes; the Inner Circle; Magic; Parselmouths; Petrification; the Price; Prophecies fulfilled only because someone tries to prevent them; the Resurrected Hero; Ritual of Desecration; (Harry's) Scar; Things Bought at Too High a Cost; Trolls; the Ugly Duckling; the Unbreakable Vow; Underground Adventures; the Unwanted Child

Tom Tit Tot — the taboo/true Name

Trelawney, Sybill — the taboo/true Name; Prophecies fulfilled only because someone tries to prevent them; reading the Tea Leaves

Tristan — Folklore, Literature…; Love Conquers All; the Unbreakable Vow

Tudor, Henry — see Henry VII

Túrin Turambar *(Tolkien)* — Prophecies fulfilled only because someone tries to prevent them

Twain, Mark — Prophecies fulfilled only because someone tries to prevent them

Urashima, the kindly fisherman — Old Age

Usdent/Utant, Tristan's hound — Love Potions

Uther, father of Arthur — Transfiguration

Vablatsky, Cassandra — the taboo/true Name

Väinämöinen *(Kalevala)* — the taboo/true Name

Valhalla (Norse place of the afterlife) — The Afterlife and Catching a Train

Vane, Romilda — Love Potions

Vathrúdnir, giant — Giants; the entrance to Ravenclaw House

Vector, Professor — the taboo/true Name

Vergil — Love Conquers All

Vishnu, Hindu preserver — Padma and Parvati Patil; Three

Voldemort — Introduction; Folklore, Literature…; Achilles's Choice; The Afterlife and Catching a Train; "And Give His Life as a Ransom for Many"; And Lead Us Not Into Temptation; Animagus; Blood; Cruel Parents and Unwanted Marriages; the Dark Lord; Deep Magic and Deeper Magic; Dragons; the Healer-King; Horcruxes; Immortality; the Inner Circle; Killed His Father and Married His Mother; Magic; Nagini; the taboo/true Name; Peacocks; Two-Faced Figures *as embodiment of evil* — Good and Evil; Magic; the Mark of Cain; the taboo/true Name; Neither Can Live While the Other Survives; the Price; Prophecies fulfilled only because someone tries to prevent them; Seven; the Soul; Things Bought at Too High a Cost; Underground Adventures; Which Side Are You On?; Wizards and Wizardry

Vortigern, King of Britain — the Chamber of Secrets; Hengist of Woodcroft; Merlin

Vortimer, son of Vortigern — Hengist of Woodcroft

Wandering Jew — the Mark of Cain

Warbeck, Perkin — Cats

Washer at the Ford — the Grim

Weasley, Arthur ("Mr. Weasley") — Nagini

Endnotes

For the sources cited in the endnotes, see the Bibliography.

1. J. K. Rowling, *Harry Potter and the Sorcerer's Stone* (American edition), Arthur A. Levine Books, 1997, p. 65.
2. Patricia Meyer Spacks, "Power and Meaning in *The Lord of the Rings,*" **Isaacs & Zimbardo**, p. 82.
3. **Tolkien-Fairy**, pp. 26–27.
4. **Harmin**, p. 17.
5. **Granger**, p. 127.
6. **LeGuinNight**, p. 136.
7. **Clute/Grant**, p. 341.
8. **Granger**, p. xii.
9. **Kirk**, p.47.
10. Rowling, in her first two years of college, took Greek and Roman studies, and particularly enjoyed their mythology, but dropped the subject after two years because her overall college results were not very good; **Kirk**, p. 45.
11. **Harmin**, p. 90.
12. **Rowling & Fraser**, pp. 30–31.
13. **Baggett & Klein**, p. 160.
14. **Colbert**, p. 57.
15. **LeGuinNight**, p. 44.
16. **Spartz & Schoen**, p. 31.
17. **RankEtAl**, p. 3.
18. **Clute/Grant**, p. 567.
19. **BriggsFolk-Tales**, pp. 341–342.
20. **BriggsFolk-Tales**, pp. 331–333, derived from the Hereford version found in **Leather**, pp. 174–176, but itself derived from print.
21. **Lang**, pp. 136–140.
22. **Shippey-Author**, pp. 182–187.
23. **Newman**, pp. 11–16.
24. **Tong**, pp. 111–113.
25. **Lüthi**, pp. 139–140.
26. **LeGuinNight**, p. 87.
27. **Baggett & Klein**, p. 50.
28. *Odyssey* I.1; **HomerOdyssey/Fagles**, I.1, p. 77.
29. *Odyssey* V.182; **HomerOdyssey/Fagles**, V.202, p. 158.
30. **Mercantante & Dow**, p. 120.
31. *Odyssey* I.87; **HomerOdyssey/Fagles**, I.103, p. 80.
32. *Odyssey* I.96–212; **HomerOdyssey/Fagles**, I.112–247, p. 80–84.
33. *Odyssey* V.382; **HomerOdyssey/Fagles**, V.421, p. 164.
34. *Odyssey* XXI.1–3; **HomerOdyssey/Fagles**, XXI.1–3, p. 424. "Bending bow as test" is Thompson D1651.1.

35. *Iliad* X.240–243; **HomerIliad/Fagles**, X.281–284, p. 284. Odysseus prays to Athena for help in X.277–278; **HomerIliad/Fagles**, X.325–326, p. 285.
36. **Grimal**, pp. 321–322.
37. W. H. Auden, "The Quest Hero," **Isaacs & Zimbardo**, p. 54.
38. Marion Zimmer Bradley, "Men, Halflings, and Hero Worship," **Isaacs & Zimbardo**, p. 126.
39. Auden, "The Quest Hero," **Isaacs & Zimbardo**, p. 55.
40. **Ellis**, pp. 208–210.
41. **Card-Miracles**, pp. 2–3.
42. Marion Zimmer Bradley, "Men, Halflings, and Hero Worship," **Isaacs & Zimbardo**, p. 124.
43. Marguerite Krause, "Harry Potter and the End of Religion," **Lackey**, p. 65.
44. **BakerDictionary**, p. 400.
45. **Nigg**, p. 134.
46. **Christie-Murray**, p. 87.
47. **Clifton**, p. 111.
48. **Christie-Murray**, p. 87.
49. **Granger**, p. 170.
50. **Granger**, p. 172, quoting Jill Lepore in *The New Yorker*.
51. **Frye**, pp. 33–35.
52. **Waltz-Orfeo**, p. 7.
53. **OxfordMind**, pp. 404–405.
54. **Bettelheim**, p. 36.
55. **Frith**, pp. 102–104.
56. **LeGuinNight**, p. 79.
57. **LeGuinNight**, p. 61.
58. **LeGuinNight**, pp. 59–61.
59. **Shippey-Road**, p. 265.
60. **Lupack**, p. 434. This strikes me as rather a stretch, at least based on the version of the tale in Malory.
61. **Clute/Grant**, pp. 526–527.
62. **Grimal**, p. 6; **Seyffert**, p. 3.
63. **SykesKendall**, p. 10.
64. **Cotterell**, p. 240.
65. **Jekyll**, p. 1.
66. **Jekyll**, pp. 9–10.
67. **Opie & Tatem**, p. 368.
68. **Opie & Tatem**, p. 117.
69. **Simpson & Roud**, p. 339.
70. **Larousse**, p. 400.
71. **Pickering**, p. 273.
72. *Odyssey* XI.29–30; **HomerOdyssey/Fagles**, XI.33, p. 250.
73. **Mercantante & Dow**, pp. 639–640; **Pickering**, p. 210.
74. **BakerDictionary**, p. 164.
75. **Cohen-LSRail**, pp. 619–614.
76. **Speake**, p. 17.
77. **Speake**, p. 18.
78. **LarousseBiog**, p. 17.
79. Acts 12:1–23.
80. Acts 25:13–26:32.
81. *Coriolanus,* Act I, scene i.
82. **Wedeck & Schweitzer**, p. 12.

83. **LarousseBiog**, p. 17. The best online source I have found for information about Agrippa is Charles Nauert, "Heinrich Cornelius Agrippa von Nettesheim," *The Stanford Encyclopedia of Philosophy* (Summer 2011 Edition), Edward N. Zalta (ed)., URL = <http://plato.stanford.edu/archives/sum2011/entries/agrippa-nettesheim/>.

84. **Colbert**, p. 198.

85. **Larousse**, p. 15.

86. **Clute/Grant**, pp. 25–26.

87. **Larousse**, p. 286.

88. **Seyffert**, p. 452. See also the chapter on Folklore.

89. **Magnusson**, p. 123; **Mercantante & Dow**, p. 798; **Pickering**, p. 276.

90. **Clute/Grant**, p. 767.

91. **Henderson & Oakes**, pp. 129–132.

92. Found in Chapter 34 of *The Deathly Hallows*.

93. **TolkienLetters**, p. 233.

94. **Shippey-Author**, pp. 112–160 (the chapter *The Concepts of Evil*); the section on the Lord's Prayer and temptation is on pp. 141–143.

95. On the Nibelungen Ring see, e.g. **Mercantante & Dow**, p. 739, although a lot of this is Wagner rather than genuine tradition.

96. **Grant & Hazel**, p. 264.

97. **Grimal**, p. 329.

98. **Grimal**, p. 379. This tale has had many imitations, including one by a modern fantasist: C. S. Lewis used it as the basis of *Till We Have Faces*.

99. From Asbjornsen and Moe; for a convenient English version see **Lang**, pp. 19–29.

100. **Bettelheim**, pp. 295–297.

101. **Waltz-Orfeo**, p. 56.

102. **Bettelheim**, p. 300.

103. **Alcock**, pp. 45–48; **Brengle**, p. 7.

104. **Sands**, p. 325.

105. **Mercantante & Dow**, p. 164, and I'm sure you can find plenty of texts of *Beowulf* yourself.

106. "Robin Hood's Death," **Child** #120, volume III, pp. 102–107; "A Gest of Robyn Hode," **Child** #117, volume III, pp. 39–78; for the actual death, with interpretation, see **Waltz-Gest**, pp. 104–106.

107. **Clute/Grant**, p. 942.

108. **Jackson**, pp. 240–241.

109. **Shippey-Author**, p. 31.

110. **Ledgard**, p. 89.

111. **Child** #113, volume II, p. 494, or see the much fuller discussion by Alan Bruford in **Lyle**, pp. 41–66.

112. **Hardwick**, p. 231.

113. **Wimberly**, pp. 61–63.

114. **Pickering**, pp. 191–192; **Larousse**, pp. 298–299; **Jackson**, p. 391.

115. **Kronzek**, p. 4.

116. **InterpretersDict**, volume III, p. 566, entry "Number."

117. **Ifrah**, p. 254.

118. **SuetoniusGraves**, p. 236.

119. **Ifrah**, p. 256.

120. **Reagin**, pp, 47–48.

121. **Benet**, p. 3.

122. **Larousse**, p. 3.

123. **Reagin**, pp. 50–51. The whole explanation is a good deal more complicated than that outlined above, and really needs to be read to be understood.

124. **Reagin,** p. 49.
125. **Rose,** p. 78.
126. **Reagin,** p. 46.
127. **Hazlitt,** p. 3.
128. Suetonius, "Life of Gaius," LV; **SuetoniusLoeb,** pp. 498–499.
129. **OxfordCompanion,** p. 467.
130. **Wolffe,** pp. 270–271.
131. **OxfordCompanion,** p. 468.
132. **Wolffe,** p. 271.
133. **Wimberly,** p. 64; **Westwood & Simpson,** p. 280.
134. **Douglas,** p. 142.
135. **Williams,** p. 10.
136. **Larousse,** p. 50.
137. **O hOgain,** p. 31.
138. **Kronzek,** p. 20.
139. **Pickering,** p. 24.
140. **Alexander, Marc,** p. 13.
141. **Mercantante & Dow,** p. 143.
142. **Rose,** p. 61.
143. **SykesKendall,** p. 30.
144. **Jones,** p. 78.
145. **Cooper,** p. 14.
146. **Liddell & Scott,** p. 230.
147. Most of the information in this section is from **Tatar-Annotated**; additional examples can be found in **Zipes**.
148. **Baring-Gould-Mother,** p. 17.
149. **Simpson & Roud,** p. 247.
150. **Baring-Gould-Mother,** p. 15.
151. **Scott,** p. 209.
152. J. R. R. Tolkien thought the runes came from the Goths; **Tolkien-Sigurd,** p. 22.
153. **Bethard,** p. 135.
154. This and other data about bright stars are from **Ridpath,** p. 554.
155. **Hesiod & Theognis,** p. 11.
156. **Ridpath,** p. 448.
157. J. K. Rowling, *Harry Potter and the Goblet of Fire* (American edition), Arthur A. Levine Books, 2000, p. 642.
158. From the Old French "Perceval," quoted on p. 225 of **Loomis**.
159. **Wimberly,** p. 19.
160. **Pickering,** p. 39.
161. **Pickering,** p. 38.
162. **Pickering,** p. 38.
163. **Child,** volume III, p. 239.
164. **Child** #155, volume III, pp. 243–253. Child's notes on pp. 234–235 mentions various ways in which the murdered child communicates.
165. **Wimberly,** pp. 81–82, citing as evidence Child #90, "Jellon Grame."
166. **Bettelheim,** p. 300; **Larousse,** p. 70; **Wimberly,** p. 81.
167. **BriggsFairies,** p. 29.
168. **Hardwick,** p. 170.
169. **Alexander, Marc,** p. 27; **Simpson & Roud,** p. 29.
170. **Simpson & Roud,** p. 29.
171. **Leather,** pp. 47–48.
172. **Harland & Wilkinson,** pp. 49–50.

173. BriggsFairies, pp. 218–219.
174. BrownM, p. 216, citing a reference of Child's that I cannot trace.
175. Frazer, pp. 706–707.
176. Williams, pp. 49–50.
177. Simpson & Roud, p. 30.
178. Williams, p. 50.
179. Simpson & Roud, p. 30.
180. Larousse, p. 458.
181. Thompson-Folktale, p. 250.
182. Larousse, p. 458; Pickering, p. 318.
183. Simpson & Roud, p. 36.
184. Lindahl Et Al, p. 438.
185. Larousse, p. 45; Pickering, p. 21.
186. Opie & Tatem, p. 45; Leather, pp. 18–19.
187. Opie & Tatem, p. 45.
188. Wimberly, p. 351.
189. Larousse, p. 458.
190. Wimberly, p. 58, quoting Gomme.
191. Mercantante, p. 20.
192. Cooper, p. 41.
193. Snorri/Young, p. 32, 33, 53. From Snorri's *Gylfaginning,* "The Deluding of Gylfi,"
194. Cooper, p. 42.
195. Jackson, p. 508.
196. Ellis, p. 57; of these, "puss" has been adopted into English — although others have tried to derive "puss" from Egyptian or other sources (**Cooper**, p. 41).
197. Cooper, p. 42.
198. Grimal, p. 89.
199. Seyffert, p. 123.
200. Grimal, p. 89.
201. Grant & Hazel, p. 84.
202. Seyffert, p. 416.
203. Clute/Grant, p. 581, article on "Liminal Beings."
204. Geoffrey/Evans & Dunn, VI.17, p. 132.
205. Geoffrey/Evans & Dunn, VI.19, p. 135, and after.
206. Baring-Gould-Myths, pp. 171–173.
207. Clute/Grant, p. 873.
208. Mercantante & Dow, p. 323.
209. Jackson, p. 531; a detailed retelling is in **Baring-Gould-Myths**, pp. 51–61.
210. Lupack, p. 298.
211. Grimal, p. 95.
212. Larousse, p. 108.
213. Gerritsen & van Melle, p. 64.
214. Mercantante & Dow, p. 237.
215. *Odyssey* X.237–243; HomerOdyssey/Fagles, X.261–268, pp. 237–238.
216. Grimal, p. 99.
217. Larousse, p. 115.
218. Grant & Hazel, pp. 266–267.
219. Grimal, p. 99.
220. Larousse, p. 116.
221. Grant & Hazel, p. 91.
222. Grimal, p. 419.
223. Grant & Hazel, p. 324.

224. **Grimal**, p. 100.
225. **Ellis**, p. 64.
226. **SykesKendall**, p. 48.
227. **Larousse**, p. 116.
228. **Rose**, p. 33.
229. **O hOgain**, p. 85.
230. **O hOgain**, p. 86.
231. **O hOgain**, p. 87.
232. **BriggsFairies**, p. 329.
233. **Alexander, Marc**, p. 218.
234. **BriggsFairies**, p. 328.
235. **Simpson & Roud**, p. 279.
236. **Simpson & Roud**, p. 279.
237. **BriggsFairies**, p. 328.
238. **BriggsFairies**, p. 330.
239. **Gardner/Chickering**, p. 178, verse 2.
240. **Laws**, p. 179, lists the songs, with descriptions on pp. 180–200.
241. Laws M25; **Laws**, p. 192.
242. Laws M13; **Laws**, pp. 186–187.
243. Laws M15; **Laws**, pp. 187–188.
244. **Child** #272; volume V, pp. 66–67.
245. Laws M20; **Laws**, pp. 189–190.
246. Laws M35; **Laws**, p. 198.
247. Laws M34; **Laws**, pp. 197–198.
248. Laws M30; **Laws**, pp. 194–195.
249. Laws M36; **Laws**, p. 198.
250. **Simpson & Roud**, p. 241.
251. **Zipes**, pp. 581–583.
252. **Clute/Grant**, p. 250.
253. **Chaucer/Benson**, p. 905.
254. **Granger**, p. 180.
255. **Speake**, p. 328.
256. **ApostolicFathers**, p. 64.
257. **Grimal**, p. 79.
258. **Pickering**, p. 132.
259. **Loomis**, pp. 113–115.
260. **Ellis**, p. 56.
261. **O hOgain**, p. 151.
262. **Jackson**, p. 112.
263. **Loomis**, p. 59.
264. **Mabonagi/Gantz**, p.72.
265. **Mabinogi/Ford**, p. 63.
266. **Moorman**, pp. 101–102.
267. **Moorman**, p. 28.
268. **Geoffrey/Evans & Dunn**, p. 188; the reference is to section IX.4 of Geoffrey. The name "Rhongomyniad" is from *Culhywych and Olwen* in *The Mabinogion;* **Lupack**, p. 468.
269. **Larousse**, p. 240; **Pickering**, p. 148.
270. **Grant & Hazel**, p. 274; **Larousse**, p. 240; **Seyffert**, p. 473.
271. **Larousse**, p. 393.
272. **Williams**, p. 13.
273. **SykesKendall**, p. 43.
274. **Lupack**, p. 91.

275. **Pickering**, p. 148.
276. **Noel**, p. 65, based on Snorri's *Prose Edda.*
277. For an example, see the tale of Fortunatus, **BriggsFolk-Tales**, A.II, pp. 245–249.
278. See the extended discussion in **Shippey-Author**, pp. 130–136; also the footnotes to GOOD AND EVIL.
279. **Knight**, p. 69.
280. **Duriez**, p. 94.
281. J. K. Rowling, *Harry Potter and the Goblet of Fire* (American edition), Arthur A. Levine Books, 2000, p. 657.
282. **Gardner**, p. 27 n. 10.
283. **Simpson & Roud**, p. 96.
284. **BriggsFairies**, p. 103.
285. **Waltz-Gest**, p. 3.
286. **Rose**, p. 88.
287. The *Inferno,* III.9. **Dante/Ciardi**, p. 42, renders "Abandon all hope ye who enter here."
288. *Odyssey* XI.36–27; **HomerOdyssey/Fagles**, XI.41–43, p. 250.
289. **OvidMetamorphoses/Innes**, p. 225 (beginning of Book X), and see under the LAKE and LOVE CONQUERS ALL.
290. **Shippey-Author**, pp. 282–283.
291. **Snorri/Young**, pp. 56, from Snorri's *Gylfaginning.*
292. **Kittel**, volume III, p. 629.
293. **Pickering**, p. 83.
294. **Waltz-Orfeo**, p. 50.
295. **Gerritsen & van Melle**, pp. 24–25.
296. **Beahm**, p. 11.
297. **Larousse**, p. 148.
298. J. K. Rowling, *Harry Potter and the Order of the Phoenix* (American edition), Arthur A. Levine Books, 2003, pp. 103–104.
299. **Liddell & Scott**, p. 330.
300. **Partridge**, p. 239.
301. For the list of dragon names, see **Jones**, p. 1, who lists several others in addition to these.
302. **Cooper**, p. 81.
303. **Noel**, p. 154.
304. **Tolkien-Beowulf**, p. 109; cf. **Shippey-Road**, p. 81. The tale of Fafnir is also in **BrownN**, pp. 171–173, in a more Norse form; her version makes it clear how much the story inspired Tolkien.
305. *Beowulf,* lines 2714–2715; **Beowulf/Chickering**, p. 213; **Beowulf/Heaney**, p. 68.
306. For this idea see **Jones**, p. 4.
307. **Hooke**, p. 17; compare **Cooper**, p. 81, which more guardedly says that the various stories are "counterparts."
308. **Kittel**, volume II, p. 281.
309. *ibid.*
310. **InterpretersDict**, volume I, p. 868, entry "Dragon."
311. **Jones**, pp. 121–121.
312. **Finlay**, pp. 176–179.
313. **Gilliver, Marshall, & Weiner**, p. 104.
314. **Rowling & Fraser**, p. 55.
315. **Benet**, p. 19, although a connection to the Celtic root "alp" for "cliff" has also been suggested.
316. **Lupack**, pp. 465–466.
317. **Ellis**, pp. 42–43.
318. **SykesKendall**, p. 39.

319. E.g. **Kronzek**, p. 75.
320. **Gilliver, Marshall, & Weiner**, pp. 104–107.
321. **Simpson & Roud**, p. 105.
322. **Pickering**, p. 93.
323. **Larousse**, p. 206.
324. There are three versions in **BriggsFolk-Tales**, pp. 316–322. Interestingly, not all of these involve the actual golden goose; some simply show Jack stealing treasure.
325. **Pickering**, p. 98.
326. **Benet**, p. 348.
327. **Larousse**, p. 164.
328. **Benet**, p. 348.
329. **Grant & Hazel**, p. 166.
330. **Clute/Grant**, p. 305.
331. Adam–Troy Castro, "From Azkaban to Abu Ghraib," **Lackey**, p. 120.
332. **Larousse**, p. 170.
333. **Alexander, Marc**, p. 90.
334. **Tolkien-Fairy**, p. 4.
335. **Simpson & Roud**, p. 115.
336. **Opie & Tatem**, p. 146.
337. **O hOgain**, p. 206.
338. **Alexander, Marc**, p. 90.
339. **Waltz-Orfeo**, pp. 19–20.
340. **Waltz-Orfeo**, p. 22.
341. "Thomas Rhymer," **Child** #37, text C, stanza 13, volume I, p. 325; cf. **Tolkien-Fairy**, p. 5.
342. **Simpson & Roud**, p. 118.
343. **Pickering**, p. 103; **Simpson & Roud**, p. 118.
344. **Simpson & Roud**, p. 118.
345. **Benet**, p. 1082.
346. J. K. Rowling, *Harry Potter and the Half-Blood Prince* (American edition), Arthur A. Levine Books, 2005, p. 187.
347. **Simpson & Roud**, p. 218.
348. **Shippey-Author**, pp. 145–146.
349. **Ellis**, p. 99.
350. **Pickering**, p. 107.
351. **O hOgain**, p. 238.
352. **O hOgain**, p. 239.
353. **O hOgain**, p. 242.
354. **Grant & Hazel**, p. 86.
355. **VirgilLoeb**, pp. 230–231.
356. **Jackson**, p. 246.
357. **Grant & Hazel**, p. 86.
358. **Larousse**, p. 286.
359. **Lang**, pp. 342–373.
360. **Lang**, p. 344.
361. **Clute/Grant**, p. 503.
362. The *Inferno*, I.3; **Dante/Ciardi**, p. 28.
363. **Gawain/Tolkien & Gordon**, p. 20.
364. **Gawain/Tolkien & Gordon**, p. 229.
365. **Gawain/Tolkien**, p. 41.
366. **Shippey-Author**, pp. 82–84.
367. **Simpson & Roud**, p. 385.
368. **Simpson & Roud**, p. 393.

369. **Pickering**, p. 313.
370. Mark 12:42–44; parallel Luke 21:1–4.
371. **Grimal**, p. 243.
372. **Rose**, p. 126.
373. **SykesKendall**, p. 76.
374. **Haddawy**, pp. 42–44.
375. **Larousse**, p. 200.
376. J. K. Rowling, *Harry Potter and the Deathly Hallows* (American edition), Arthur A. Levine Books, 2007, p. 98.
377. **Rose**, p. 126.
378. **BriggsFairies**, p. 186.
379. **Williamson**, p. 12.
380. **Simpson & Roud**, p. 147.
381. **Williamson**, p. 12.
382. **Kronzek**, p. 95, adds another group, the "Gibborim." But "Gibborim" are not mentioned in the Bible; the root *gibor* means simply "mighty"; "Gibborim" should be called "mighty men" (which is the term usually used in the King James Bible).
383. **Bennett & Gray**, p. 150.
384. **Bennett & Gray**, p. 126.
385. **Jackson**, p. 154.
386. *The Poetic Edda*, "Vafthrudnir's Sayings," 54.3–4; **EddaLarrington**, p. 48.
387. **O hOgain**, p. 49; **Gawain/Tolkien & Gordon**, p. xv.
388. **Grant & Hazel**, p. 342.
389. **Henderson & Oakes**, p. 89.
390. **Mabinogi/Ford**, p. 123, etc.
391. **Jackson**, p. 76.
392. **Ellis**, p. 111.
393. **Wimberly**, p. 149.
394. *The Winter's Tale*, IV.iv.81–82; see also line 98.
395. "Sir Thopas," ninth stanza; line 762 of Fragment VII of the *Canterbury Tales*; **Chaucer/Benson**, p. 214. It is curious to find Chaucer mentioning the plant only in "Sir Thopas," which is a mock-romance.
396. **Ault**, p. 72, quoting the 1584 book *A Handful of Pleasant Delights*.
397. **Opie**, p. 375.
398. **Wimberly**, p. 149, quoting "Sweet William's Ghost," Child #77, volume II, p. 230 — text B, seventh stanza.
399. **Wimberly**, p. 152.
400. **Wimberly**, p. 34.
401. **Ellis**, p. 216.
402. **Benet**, p. 434.
403. **HouseholdTreasury**, pp. 133–135.
404. **Alexander, Marc**, pp. 195–196.
405. **Lupack**, p. 120; it appears Bulwer-Lytton used this name because it is found in French romances.
406. **Benet**, p. 435.
407. **Pickering**, p. 121.
408. **Simpson & Roud**, pp. 145–146.
409. **Larousse**, p. 203.
410. Quoted from the Prefatory Letter to *The Rape of the Lock* on p. 439 of **Benet**.
411. **Simpson & Roud**, p. 146.
412. **Shippey-Road**, p. 293.
413. **Shippey-Author**, p. 87.

414. **Liddell & Scott**, p. 766.
415. **Simpson & Roud**, p. 146.
416. **Larousse**, p. 204.
417. **Rose**, p. 129.
418. **Alexander, Marc**, p. 110.
419. e.g. **LewisMere**, pp. 33–36 (Book II, chapter 2).
420. **Mercantante & Dow**, p. 725.
421. Marguerite Krause, "Harry Potter and the End of Religion," **Lackey**, p. 62.
422. **Williams**, p. 59.
423. **Pickering**, p. 126.
424. **Benet**, p. 461.
425. **Grimal**, p. 166.
426. **Gerritsen & van Melle**, p. 15.
427. A reproduction of the image is in **Gerritsen & van Melle**, p. 18.
428. **Larousse**, p. 210.
429. **Mercantante & Dow**, p. 388.
430. **Gardner**, p. 94 n 11; the reference, according to **Mercantante & Dow**, p. 388, is to canto 29 of the *Purgatorio.*
431. **Gardner**, p. 94 n 11.
432. **Pickering**, p. 74.
433. **Alexander, Marc**, p. 64.
434. **BriggsFairies**, p. 173; **Alexander, Marc**, pp. 65, 96; cf. **Simpson & Roud**, p. 397, entry on "wraiths."
435. **Rose**, p. 32.
436. **Alexander, Marc**, p. 15.
437. **Pickering**, p. 311.
438. **BriggsFairies**, pp. 19–20.
439. **Rees**, p. 326.
440. **BriggsFairies**, p. 14.
441. **Pickering**, p. 117.
442. **Simpson & Roud**, pp. 308–309.
443. **Simpson & Roud**, p. 157. The title "church grim," although not used by Rowling, is common in folklore, and is the equivalent of Swedish *kirkegrimm;* **BriggsFairies**, p. 205.
444. **Arrowsmith**, p. 53.
445. **Rose**, p. 181.
446. **Simpson & Roud**, p. 390.
447. **Swanton**, p. 258, with other early references in the notes.
448. **BriggsFairies**, p. 206.
449. **Rose**, p. 4.
450. **Larousse**, p. 214.
451. **Pickering**, p. 130.
452. **O hOgain**, p. 283.
453. **Stone**, p. 65.
454. **O hOgain**, pp. 58–59.
455. **O hOgain**, p. 283.
456. **Simpson & Roud**, p. 161.
457. line 141; **Gawain/Tolkien & Gordon**, p. 5. Glossed on p. 178 as an ogre or giant, and derived from Old English *eoten.*
458. **Gilliver, Marshall, & Weiner**, p. 119.
459. **Grant & Hazel**, p. 342.
460. **Mabinogion/Gantz**, p. 136, etc.
461. **Jackson**, p. 154.

462. **EddaLarrington**, p. 61.
463. **Jackson**, p. 156.
464. **Hooke**, p. 132.
465. **Wise Et Al**, p. 246.
466. **Wise Et Al**, p. 247.
467. **Alexander, Marc**, p. 123, has both an article and a picture.
468. Details, if you must, are in **Pickering**, p. 133, and **Simpson & Roud**, p. 165; **Baring-Gould-Myths**, pp. 225–226, gives some variations.
469. **Larousse**, p. 217; **Opie & Tatem**, p. 100.
470. **Simpson & Roud**, p. 165.
471. The full account, with the language modernized, is found in **Storey**, pp. 199–209.
472. **Simpson & Roud**, p. 165; **Baring-Gould-Myths**, p. 227, gives a tale of how this might have been discovered.
473. **Wimberly**, p. 82.
474. **Wimberly**, p. 92.
475. **Rose**, p. 2.
476. **Norwegian**, pp. 97–101.
477. **Gawain/Tolkien**, p. 32, translating Stanza XIX of *Sir Gawain and the Green Knight.*
478. **Gawain/Tolkien & Gordon**, pp. xv–xvi.
479. A list is on pp. xvi–xvii of **Gawain/Tolkien & Gordon**.
480. **Lang**, p. 92.
481. **Haskins**, pp. 64–68.
482. **Noel**, p. 72, citing Grimm.
483. **OxfordCompanion**, p. 922.
484. **Cooper**, p. 214.
485. **OxfordSaints**, p. 243; **Watkins-Saints**, pp. 109–110.
486. **OxfordCompanion**, p. 463.
487. **Benet**, p. 494.
488. **Mercantante & Dow**, p. 416.
489. **Lupack**, pp. 451, 469. The reference is to Book VI, chapter 12 of Geoffrey's *History;* cf. **Geoffrey/Evans & Dunn**, pp. 124–125, where the woman's name is given as "Ronwen."
490. J. K. Rowling, *Harry Potter and the Deathly Hallows* (American edition), Arthur A. Levine Books, 2007, p. 412.
491. **Knight & Ohlgren**, p. 639.
492. **Knight & Ohlgren**, p. 640.
493. **Head**, p. 38.
494. **Knight & Ohlgren**, p. 647.
495. **Knight & Ohlgren**, p. 649.
496. **Head**, p. 25, etc.
497. Probably; there is one tradition that she later had a son Nicostratus; **Grimal**, p. 175.
498. *Odyssey* IV.12–14; **HomerOdyssey/Fagles**, IV.14–17, pp. 124–125.
499. **Grant & Hazel**, p. 182.
500. **Grimal**, p. 199.
501. **Grimal**, p. 199; **Seyffert**, p. 288.0.
502. **Grant & Hazel**, pp. 341–342.
503. "Argus has eyes all over body" is Thompson Types F512.2.2, D1961.
504. **Grant & Hazel**, p. 52.
505. **BriggsFairies**, p. 221.
506. **Benet**, p. 506.
507. **Benet**, p. 851; **NewCentury**, p. 873, says that the earliest manuscripts are from the eighth century, making the date of translation uncertain.
508. **Colbert**, pp. 38–39.

509. Larousse, p. 227.
510. Benet, p. 506.
511. Greene, p. 91.
512. LeGuinNight, p. 51.
513. Clute/Grant, p. 309.
514. Reagin, p. 78.
515. Reagin, p. 78, which notes that this is the first stage of alchemical learning.
516. BriggsFairies, p. 355.
517. Tolkien-Fairy, pp. 15–17, esp. n. 11.
518. Baring-Gould-Myths, p. 260.
519. Summarized from the examples on pp. 774–782 of Frazer.
520. Frazer, p. 775.
521. Burne, p. 345.
522. Frazer, pp. 775–776.
523. Child #39, volume I, pp. 335–358; the "tiend" (tithe) to hell is in verse 24 of the "A" version (p. 342), verse 23 of the "B" text (p. 344), verse 28 of the "G" text (p. 350), and verse 32 of the "I" text (p. 354).
524. Larousse, pp. 82–83.
525. Pickering, p. 44.
526. Alexander, Marc, p. 36; Simpson & Roud, p. 36.
527. Pickering, p. 44.
528. Wells, p. 17.
529. Simpson & Roud, p. 36.
530. Alexander, Marc, p. 36.
531. Simpson & Roud, p. 36.
532. Mercantante & Dow, p. 194; Simpson & Roud, p. 36.
533. Wimberly, pp. 209–210; Alexander, Marc, p. 23.
534. Ranke, #13, p. 31.
535. Ranke, #16, p. 33.
536. Simpson & Roud, p. 397.
537. Flanders & Olney, p. 58.
538. Grimal, p. 441.
539. Jackson, p. 219.
540. Benet, p. 867.
541. Pickering
542. BriggsFairies, p. 232.
543. "Sir Orfeo," line 70; Waltz-Orfeo, p. 19, and especially n. 111, pp. 79–80.
544. J. K. Rowling, *Harry Potter and the Half-Blood Prince* (American edition), Arthur A. Levine Books, 2005, p. 62.
545. Child #78, volume II, p. 237, verse 4 of text "C."
546. Clute/Grant, pp. 220–221.
547. Clute/Grant, p. 272.
548. Clute/Grant, p. 853.
549. Mercantante & Dow, p. 500.
550. Rose, p. 176.
551. Douglas, p. 113; Pickering, p. 177.
552. Douglas, p. 114.
553. Larousse, pp. 256–257.
554. Douglas, p. 115.
555. Alexander, Marc, p. 153.
556. Mercantante & Dow, p. 502.
557. Pickering, p. 160.

558. **Rose,** p. 63.
559. **Williams,** p. 71.
560. **Larousse,** pp. 256–257.
561. **Douglas,** p. 116.
562. **Benet,** p. 790; **Grant & Hazel,** p. 252; **Grimal,** p. 306; **Seyffert,** p. 424.
563. **Grimal,** p. 307.
564. **Grimal,** p. 307.
565. **Grant & Hazel,** p. 252; **Grimal,** p. 307.
566. **Grant & Hazel,** p. 252; **Grimal,** p. 307; **Seyffert,** p. 425.
567. **Grant & Hazel,** p. 253; **Grimal,** p. 308.
568. **Grimal,** p. 308; **Seyffert,** p. 425.
569. **Grimal,** p. 46.
570. **Grant & Hazel,** p. 256. This is the subject of Æschylus's *Agamemnon,* and its aftermath the subject of the whole *Orestia;* cf. **Æschylus/Vellacott,** pp. 12–32.
571. **Grant & Hazel,** p. 350.
572. **Grant & Hazel,** p. 98.
573. **RankEtAl,** p. 18.
574. **Lupack,** pp. 461–462.
575. **Grimal,** p. 308.
576. **Grimal,** p. 313.
577. *Beowulf,* starting around line 1390, where Beowulf vows to kill the creature; **Beowulf/Chickering,** p. 128; **Beowulf/Heaney** inserts a section head, "Beowulf Fights Grendel's Mother" on p. 37 following line 1382.
578. **Grant & Hazel,** pp. 258–259.
579. See *Sir Orfeo,* lines 429–471, or the translation in **Waltz-Orfeo,** pp. 23–24; see also LOVE CONQUERS ALL.
580. For the text, see **Wimberly,** pp. 135, 326–327; it is not in the text on pp. 485–486 of **Child,** volume I.
581. **Mercantante & Dow,** p. 725.
582. **O hOgain,** p. 308.
583. **O hOgain,** pp. 308–309.
584. **Pickering,** p. 171.
585. **BriggsFairies,** p. 264.
586. **Benet,** p. 628.
587. **Rowling & Fraser,** p. 39.
588. Thanks to the late Sam Hinton for this information.
589. **Benet,** p. 434.
590. **Percy/Wheatley,** p. 319.
591. **Percy/Wheatley,** p. 318.
592. **VirgilLoeb,** p. 74. There is some variation in the verb; the manuscript M of the fifth century reads *vincit,* which is followed by the Loeb text; R, of about the same date, has *vicit.*
593. **Chaucer/Benson,** p. 126.
594. See under DOOR OF DEATH.
595. See *Sir Orfeo,* lines 497–596, or the translation in **Waltz-Orfeo,** pp. 24–25; also the LAKE.
596. **Jackson,** p. 231.
597. **Jackson,** p. 573.
598. **Larousse,** p. 281.
599. **Lupack,** pp. 435–436.
600. **Lupack,** p. 451.
601. **Spartz & Schoen,** p. 71.
602. **Stevens,** p. 101.
603. **Knight,** p. 68.

604. Baggett & Klein, p. 82.
605. Thompson-Folktale, p. 70.
606. Reagin, p. 10.
607. Larousse, p. 288.
608. Larousse, p. 288.
609. Mercantante & Dow, p. 571.
610. Pickering, p. 185.
611. Simpson & Roud, p. 224.
612. Stevens & Klarner, p. 63.
613. Stevens & Klarner, p. 64.
614. Larousse, p. 268.
615. Mercantante & Dow, p. 572.
616. Kronzek, p. 178.
617. Liddell & Scott, p. 866.
618. For the term see Clute/Grant, pp. 2–3.
619. Goldstein, p. 41.
620. Pickering, p. 318.
621. Knight, p. 65.
622. Lacy, p. 382.
623. Lupack, p. 329.
624. Ellis, p. 165.
625. Skene, p. 462.
626. Skene, p. 478.
627. Lupack, p. 330.
628. Lupack, p. 331.
629. Stone, p. 60.
630. Pickering, p. 285; Stone, pp. 58–60; Mabinogi/Ford, pp. 159–164, has both the full text of the story and a useful introduction and summary.
631. Grimal, p. 403; according to Grant & Hazel, p. 312, they resembled Harpies.
632. BriggsFairies, p. 290.
633. Stone, p. 111.
634. InterpretersDict, volume 1, p. 305, entry "Atargatis."
635. SykesKendall, p. 20, mentions the equation but clearly regards it as dubious.
636. Mercantante & Dow, p. 118.
637. InterpretersDict, volume 1, p. 756, entry "Dagon."
638. Mercantante & Dow, p. 266.
639. Hertzberg, p. 53.
640. McCarter, pp. 121–122.
641. SykesKendall, p. 135; Saggs, p. 140.
642. Saggs, pp. 316–317; also pp. 72, 74, etc.
643. Stone, p. 237.
644. Ellis, p. 160.
645. Gerritsen & van Melle, p. 64.
646. Child #289, volume V, pp. 148–152.
647. Child #289, text C, volume V, p. 150.
648. Simpson & Roud, p. 234.
649. Larousse, p. 300; Mercantante & Dow, p 596; Pickering, p. 193. "Mermaid Captures" is Thompson B81.13.11.
650. BriggsFairies, p. 289.
651. Alexander, Marc, p. 193.
652. Rose, p. 137.
653. BriggsFairies, p. 287.

654. BriggsFairies, p. 290.
655. Arrowsmith, p. 115.
656. Arrowsmith, p. 118.
657. OxfordFairyTales, pp. 317–318.
658. Grimal, p. 271.
659. Cornfeld, p. 213.
660. Grant & Hazel, p. 235.
661. Tatar-Classic, p. 83, following the Grimm text.
662. Newman, pp. 105–111.
663. Opie & Tatem, p. 252.
664. Pickering, p. 196; cf. Gerritsen & van Melle, p. 214.
665. Simpson & Roud, p. 241.
666. Tatar-Annotated, pp. 70–71.
667. Benet, p. 741.
668. OxfordFairyTales, p. 324.
669. Moorman, p. 91; Stone, p. 60.
670. Alexander, Marc, p. 196.
671. Lupack, p. 462.
672. Benet, p. 741.
673. Larousse, p. 309; Alexander, Marc, p. 196.
674. Lupack, p. 462.
675. Pickering, p. 200.
676. Steindorff & Seele, pp. 150–151.
677. Aristophanes & Menander, p. xi.
678. Mercantante & Dow, p. 616.
679. Kronzek, p. 192.
680. Knappert, p. 176.
681. Stevens & Klarner, p. 97.
682. Ledgard, p. 84.
683. Rose, p. 229.
684. Stevens & Klarner, p. 91.
685. Stevens & Klarner, p. 93.
686. Larousse, p. 317; Williams, p. 40.
687. Wimberly, p. 303, citing the same text as in the preceding note.
688. Grimal, p. 145.
689. Æschylus/Vellacott, p. 17.
690. Æschylus/Vellacott, pp. 14, 33–36.
691. Wimberly, p. 2.
692. McCarter, pp. 417–418.
693. InterpretersDict, volume I, p. 857, entry "Divination."
694. Grimal, p. 315, and see the entries on the Door of Death and Love Conquers All.
695. SykesKendall, p. 29; for an English text of the tale, see Snorri/Young, pp. 80–84.
696. Mercantante, p. 73.
697. Emsley, p. 393.
698. Pickering, p. 218.
699. Simpson & Roud, p. 265.
700. Larousse, p. 331.
701. Pickering, p. 218.
702. "Squire Per" is in Norwegian, pp. 122–127; "Puss in Boots" is found in Lang, pp. 141–147.
703. Grimal, p. 441.
704. Newman, pp. 85–92.

705. Williamson, pp. 6–10.
706. Mercantante & Dow, p. 671.
707. Goldstein, p. 26.
708. Simpson & Roud, p. 270; Mercantante & Dow, p. 671.
709. *Hamlet,* IV.v.42, p. 1173 in the Riverside edition.
710. Cooper, p. 181.
711. Pickering, p. 223.
712. Alexander, Marc, p. 210.
713. Cooper, p. 181.
714. Livo & Cha, pp. 61–63.
715. Mercantante & Dow, p. 670.
716. Eberhard, pp. 221–222.
717. Larousse, p. 338.
718. Plutarch, *Life of Themistocles,* 12.1; PlutarchAthens, p. 89.
719. Simpson & Roud, p. 270; Opie & Tatem, pp. 295–296.
720. *The Parliament of Fowls,* line 343; Chaucer/Benson, p. 390.
721. Pickering, p. 223.
722. Crump, p. 63; Wedeck & Schweitzer, pp. 444–445.
723. Jaffe, p. 16.
724. Darrow, pp. 4, 11.
725. Darrow, p. 254.
726. Jaffe, p. 13.
727. Jaffe, pp. 16–17.
728. Jaffe, p. 17.
729. Jaffe, p. 14.
730. Asimov, p. 71.
731. Jaffe, p. 18.
732. Jaffe, p. 19.
733. Asimov, p. 72.
734. Timbrell, p. 313.
735. Grant & Hazel, p. 340.
736. Larousse, p. 393.
737. Grant & Hazel, p. 223.
738. Lüthi, p. 67.
739. Jackson, p. 161.
740. Thompson-Hundred, p. 304.
741. Knappert, p. 187.
742. Knappert, p. 193.
743. Seyffert, p. 279.
744. Grimal, p. 58.
745. Larousse, pp. 342–343.
746. Eberhard, p. 229.
747. Opie & Tatem, pp. 300–301.
748. Mercantante & Dow, p. 687.
749. Cooper, p. 186.
750. Pickering, p. 226.
751. Colbert, p. 167.
752. Pickering, p. 217.
753. Grimal, pp. 244, 277.
754. Simpson & Roud, p. 386.
755. BriggsFolk-Tales, pp. 290–295.
756. Thompson-Folktale, p. 259.

757. Grimal, p. 164.

758. Grant & Hazel, p. 274.

759. Lupack, p. 116.

760. SykesKendall, p. 191.

761. Crosland, p. 23.

762. Crosland, p. 11.

763. Crosland, p. 3.

764. "λιθον τον ου λιθον"; Crosland, p. 22.

765. Digital Index of Middle English Verse #3728. http://www.cddc.vt.edu/host/imev/record.php?recID=3728. Site checked March 31, 2013. I do not believe this is where I first found this verse, but I cannot determine where I learned of it.

766. lines 1428–1481; Chaucer/Benson, p. 281.

767. Chaucer/Benson, p. 948.

768. Chaucer/Benson, p. 947.

769. Reagin, pp. 73–76.

770. Translated on p. 76 of Reagin.

771. Child #39; for details, see note 523.

772. Emsley, p. 258.

773. The alchemists recognized three substances as "principles:" sulfur, mercury, and salt; Darrow, p. 9.

774. Emsley, p. 412.

775. Emsley, p. 258.

776. Bradley, p. 290.

777. Mercantante & Dow, p. 699.

778. *Pearl,* lines 430–431 (Part VIII; Stanza 36); PearlVantuano, p. 420.

779. *The Book of the Duchess,* lines 981–984; Chaucer/Benson, p. 342.

780. Pickering, p. 229.

781. Eberhard, pp. 234–235.

782. Liddell & Scott, p. 1570, item V.

783. Cooper, p. 189.

784. TacitusAnnals, VI.27f.; pp. 213–214.

785. Frankel, pp. 15–17.

786. Parmelee, p. 203.

787. Spartz & Schoen, p. 133.

788. Granger, p. 206.

789. NewCentury, p. 876.

790. Thanks to Elisheva Rosenberg for researching this information on Russian-language web sites.

791. Benet, p. 866.

792. Domesday, p. 254; also p. 1389.

793. Child #10;.

794. Pickering, p. 217.

795. Grant & Hazel, p. 294.

796. Tolkien, *The Lord of the Rings,* Book VI, Chapter IX, "The Grey Havens." It is about two pages from the end of the book; p. 309 in the Houghton Mifflin hardcover edition of *The Return of the King.* It is also notably quoted by W. H. Auden on p. 61 of Isaacs & Zimbardo.

797. Beahm, p. 11.

798. Thanks to Katryn Conlin for pointing this out to me.

799. Clute/Grant, p. 831.

800. **Campbell**, p. 30; also quoted by **Huttar**, p. 119, who leaves out some of Campbell's excessive dependence on psychological theories which now appear to be false.
801. J. K. Rowling, *Harry Potter and the Prisoner of Azkaban* (American edition), Arthur A. Levine Books, 1999, p. 290; the point is brought out on p. 249 of **Dickerson & O'Hara**.
802. **RankEtAl**, pp. xxviii–xxix.
803. **Campbell**, pp. 30–31.
804. **Jackson**, p. 465; **RankEtAl**, p. 19.
805. **Grimal**, p. 11; **RankEtAl**, p. 21.
806. **Herodotus**, Histories I.106fff., pp. 85–87, etc.; cf. **RankEtAl**, pp. 22–32.
807. **O hOgain**, p. 163.
808. **Gerritsen & van Melle**, pp. 47–49.
809. **Josephus/Thackeray**, II.ix.2 / II.205fff.; pp. 252–255.
810. **Shippey-Road**, p. 255.
811. From Tolkien's *Narn I Hîn Húrin,* printed variously in *Unfinished Tales* and *The Children of Húrin;* the quotation here is from p. 49 of the 1980 Houghton Mifflin edition of the *Unfinished Tales.* This is about four pages into the tale.
812. **Speake**, p. 214.
813. **Clute/Nicholls**, p. 1227.
814. **VirgilMcKail**, p. 105. The quote is from Book VI, line 49..
815. For a summary of this, see **Hartman & Di Lella**, pp. 286–287, or my own *The Bible in History* e-book (the information on the Seleucid and Ptolemaic kingdoms).
816. **Asimov**, p. 40.
817. **Asimov**, p. 41.
818. **Crump**, p. 30.
819. **Porter**, p. 567, gives a diagram.
820. **Porter**, p. 568.
821. **Pickering**, p. 236.
822. **Williams**, p. 62.
823. **Haskins**, pp. 77–79.
824. **Larousse**, p. 357; **Pickering**, p. 235.
825. **Cooper**, p. 198.
826. **Liddell & Scott**, p. 573.
827. **Cooper**, p. 198.
828. **Grimal**, p. 407.
829. **Grant & Hazel**, pp. 314–315.
830. **Loomis**, pp. 46–53.
831. **Clute/Grant**, pp. 441, 812–813.
832. Based on the translation in **Bradley**, p 373. Bradley tries to capture the language of the original; I have simplified it by eliminating the elaborate analogies.
833. **Sokolov**, p. 284. I believe the answer is "four."
834. **Jackson**, p. 154.
835. **Larousse**, p. 366.
836. **BriggsFairies**, p. 339.
837. **Williams**, p. 92.
838. **Arrowsmith**, p. 47.
839. **InterpretersDict**, volume IV, p. 843, entry "Wild Ox."
840. **Cooper**, p. 10.
841. **Grant & Hazel**, p. 202.
842. **Grimal**, pp. 229–230.
843. **Cooper**, p. 202.
844. **Frankel**, pp. 14–15.
845. **Grimal**, p. 385.

846. **Grimal**, p. 387.
847. **Grant & Hazel**, p. 301.
848. **Grant & Hazel**, p. 300.
849. **Seyffert**, p. 543.
850. **Grant & Hazel**, p. 301.
851. **Grimal**, p. 389.
852. **Benet**, p. 945.
853. **Grimal**, p. 341.
854. **Henderson & Oakes**, pp. 15–16; **Hooke**, pp. 39–41.
855. **Henderson & Oakes**, pp. 25–26; **Hooke**, pp. 67–68; **Mercantante**, pp. 73–74, 113–114.
856. **Kennedy**, pp. 608–609, 627–628.
857. **Tatar-Annotated**, pp. 158–171; for related English tales, see **BriggsFolk-Tales**, pp. 283, 378–379, 414, 441–443, 472–474. "The Juniper Tree" is Grimm tale #47.
858. **Wimberly**, p. 71.
859. **BrownN**, pp. 128–131.
860. For texts of both the Ovidian and Virgilian accounts, see **Waltz-Orfeo**, pp. 11–13.
861. **Gerritsen & van Melle**, p. 9.
862. List from **Noel** p. 73; for Odin's self-hanging see also **SykesKendall**, p. 145.
863. **Clute/Grant**, pp. 813–814.
864. **Grant & Hazel**, p. 63; **Grimal**, p. 438.
865. **Alexander, Marc**, p. 142.
866. **Waltz-Orfeo**, p. 4.
867. **Lupack**, p. 83.
868. **Waltz-Orfeo**, p. 5.
869. **Stevens**, p. 46.
870. **Waltz-Orfeo**, p. 7.
871. **OxfordSaints**, p. 301.
872. **Mercantante & Dow**, p. 756.
873. **Cooper**, p. 205.
874. **Benet**, p. 982.
875. **Bennett & Gray**, p. 158.
876. **Lupack**, p. 450.
877. **Moorman**, p. 108.
878. **Grimal**, p. 305.
879. **Pickering**, p. 36.
880. **Beowulf/Chickering**, pp. 80–81.
881. **Bradley**, pp. 355–356, quoting "The Whale," a translation in the *Exeter Book* of the bestiary known as the *Physiologus;* the Old English is on folios 96a–97b of the *Exeter Book.*
882. **Larousse**, p. 386.
883. **InterpretersDict**, volume IV, p. 639, entry "Tiamat."
884. **ANET**, pp. 31–34.
885. **Moscati**, p. 69.
886. **Stone**, p. 117.
887. **InterpretersDict**, volume III, p. 116, entry "Leviathan."
888. **Pope**, p. 276.
889. **Graves & Patai**, p. 47.
890. **Graves & Patai**, p. 48.
891. **Jones**, p. 90; compare **Noel**, p. 155.
892. **InterpretersDict**, volume 4, pp. 294–295, entry "Seven."
893. **BakerDictionary**, p. 483.
894. **BakerDictionary**, pp. 482–483; **LewisMere**, pp. 60–63, explains the Cardinal virtues well, and takes on the other three on pp. 100–117.

895. Alexander, Marc, p. 29.
896. Eberhard, pp. 270–271.
897. Haskins, p. x.
898. Grant & Hazel, pp. 155–156.
899. See HastingsDictionary, p. 872, article *SOUL*.
900. Mercantante, p. 169.
901. Cornfeld, p. 105.
902. Cooper, p. 228.
903. Baring-Gould-Myths, pp. 82–83.
904. Baring-Gould-Myths, p. 81.
905. Opie & Tatem, p. 391.
906. Simpson & Roud, p. 353.
907. Eberhard, p. 285.
908. Williams, p. 54.
909. Clute/Grant, p. 942.
910. Henderson & Oakes, p. 34.
911. Simpson & Roud, p. 356.
912. Larousse, p. 420.
913. An English example of this is the tale of Fortunatus, **BriggsFolk-Tales**, A.II, pp. 245–249.
914. Kennedy, pp. 517, 534–535.
915. For English translation see, naturally, **OvidMetamorphoses/Innes**.
916. Grant & Hazel, pp. 340–341.
917. Gerritsen & van Melle, p. 17.
918. O hOgain, pp. 410–411.
919. Child #44; volume I, pp. 399–403.
920. Pickering, p. 285.
921. Child #39, volume I, pp. 335–358.
922. Thompson-Folktale, p. 69.
923. Zipes, pp. 347–353.
924. Thompson-Folktale, p. 259.
925. Moorman, p. 111.
926. Wimberly, pp. 34–35. Both ballads are in volume I of **Child**.
927. Larousse, p. 430.
928. Axelrod & Oster, p. 473.
929. Norwegian, pp. 139–149.
930. Norwegian, pp. 31–48.
931. Norwegian, pp. 67–76; it is also in *The Red Fairy Book*.
932. Norwegian, pp. 84–96.
933. Thompson-Hundred, p. 1.
934. Norwegian, pp. 81–83.
935. Norwegian, p. 21.
936. Norwegian, pp. 97–101.
937. Norwegian, p. 10.
938. Norwegian, pp. 122–127.
939. Lang, pp. 141–147.
940. Norwegian, pp. 150–157; **Lang**, pp. 19–29, gives another Norwegian version of this story under the title "East of the Sun and West of the Moon."
941. Pickering, p. 296.
942. Douglas, p. 109.
943. Wimberly, p. 321.
944. Grimal, p. 229.
945. Mercantante & Dow, pp. 363–364.

946. Clute/Grant, p. 972.
947. TolkienLetters, p. 232.
948. W. H. Auden, "The Quest Hero," p. 46 in **Isaacs & Zimbardo**
949. **O hOgain**, p. 265.
950. **O hOgain**, p. 144.
951. **Alexander, Marc**, p. 17, entry "Belvoir Castle witches."
952. **Wimberly**, p. 128.
953. **Child** #37; volume I, pp. 317–326. The text cited is from p. 324: Version A, stanza 7.
954. **Wimberly**, p. 129.
955. **Waltz-Orfeo**, p. 22; **Wimberly**, p. 131.
956. **Liddell & Scott**, p. 919.
957. **Larousse**, p. 437.
958. **Eberhard**, pp. 302–303.
959. **Larousse**, p. 438.
960. **Simpson & Roud**, p. 371.
961. **Larousse**, p. 438.
962. **Pickering**, p. 302.
963. **Larousse**, p. 438.
964. **Norwegian**, pp. 139–149.
965. **Mercantante & Dow**, p. 858. This later became the basis of a song, "The Unicorn," by Shel Silverstein.
966. **Granger**, p. 177.
967. **Larousse**, p. 438.
968. **Simpson & Roud**, p. 371.
969. **Granger**, p. 258.
970. **Granger**, pp. 17–20, especially p. 18.
971. **Jackson**, p. 18.
972. **RankEtAl**, p. 13.
973. **RankEtAl**, pp. 15–16.
974. **RankEtAl**, p. 43.
975. **Lupack**, p. 470; **Pickering**, p. 285; **Stone**, p. 60.
976. **Lupack**, p. 451.
977. **RankEtAl**, p. 34.
978. **RankEtAl**, p. 18.
979. **RankEtAl**, p. vii.
980. **RankEtAl**, p. 57.
981. **Tolkien & Tolkien**, p. 8, etc.
982. **Child** #54, volume II, pp. 1–6.
983. See the description in **Simpson & Roud**, p. 374.
984. **Grimal**, p. 280.
985. **Larousse**, p. 444.
986. **Mercantante & Dow**, p. 870.
987. **Axelrod & Oster**, p. 486.
988. **Mercantante & Dow**, p. 879.
989. **OxfordFairyTales**, p. 468.
990. **Larousse**, p. 405.
991. **Larousse**, p. 203.
992. **Pickering**, p. 308.
993. **Cooper**, p. 216.
994. **Larousse**, p. 446.
995. **Rose**, p. 234.
996. **SykesKendall**, p. 205; a part of the text of the tale can be found in **Colbert**, pp. 187–188.

997. **SykesKendall**, p. 124.

998. **Shippey-Author**, p. 17.

999. **Baring-Gould-Myths**, p. 31.

1000. **Jackson**, p. 112.

1001. Odyssey X.238; **HomerOdyssey/Fagles**, X.262, p. 237.

1002. **Baring-Gould-Myths**, p. 31.

1003. **Pickering**, p. 217.

1004. **EddaTerry**, p. 54.

1005. **EddaLarrington**, p. 65.

1006. **Shippey-Author**, pp. 15–17.

1007. **Child** #35, volume I, pp. 314–315.

1008. **Child** #30; **Wimberly**, p. 181.

1009. **Mabinogion/Guest**, p. 43.

1010. **Mabinogion/Gantz**, p. 106.

1011. **Mabinogion/Jones**, p. 54.

1012. **Mabinogi/Ford**, p. 98.

1013. See **Zipes**, p. 451, for the use of the wand in Perrault's version, and pp. 468–469 for the Grimm version of the tale, in which Cinderella plants a twig on the grave and waters it with her tears.

1014. *Macbeth* (Act I, scene iii, lines 32–33 [p. 1314] in the Riverside edition).

1015. **HolinshedHosley**, p. 17.

1016. Page 132 of the "tragedies" section of the First Folio.

1017. **Shippey-Road**, p. 152.

1018. **Grimal**, p. 250; **Grant & Hazel**, p. 213.

1019. **OvidMetamorphoses/Innes**, pp. 33–35, translating book I, sections 165–248 or so.

1020. **Cooper**, pp. 158–159.

1021. **Clute/Grant**, p. 1006.

1022. **Grimal**, p. 71.

1023. **Gilliver, Marshall, & Weiner**, p. 210.

1024. **Simpson & Roud**, p. 386.

1025. **Marie/Hanning/Ferrante**, pp. 100–101.

1026. *Bisclavret*, lines 3–14; **Marie/Hanning/Ferrante**, p. 92.

1027. *Bisclavret*, lines 25–26; **Marie/Hanning/Ferrante**, p. 92.

1028. **Reagin**, p. 301.

1029. **SykesKendall**, p. 176.

1030. **InterpretersDict**, volume 3, p. 436, entry "Moon."

1031. **Simpson & Roud**, p. 244.

1032. **BrownN**, p. 187.

1033. **Lupack**, pp. 225–226, 335.

1034. **BakerDictionary**, p. 230.

1035. **Rose**, p. 3.

1036. **Leach**, pp. 689; another version in **Leather**, pp. 181–184.

1037. **Simpson & Roud**, p. 392.

1038. **Mercantante & Dow**, p. 905.

1039. **Eberhard**, p. 314.

1040. **Pickering**, p. 317.

1041. **Grant & Hazel**, p. 69.

1042. **Grimal**, pp. 332–333.

1043. **Cooper**, p. 31.

1044. **Clute/Grant**, p. 432.

1045. **Pickering**, p. 381.

1046. **Westwood & Simpson**, p. 62.

1047. **Simpson & Roud**, p. 395.
1048. **Simpson & Roud**, p. 389.
1049. **Alexander, Marc**, p. 321.
1050. **Clifton**, p. 134.
1051. **Nigg**, p. 275.
1052. **Wimberly**, p. 204.
1053. **Wimberly**, p. 206.
1054. **Nigg**, p. 281.
1055. **Nigg**, p. 276.
1056. **Nigg**, p. 276.
1057. David Buchan, "Talerole Analysis and Child's Supernatural Ballads," **Harris**, p. 73.
1058. **Nigg**, p. 285.
1059. **Alexander, Marc**, p. 323; **Simpson & Roud**, p. 395.
1060. **OxfordCompanion**, p. 995.
1061. Examples in **Alexander, Marc**, p. 322.
1062. **Tatar-Classic**, p. 187; **Zipes**, p. 714.
1063. **Child** #35, volume I, pp. 314–315.
1064. **Child** #43, texts A, C, volume I, pp. 394–395.
1065. **OxfordCompanion**, p. 859.
1066. **Smith**, p. 13.
1067. **Smith**, p. 14.
1068. **SykesKendall**, pp. 216–217.
1069. **Pickering**, p. 322.
1070. **SykesKendall**, p. 216.
1071. **Pickering**, p. 324.
1072. **Larousse**, p. 468.
1073. **Mercantante & Dow**, p. 934.
1074. **Stevens & Klarner**, pp. 117–118.
1075. **MacInnis**, p. 187.
1076. **Satin**, pp. 206–207.
1077. **Satin**, p. 208.
1078. **Botkin**, p. 548.
1079. **Botkin**, p. 549.

www.ingramcontent.com/pod-product-compliance
Lightning Source LLC
Chambersburg PA
CBHW060041100426
42742CB00014B/2655